26.2 ESSAYS

AN INSPIRING NEW WORLD VIEW

BY

BOBBI GIBB

The First Woman to Run the Boston Marathon
Three Time Winner in the Pioneer Women's Division
(1966, 1967 and 1968)

The Institute for the Study of Natural Systems Press
Cambridge Massachusetts

Anniversary Edition
Copyright 2016 by Roberta (Bobbi) Gibb
All Rights Reserved

ISBN: 978-0982967522

Book Design: Y42K Publishing Services

http://www.y42k.com/publishing-services/

Books by Bobbi Gibb

Wind in the Fire
The Art of Inflation
To Boston with Love
DiMa
The Art of Meditative Running
The Art of Economics
Visions and Social Consciousness
Seven Years of Seasons
26.2 Essays

To all my friends and family who helped me on my journey.
To my parents who gave me the gift of life.
To my Beloved Son
To Roger, who will understand how truly heretical and therefore necessary this book is, to challenge the false beliefs that tear us apart and keep us captive, and to offer a new vision that sets us free and joins us together in a celebration of the beauty, wonder and miracle of Existence.
And to Future Generations.

Thank you to all you wonderful people.
May your lives be filled with happiness, health, joy, and love.

INTRODUCTION

26.2 Essays is a collection of essays on my thoughts over the years.

The first essay sets the tone and lays out the underlying insight. This insight is then applied to a multitude of human endeavors including economics, politics, religion, sociology and science.

The Essays are arranged as 26.2 points along the course of the Boston Marathon, each of which triggers the main topic of the given essay. These were compiled as separate thoughts and writing for decades and are not meant to be in chronological order.

TABLE OF CONTENTS

Introduction..5

Chapter One: Beginnings...9

Chapter Two: Life...24

Chapter Three: Colors..34

Chapter Four: Perception..44

Chapter Five: Form and Wholeness.....................................55

Chapter Six: Evolution...66

Chapter Seven: Complexity..78

Chapter Eight: Human Nature..89

Chapter Nine: Children...103

Chapter Ten: Power, Good and Evil....................................112

Chapter Eleven: Relativity..123

Chapter Twelve: Interaction...136

Chapter Thirteen: Democracy in America..........................150

Chapter Fourteen: War..166

Chapter Fifteen: Women..180

Chapter Sixteen: Economics...193

Chapter Seventeen: Cosmology..206

Chapter Eighteen: Language...219

Chapter Nineteen: Knowing..231

Chapter Twenty: Consciousness...243

Chapter Twenty-One: Health..255

Chapter Twenty-Two: Causality...267

Chapter Twenty-Three: Matter, Mass and Energy.............283

Chapter Twenty-Four: Religion..295

Chapter Twenty-Five: Information and Meaning................308

Chapter Twenty-Six: Substance..324

Chapter Twenty-Six and Two Tenths: DiMa......................336

CHAPTER ONE: BEGINNINGS

Hopkinton

Barren trees still wrapped in winter gray brush the April sky with pastel shades of mauve and lavender. People dressed in brightly colored clothes walk among the trees talking and clustering in little groups. Children dart in and out among the adults playing tag, laughing and squealing. The air pulses with excitement.

It's Patriots' Day, April 19th 1966. My mother has just dropped me off, on the outskirts of Hopkinton. I pull the hood of my blue sweatshirt up over my hair and tighten the string that holds up the khaki Bermuda shorts that I borrowed from my brother, around my waist. The Boston Marathon is about to begin.

The Marathon is a celebration of life, a celebration of the timeless ritual of the spring that has finally reached the cold rocky forests of New England. Hopkinton, where the race begins, is an old New England village built around a central green. A white church with a green roof, a cemetery with thin slate stones and huge dark Conifer trees pushing up between the stones breathes of bygone eras. A brick school building calls to mind generations of children. Large comfortable houses ring the Common.

Pre-occupied race officials dressed in suits hurry back and forth. I drink in the cool spring air, excitement fluttering like birds in my rib cage. In a flurry of white shorts and white undershirts, runners gather on the far side of the Common. Policemen backed crowds away from the rope barricades.

Next to the Common I find a little hollow smelling dank and dusty with last year's leaves. Earthen vaults with rusting doors remind me of the ammunition storage vaults my ancestors used in the

Revolutionary War almost two hundred years ago. A stonewall encloses a little hollow and forsythia adorn two granite posts which mark the old gate.

Here I crouch, wondering how many other women in history have been concealed or been made invisible. How many women have had to express their ideas, their very selves, through men. How many women warriors, statesmen, poets, authors, mathematicians, scientists have had to disguise their femininity so well that history has still not discovered. How tragic it has been for both men and women to have lost the brilliance of the female mind and the power of the female spirit. How long will it be until we reach a new balance of the female with the male principle in all aspects of self, society and culture? How long will it be until we throw off the old false beliefs and embrace a new mutual truth?

The Boston Marathon is the oldest marathon in the country, and as far as I know it is the only one. This is the seventieth running of the Boston Marathon. I am about to become the first woman ever to run the Boston Marathon. I'm wearing a new pair of boy's size six running shoes, which I had purchased in San Diego just before making the three and a half day bus trip back to New England. I had spent the night with my parents in Winchester, where I devoured huge heaps of roast beef and apple pie, half-starved after subsisting on apples and bus station chili.

I didn't start out to make a feminist statement. When I began I didn't even know that women weren't allowed to run long distance. I was just doing what I loved to do. I was unfolding my life along the path it was meant to unfold. I had trained for two years for the Boston Marathon never dreaming that it was closed to women. Two months earlier, in February, I had moved to California. From there I had written for my application to run the Boston Marathon. I had received a curt reply that women were not physiologically able to run a twenty-six and two tenths mile marathon, and furthermore, were not allowed to do so because the Marathon is a men's division race, for men only.

Here it was again: that mindless prejudice about women that had been keeping women from being full persons for centuries. Here again were the social customs, laws and false beliefs that were keeping women caged.

I saw that this was an opportunity to crash through those false beliefs and to show that women can do things never before thought possible. If I could disprove this false belief about women, I could call into question all the other false beliefs that were being used to keep women imprisoned.

"All the more reason to run," I thought to myself. I chuckled as I thought how many false beliefs would shatter as I trotted along with the men from Hopkinton to Boston, twenty-six and two-tenths miles. I want to show that men and women can run together. The old so-called war of the sexes is a waste of time.

I believe in the right and the ability of every individual to unfold in their own unique way to the best of their ability no matter what the accident of their birth. This was the message I am bringing to Boston.

The first time I had seen the Boston Marathon, two years before, I had fallen in love with it. I had been running cross-country for a year and a half with a man whom I later married. He had been running track and field at Tufts University. When he had told me that he ran five miles I couldn't believe it. I couldn't imagine anyone running five miles. I had always been a sprinter but soon I was trotting along behind him for two, three, and six miles through the woods, across frozen lakes in winter and into Boston.

When the father of one of my high school friends told me about the Boston Marathon I was amazed. "Twenty-six miles?" I had exclaimed. "How can anyone run twenty-six miles?"

"You should go out and see it," he said, and I did.

When I saw the Boston Marathon for the first time I didn't notice whether the people were men or women. I just saw people running, beautiful, exotic, elegantly powerful people running quietly with such dignity and grace. I knew these people felt the same ancient bond with the earth and with themselves as human animals as I did.

The Marathon is an expression of what it is to be human—the great endurance and courage it takes to live a life of dignity and grace. This Marathon is a celebration of the same life I feel rising within and all around. This is the vision I sought to find and express in my life. I didn't hesitate. There were no pros and cons. The decision was full-blown, already made in side of me. I was going to run in that race, to be a part of it. I set myself that challenge and began to train with no coach and no idea of how to train. I just kept running longer and longer distances day after day.

At an early age the beauty of everything had filled me with a sense of love. It was a vision I first had, as a toddler, in the peace and grandeur of the sunlight filtering down through a big chestnut tree in our backyard in Watertown. My father had been involved in the war effort. My mother had been anxious and preoccupied and, according to the custom of the day, left me alone in the room hour after hour after hour without the essential warmth, love and companionship. But I found it curiously in the patches of sunlight that fell on my little crib, and the delicacy of the edge of the curtain. I found something there—a Presence, a love, a vibrancy, a warmth, as if huge invisible hands were holding me lovingly, gently. I saw it in the beauty that everywhere revealed itself to my infant eyes. And I felt it in the presence of my grandmother who gave me the unconditional love I needed.

When finally I became sick with Whooping Cough, my Nana took me to her home and nursed me back to health. I remember cuddling in her lap with her warm loving arms around me. I remember her looking into my eyes with her eyes, brushing the hair out of my face, and taking me to see the beauties of the garden and the wonder of the catbird who would eat raisins out of her hand. I felt the warmth of her love surround me and infuse me and the sense of my own self responding.

I had the same feeling of love everywhere and beauty in everything—this incomprehensible love that fills all space and unfolds and flings itself across the sky in wild blueness, uplifting the soaring wings of birds. I felt this presence within and all around. I felt it in the sunlight that flickered down through the leaves of the chestnut tree in our back yard in Watertown. It followed me like the moon used to follow along behind the far hills and the woods as we drove in the car in the nighttime. I would look out the back window at the delicate branching trees wheeling darkly above, the tiny fragile brightnesses of stars whisking silently behind the twigs in the vast oceanic darkness of night.

All the while this larger presence, this indwelling, up-welling sense of love impressed itself on my young eyes. Seeing it all for the first time, I was filled with a sense of wonder at the beauty of it all. It filled me with little soft explosions of joy as I realized this joy over and over again in different ways.

As I grew to be ten, twelve and then into adolescence I kept this sense of life and love and wonder. I kept it in the quiet of my woodland retreats. When I saw a field open up before me, green with living grass, shimmering in the sun, caressed by the moving wind I would be filled with an overpowering up welling of joy that could only be expressed by running run full speed across the field.

I loved being outside, in nature. I spent most of my childhood in the forests near our house, avoiding the cold and dysfunctional dynamics of my family. I sought the comfort of the wind in my face and the warm sunshine on my back and the wagging tails and loving eyes of my furry canine companions. My running was a natural part of my love of life. I clambered up and down hills glorying in the beauty of it all. The woods were my solace and my refuge.

13

Here I am, having trained in solitude for two years, in front of all these people. I feel so much love for these people, for the runners and the spectators. I can feel their warmth. I feel that these runners are my brothers and these spectators my mothers and my fathers, and my sisters and my brothers, the family I have always wanted. "If I can do this I can do anything," I think.

I hear a loud bang!

Like ice melting in the spring and breaking into tumultuous white foam that speeds, racing down the rivers, to the sea, the men burst from the pen and begin that long run to Boston. I leap into their midst with the hood of my sweatshirt still concealing my femininity.

This is the beginning: The beginning of the race; the beginning of a new life for me; the beginning of a new consciousness. I think about beginnings. I think about the beginnings of life, the beginning of the world.

Creation myths abound in the rich imagination of the diverse people of the world. During the thousands of miles of cross country running I did in preparation for the Boston Marathon I had plenty of time to think about creation, beginnings, existence and the reality of earth and life. The Native American had quite a different view of the creator from the Hindus; the Taoists from the Buddhists or Muslims; or the Hebrews from the ancient Greeks.

As long as I can remember I've felt this sense of being surrounded and infused with a kind of golden love. I've felt a huge loving presence, just behind what we can see and touch and feel. This presence has been my constant companion and guide and I have followed it, wondering what it is.

This indwelling love has determined my course and informed my decisions, not only to run the Boston Marathon, but long before that. I particularly felt this presence in Nature where the clamor of distracting human events was silenced. But I also felt it in people, on the subway and in other people.

I wanted to find out what this huge loving Presence is, which I thought might be God, but it was not a God that was in books or in religions; it was the raw Creative Power of the Universe that somehow had brought all this into existence. I wanted to stand face to face with it and ask it who or what it is. So I determined to follow it and to see where it would lead.

In the summer of 1964 I saw my chance to follow this love. My parents were on sabbatical in England and they had left the family Volkswagen Bus with me. I packed up the camper and began a journey west, into the wilderness, with my Malamute puppy.

I trekked six thousand miles from Massachusetts to California and back. Every day I ran in a different place and at night I slept under the stars. This was a love affair with our country, every part of it, every open plain, every little glade and tiny winding streams, marshes, bogs and the vast up-thrustings of mountains.

I thought, "How did all this come to be? Why bother with all this vast intricate tapestry of life? Each thing made with such care. Why not one vast emptiness? Why all this wonder? Why all this activity and glory?"

Everything I saw as the road rolled on ahead of me and the scenery reeled by delighted me — the daisies dancing in the center strip, the stalks of grass moving with the wind. I wondered where and how did all of this begin? How does it continue? Each day as I ran I become overwhelmed by the sheer wordless reality of existence itself.

I watched the vast wind-driven clouds move and roll across the sky. The huge ponderous earth turned over and over — not being turned by any person. The wind blew itself. The vast forests grew all by themselves — not being put there by any person. All this wondrous nature unfolded all around me and at night the sounds of a million insects and little trilling amphibians sang me a lullaby.

15

Far above, the vast array of inter-galactic space stretched out, uncountable infinities on every side deep dark soft and safe. A feeling inside of me quietly grew, a feeling of awe that all this exists...that I exist.

As I danced along a ridge somewhere in West Virginia glorying in the gnarled knotted roots, moist mossy banks, the sensuously rounded mountains, I found myself thinking, "This wordless wonder all exists. Each thing is so exquisite it seems to be aware of itself. It speaks to me in a language beyond words. The shape of the maple leaf, like a broad flat hand, is like a letter of the alphabet. Each plant seems to be a hieroglyph of some ancient language, each knowing exactly how to form itself. How does it know what form to take? How does all of this evolve?" The huge vastness of it all hovered near in every leaf and buoyant flower as if to say, "We are. Here we are. We are alive!"

An intense aliveness, a sense of beingness, a sense of belonging to all this and that feeling of joy came to me more and more. It was like being in love but it was being in love with everything. The scent of the dank deep woods filled my nostrils. The arch of the blue sky above was my roof. All was moved by an unseen hand flowering forth from an unseen body, intricately designed by an unseen mind and yet wholly itself, moving itself, unfolding itself. In the same way I was moving myself and glorying in the feeling of racing headlong down the side of a mountain and pausing to look at a sunset at night. I would lay deep in some wooded glen feeling the utter peace that lying right on the earth itself gives you. Where did all this come from?

All of this moves itself! No one makes it go! No one moves it!

The trees grow. The birds sing. The clouds move. The sun shines. The earth turns. Nature moves itself, and, in some grand vast highly coordinated, intricately related, incomprehensible way, unfolds itself. There is no boss somewhere, no engineer making it go.

The intelligence that unfolds all this wonder is not some architect, builder off somewhere else. Rather the intelligence is implicit internally in Nature. It is not that there is a separate supernatural head somewhere designing and directing all this unfolding. Rather, it's doing it itself, from within itself. The head is the body and the body is the head. Nature's intelligence is intrinsic.

Out across the Great Plains, one night I lay down in a nest of grass and imagined myself a tiny water droplet hanging off the bottom the earth looking down into infinite space into billions of galaxies and stars. That same feeling took my breath away:

This has no end! There is no outside to the Universe of all that exists!

Anything that exists outside all-that-is is immediately part of all-that-is by definition. It's not that existence floats like a ball or sphere in a huge empty space that surrounds it. Existence is all there is. There is no space or time or anything outside of it, not even nothing. All that exists has no outside boundary; there is no outside to all that exists. It is a paradox; it is impossible to think of an object with no outside boundary.

The next day I ran across the prairies. Fields of grass were blowing in the wind and shining in the sun. I had discovered that the world is intrinsically self-active and self-unfolding and that there is no outside to all-that-is. Yet something still was missing. What? Something was pulling me ever Westward, across Nebraska, into Colorado and up into Wyoming. There I stopped briefly to visit Debby, my high school friend, whose father had first told me about the Boston Marathon.

From there I pushed on deeper into the mountain wilderness, into the Snowy Range. There, the sense of Divine Presence became stronger and stronger until it consumed and infused me with its power.

The same power and presence that I'd always felt around me, delicately dancing in the leafy sunshine, now took on a different, deeper, more powerful tone. Here, the huge up-thrusting mountains broke the surface of the earth into jagged fragments.

I felt within and all around me the overwhelming, physical presence of what we call God, the Divine Creator, in the act of creating all-that-is into existence right here and now. This Presence was not something separate and apart, as a supernatural being, but rather, was something entirely natural and fully present, intrinsic in the physicality of all-that-exists.

I understood that the reality we think we see, feel, taste, hear, smell, and touch is not what is really out there in the so-called objective world. Rather, we know only our interaction with whatever is there from our own point of view. We know only our perceptions and conceptions of what it is. We never know it objectively, only subjectively.

Each day I ran across the planet earth marveling in its magnificent landscapes, the sculptured canyons of Utah and the mountains and broad valleys of Nevada.

I continued to think.

Where does this Creative Power of all-that-is come from? What goes on creating all this? If the earth was created out of chunks of matter falling together and those chunks of matter were created out of intergalactic dust falling together, and that intergalactic dust was created out of the explosion of other stars, in one huge vast cycle. Where did the matter come from? Where did the energy come from? If it precipitates out from background and disappears back into background, where did the background come from?

One night, standing on a mountaintop in Nevada, looking out into the velvety blackness at infinites of stars I thought, "How does all this wonder and beauty come to exist? Why bother with all this? Why not just one big void?"

Historically, people have thought of the Creator as a man-like deity who created the world the way an architect creates a building or the way a watchmaker creates a watch.

However, to the contrary, I'd seen that what we call the God or the Divine Creator is fully present in all-that-exists and is not a separate, supernatural being, but is fully natural, and imbedded in the intrinsic nature of everything.

So I said, "Okay, then what creates that Creative Power?

An even greater Creative Power?

And then I ask, "Well then, what creates that Creative Power?

An even greater Creative Power? This makes no sense. This can't possibly be right.

Suddenly an astounding feeling washed through me. *This Creative Power must create Itself, since there is nothing else to create it. All-That-Exists in its fundamental Being must be the Creative Power of all-that-exists, and It must be continuously creating Itself in to being in a dynamical process of self-existing through which it creates and maintains its own existence from within.*

All-That-Is creates even its own power to create itself. All-that-Is must contain its own power to exist. All-That-Is must create and maintain itself in existence within itself. There is no external creator. The All-That-Exists, therefore is Itself what we have called the Divine Creator. The Divine Self-Creator is continuously creating itself as All-That-Exists. This is what Nature, in its largest sense, is: The Divine All-That-Is, continuously creating Itself into being as All-That-Is.

But All-That-Exits isn't what we think it is or what we perceive. We perceive and conceive our own subjective experiences of our interactions with whatever exists out there. We can never know it directly, yet it is all we know because we ourselves are it creating itself as us.

This has to be, since there exists nothing outside of, or besides, All-That-Exists. *Its power, to exist and its power to create itself, arises solely within itself.*

My entire body trembled with excitement. A feeling of intense love overwhelmed me.

God is not an external, supernatural head or king somewhere telling everything what to do:

The Divine Being is not contained or localized somewhere, but rather

19

the entire Cosmos of all that exists is Divine!

All-That-Exists is the Divine Self-Creator and the Divine Self-Creator is all that is. It must be creating Itself because there is nothing else to create it. There is no other alternative.

This revelation, of a Divine Self-Creating-Self-Existing, filled me with a feeling of awe beyond anything I had ever experienced. I was face to face with the Creator, and I'd found the Divine Self-Creating-Self-Existing. Why had I been cheated for so long into thinking there was some king somewhere that had created a mindless mechanical world? That isn't the truth at all. It isn't a mechanical world. It is a world rich with its own self-creativity and self-activity. This Universal Self-Creativity is the holy miracle, that which we have called Divine. This Divine Nature is reality unfolding. The miracle of its Self-Creativity continued to fill me with awe and wonder as it seeped deeper and deeper into my consciousness.

In the following days my sense of the Divine and of Nature merged into one as I contemplated this blade of grass, exquisitely green, quivering in the wind creating itself out of this Self-Creating Substance, this wind, which caresses the grass, this dirt out of which the grass arises, this speck of sand, every molecule, this whole earth, every human being is Divine, all holy, all in perfect harmony. All are forms of this Self-Creative Being. I let myself feel this Self-Creative Oneness, which is beyond all cause and effect and transcends all duality.

"This is the meaning of the Virgin Birth," I thought, "the Mother giving birth to Herself, the ultimate paradox, the Divine Mystery."

Although it is beyond all words and all descriptions, I began to find a word for it. I called it the Divine Self-Creating Matrice, DiMa, to make clear to myself that it wasn't just our idea of a material universe but it includes immaterial quantities like motion, organization, pattern, principle and natural law. Reality is the Divine Self-Creative Presence unfolding itself. It must create itself because there is nothing else to create it. What a wild revelation! It delighted me. I saw everything as partaking in this Divine Self-Creative Nature.

Nature is this Divine Self-Causality. Its Self-Creating creates all time and all space, everywhere simultaneously, not from some point or some place, but right here now at every point, at every place, at every time. It creates all energy, all motion, all form out of Itself. Each thing, each motion is part of the creative self–activity of the whole. Each thing is holy. Each thing is miraculous. Thou grass, thou tree, thou sky, thou person, all manifesting this mysterious incomprehensible Self–Creative Oneness. This is the elusive enigmatic present moment out of which and into which reality unfolds.

Each form is a manifold of this Self-Creative Oneness. It sees Itself with our eyes. It thinks Itself with our mind. It blows Itself as the wind. It sparkles Itself as light on the water, which is Itself as water. We are all forms of this one Self–Creative Beingness — the Divine Self-Creating Matrice, DiMa. I began to see Her everywhere hovering in the air, glinting in the sunlight. I could feel Her within me. DiMa the Self-Creating One. I saw that "being", the ultimate noun, is a verb, and that everywhere this Ultimate Substance is creating Itself out of Itself with exquisite care and perfection that can only come from a love beyond our comprehension, from a transcendent caring so vast, so perfect that to realize it is to be transformed forever.

Here was that Presence I had been sensing, that vision I had had under the chestnut tree so long ago. I let myself feel the Presence and reality of this Self-Creativity going on all around me, right here in the present moment. Every time I let myself realize that there is no outside to the system, I felt the pang of joy.

I would come into the present moment and ask, "How does all this come to be?" And I would answer, "It creates itself." Then I would ask, "But how does it create itself, until it exists to create itself?" And I would be face to face with the ultimate Divine Paradox and at that point I would be thrown beyond what I could think and I would be filled with an immense joy. I would feel every cell of my being creating itself as the Divine Self-Creator creating Itself as me, and I would know that I and every other person and the whole of existence is part of the totality of the Divine Self-Creating Miracle that is continuously bringing Itself into Being right here now.

This Self-Creative Oneness is the ultimate paradox and mystery, the fundamental nature of reality. I felt close to something very big and very dear. All of Nature is a miracle so vast as to be entirely unseen. The whole universe is the Divine Self-Creative Matrice unfolding itself in myriad forms, all intricately related. There is no split between Nature and the Divine. All of Nature is this multitudinous, interconnected, unfolding Divine manifold.

"And what does It create Itself out of?" I wondered:

"There is nothing besides Itself to create Itself out of. Therefore this Divine Self-Creating creates Itself out of Itself."

"What is it that creates all this?

"There is nothing except Itself to create It." Therefore it creates its own creativity. It creates even Its own ability to create."

"And what does it create Itself into?"

"It creates Itself into Itself because there is nothing other than Itself."

"This is the Holy Trinity," I thought. It creates Itself out of Itself. It creates Its own Self-Creativity and it creates Itself into Itself. It's a paradox. It's impossible to think. How can it be that what is doing the creating is also that which is created? It transcends our human ability to conceive. It's an effect that causes its own effect. It's a cause that's the effect of its own cause. Our linear sense of cause and effect breaks down and yet this must be true.

Each time I would approach this Ultimate Paradox I would be filled with an intense sense of love and joy, a sense of belonging, of being absolutely loved and of loving the whole of everything all at once. Its beauty and mystery would infuse me and everything I saw was filled with a sweet golden love like warm honey. I felt safe and at home in the universe; its transcendent beauty and absolute perfection immanent.

This was the presence that had always been with me. It was this Presence that I had followed into the wilderness and now I see what it is. This is the Garden of Eden, the Kingdom of God—this awareness of this Divine-Self-Creating, Self-Existing unfolding Itself from within, on all sides and within us.

CHAPTER TWO: LIFE

Celebration

The race is newborn, only a few minutes old. We run breathing together; the sound of our feet tapping on the pavement is like spring rain on the roof. The Boston Marathon is a celebration of life— A celebration of the return of life after the long, cold, dark winter of New England.

"Is that a girl?" I hear one of the men say.

"Yes, I think it's a girl."

"Hey! There's a girl running!"

"Is there a girl running?"

I turn around and smile. "It is a girl!" they exclaim delightedly.

"It's a girl!"

One tall lanky man from Connecticut is running next to me. He says wistfully, "I think it's great that you're running. I wish my wife would run."

I sense a loneliness and incompleteness in these men as if they want to share their love for running with the women they love.

The men are taking off their tee-shirts and tossing them into the crowds. People are tying their jackets around their waists. I feel the uncomfortable prickle of heat building up under my sweatshirt.

"I'm getting hot in this sweatshirt," I confide to the tall man running next to me. "But I'm afraid if I take it off and they see I'm a woman they'll throw me out, because women aren't allowed to run."

"Go ahead, take it off," the man on the other side of me says over hearing my comment.

"Yeah, it's a free road." says another

"Besides we won't let them throw you out," the tall man replies.

For a moment the brilliant patchwork of colors of the crowd and the road disappears as I pull the sweatshirt over my head. I'm engulfed in the intimate, comforting, muffled world inside the sweatshirt, with its soft familiar fabric.

As if being born, I emerge into the bright, thin air. The sweatshirt falls to the side of the road, like a spent cocoon.

Now the crowds can see I'm a woman and the applause crescendos:

"It's a girl! At a go girlie! You can do it! Hey there's a girl running!"

I can hear the chatter all around me expanding outwards like the ripples around a rock thrown into a still pond on a summer's afternoon.

These men are my brothers. I feel their respect. There's no hint of man versus woman, but rather, a quiet confirmation that men and women can share the joys and challenges of life together. It is not women running against men, but a woman running with men and the men loving it.

This idea of birth into a new life, sends my mind soaring back to Vermont and the Green Mountains, where my first baby boy was born.

 I remember the moist, fern-covered valleys, the scent of deep, sweet wet soil. Millions of past years are still present in the quiet air and in the carved valleys of layers of fossil-filled rock, once a warm shallow seabed, now a summer jungle left behind by the last ice age. Here are the steaming valleys of dinosaurs, where slate and marble metamorphosed under the warm, marshy seabeds. Here is where the ocean gave birth to the first life on earth.

"What is life?" I had wondered as a child. In high school I took my first biology course in ninth grade. Mr. Curtis, our biology teacher, has said that no one knew what made life living. So I began to think about it.

What is it about living systems that makes them living?

Seeking an answer, I had run up into the woods, with the neighborhood dogs. I was determined that I would think until I solved this riddle, so I sat in a field, for an entire day, looking at a piece of moss and concentrating. It was a complete mystery to me. What is it that makes life alive?

The vibrant green moss glistened, as the earth turned, under the sun. I looked at every detail: the dainty, green frills, the tiny, reddish stalk. I leaned close and smelled its pungent, moist breath.

I touched its delicate form. How does it do what it does? What does it do? How is it different from a stone? I could feel my mind working. What am I not seeing?

After hours of thought, I felt a tingling in my solar plexus that let me know that some thought was emerging. I waited until, with a thrill, suddenly it came bubbling up into my conscious mind. I saw what the living moss is doing:

It is building itself! A living system is building itself from the molecules and energy of its environment!

It would be as if one day, you turned the corner into your street after a hard day of work, and there on the corner was a house, but this was not the ordinary house. You screeched on the brakes and stopped in amazement. The lumber was flying up from the piles; two-by-fours were arranging themselves in neat rows next to each other eighteen inches on center; wall boards were rising, affixing themselves to the walls; the shingles were unwrapping themselves, flying up the outside of the house, nailing themselves in orderly array to the outside of the house; window frames were placing themselves in windows; joists were swung into position. It would be unbelievable; a miracle. The entire press would be there with TV cameras. All the dignitaries, the President, the Pope himself — all would hail this as a most extraordinary, miraculous occurrence.

26

More than that, this living house is building the workmen who build it. And it even builds the plans by which it organizes itself.

It was this same circularity that I had discovered on my westward journey, in 1964, that characterizes all of existence. That which exists creates and sustains itself, and in so doing it is, in fact, what we have called the Divine Creator. It is Divine since we have defined the Divine to be that which creates and sustains existence, so if Nature designs, creates and sustains itself then it is the ultimate Divine that we have been seeking.

When I got to MIT in the early 70's I discovered that Humberto Maturana, and Jerry Lettvin, were working on models of living systems as automatons, with cybernetic feedback or servo loops. I would sit around Jerry's lab with a bunch of grad students and colleagues. Jerry was one of the most warm-hearted, open people I had ever met and his office was a place where people congregated, drawn to him, as I was.

I wondered if they were talking about what I had seen in the moss, in 1957.

Humberto and his colleagues wrote computer programs. They then let the computer iterate the rule over and over. What appeared on the computer screen were little squares of dark and light that (spontaneously) took on different configurations in various patterns.

These patterns organized themselves, it was thought, because they had not been designed by anyone. The patterns emerged out of the continuous reapplication of the rule to the results of the last outcome. They called this self-organization, or autopoesis, and used it for a model for living systems, saying that the operation of the living system produced its own organization, in a way similar to the way that the computer program, through its operation, produced its own spontaneously emerging organizations of dots.

But I could see that it was a different concept of self-organization than I had seen in the moss because the parts on the computer screen

27

were not actually interacting with each other in a real dynamic way. The patterns arising in the squares on the computer screen were the result of the computer program, not of their own intrinsic power of self-organization.

True, no one designed the specific patterns that emerged in that particular sequence on the screen. But someone wrote the computer program that laid down the rule, which defined the relationships between functions that allowed the patterns to emerge. The patterns were essentially graphs of functions that described relationships between parameters. When you write it as an equation, it is a rule. When you graph it visually, it is a design or pattern. The equation $x=y$ is rule. Its graph is a straight line, i.e. a design or pattern (an organization of dots), which you can see on the paper or on the computer screen.

It was just that there was enough indefiniteness in the outcome of each experiment, specified by the rule, that no one knew in advance what specific pattern would be generated on what specific outcome. These outcomes could compile to form a kind of dynamic stability, or spontaneously repeating configurations, having certain characteristics, like closure.

What, then, is this "self-organization"? I wondered.

What is "organization?"

"Organization" can mean: 1. A pattern, as in the organized squares in the quilt make a lovely pattern; 2. An actual organized entity, as in our organization donates to the charity; and/or 3. The act of organizing, such as, she organized the room. It was these different meanings of the word, organization, to which systems designers, I thought, were referring when they distinguished, design (adjective), structure (noun), and process (verb).

So what does "self-organization" mean?" I wondered. It too has this ambiguity. It can mean: the organizational pattern; the actual organized entity; and/or the act of organizing.

Which meaning did Humberto mean?

To systems designers, the organization was a set of patterns of interrelations among components, which can be built from electronic parts as well as from organic molecules.

Self-organization then was a set of patterns that is arising spontaneously from the operation of the system itself.

Something bothered me about this.

The living system isn't just organizing itself into patterns. It is organizing itself into existence as a system.

The very existence of a living system as a system is its continuous process of organizing the energy and molecules of its environment into itself.

You have a pile of lego toy blocks on the floor. They are not capable of organizing themselves into anything. They need a child to build them into houses, trucks, bridges and towers. You have a pile of molecules on the table. They don't just jump up and organize themselves into a living system. Yet living systems are made of molecules. How does this happen?

I could see that the self-organization that leads to a living system is an entirely different type of process than the organization of a machine, or a computer program. In the case of living systems, there is no rule written by computer experts that defines the set of patterns that can emerge. If there is a "rule" written in nature which creates a series of spontaneously self-emergent patterns, what sort of thing would this rule be? Where and how would it exist?

The individual legos do not contain the pattern or design of the whole organization that they are making. Indeed the legos can be arranged in myriad designs or organizational structures, a house, a plane, a dog, a cat, a human being.

True, the shape of the lego both limits and makes possible their joining to form an organizational structure, but the individual shape of the lego does not specify the structure of which it is a part.

Since there is nothing in the individual lego to specify the design of the whole of which it becomes a part, then where is the design of the whole organized structure, and how does it impress itself on, or become incorporated as, the design of the whole entity which is formed or forms itself? In nature there is no child putting the legos together into a design.

When I asked professors in the biology department about what organizes the living creature. I was told that the DNA, the genetic material, accounts for the organization of the living organism. And the RNA transcribes the organizational pattern that is translated into the actual proteins of the cell.

But something bothered me about this. In the embryo, the cells aren't creating the design or pattern of organization, anew. They are simply translating the pattern already specified in the DNA into protein molecules and a host of other molecules in the process of building themselves.

I could see that the DNA is the genetic memory of the cell. Encoded in its sequences of adenine, cytosine, guanine and thiamine base molecules that are the sequences for the manufacture of protein molecules.

It was clear to me that, although these DNA base molecules store the information necessary for the cell to make specific proteins, it is the cell that makes the protein. That is, the DNA does not account for the intrinsic self-activity of the cell. Nor does the DNA account for the pattern that it encodes.

It's not that the DNA actively organizes the passive components of the cell into a living system. It's that the cell as a whole is the active force using the DNA, which also participates in the self-activity of the whole, to remember how to organize itself. The Deoxyribonucleic acid is the servant of the cell as a whole, not vice versa.

But what is this cell as a whole that is acting? What is this intrinsic whole activity of the embryo, this unfolding activity by which it puts itself together?

What is this internal activity by which the organism organizes itself and maintains its dynamic structure?

What was missing in these computer simulations, I had realized, was the intrinsic spontaneous self-activity of the living cell, the living organism. The cell is spontaneously self-active from the inside. In a living system it is the cell as a whole, the organism as a whole, which acts to organize itself. The living system in effect is creating itself from the materials and energy of its environment.

The dots on the computer screen, in contrast, have no intrinsic self-activity and therefore don't act to organize themselves, rather their patterns are the result of the action of something other than themselves. Nor does the pattern, which is emerging on the screen, act in some way to incorporate the dots into itself, as does a living system.

But this internal self-formative activity of living systems isn't just a chaotic random motion, like molecules of gas. It is ordered in space and time. It orders itself in space and time. It is an organized self-activity through which the organism continuously forms itself as an existent entity, in time and space.

This intrinsic push to become itself, to exist as itself, arises spontaneously within. This is what a man-made design, no matter how complex, can never do. A machine, even the most sophisticated electronic computer, can never have that intrinsic self-activity through which the living organism organizes itself into existence. It always depends on the activity of something other than itself to design and build it.

Everyone was looking at the patterns of organization for an explanation of the living quality of living systems. But, I could see that the patterns of organization emerging in living systems do not explain this intrinsic autonomous self-activity by which the living system creates itself into existence.

But what is this inner, autonomous, spontaneous self-formative activity of living systems? How does it exist?

It is inexplicable if we think of a purely mechanistic, material world. I had discovered the fundamental nature of nature to be this circular self-creativity, in which all that exists brings itself into existence and maintains its existence through the intrinsic, paradoxical act of self-creating, self-existing. My view is entirely unheard of in science. I had seen how this concept of the intrinsic self-creating-self-existing of the whole of existence bestows on nature the powers and abilities that traditionally had been ascribed to a supernatural, separate deity. Thus, the living system partakes of the divine self-creating of the Divine Self-Creating, Self-Existing Miracle that is All-That-Is.

What has designed existence capable of evolving itself into living systems? There is nothing besides All-That-Is, therefore All-That-Is has designed itself capable of evolving living systems and this ability must be fundamental to the universe.

A living system is simply a system that is capable of building itself and dynamically sustaining itself utilizing the materials and energies of its environment. This capacity to self-build, to self-sustain, to self-organize, under appropriate conditions, is, I believe, fundamental to the universe.

I had no doubt that living systems abound in the universe wherever conditions allow.

We ourselves are living systems that have evolved from complex chemical reactions that still take place throughout our bodies. Our bodies build themselves autonomously from the elements that have evolved in the cores of supernovas. We are the Matrice becoming itself as the living systems that are us.

So this is why life is a different type of system than computer generated designs, because it is forming itself through its own innate self-activity from parts that interact to form themselves into systems that don't exist until the parts come together, but the parts do not

32

come together until the system exists in which they interact to form the system that comprise themselves. Here again is the paradoxical self-active-self-creative interactivity that I had discovered characterizes All-That-Exists.

CHAPTER THREE: COLORS

Balloons

The moving arms and legs of running men engulf me. Faces, gripped with concentration, surround me. I feel my own arms and legs unfold after the long bus trip.

My legs are restless and welcome the motion. I feel like a bird in flight doing what is most natural for me to do, and here I am surrounded by other runners who feel the same pleasure in running as I do.

People dressed in brightly colored jackets and children with brightly colored balloons watch us run by. I notice the vibrant colors, reds, greens, blues, purples and oranges. My entire surrounding seems to be a patchwork of brilliant colors and cheering faces. The crowds of people are yelling and cheering. The sky is intense blue.

My arms and shoulders begin to loosen up to the rhythmic gait. My body begins to sing. I am at home and all these people are my family. I look again at the colored patchwork, the spectators, the vibrant colors on the balloons.

I was fascinated with neuroscience and curious about how the brain works. In 1972, I interviewed for the position at MIT with Jerry Lettvin, the great neuroscientist. After listening to my qualifications in science, philosophy and mathematics, he still seemed to hesitate as if he were looking for something more. Then he had asked me if I had done anything unusual, anything that demonstrated my ability to think outside the box, any new insights I'd had. I said I was the first woman to have run the Boston Marathon in 1966. His face lit up and he threw his arms up in delight and exclaimed that of course he would take me on!

Jerry had taken over the lab where Warren McCulloch and his colleague Pitts had studied the nervous system. He would take me on he said as his "autodidact," he said. That means self-teaching. My job was to ask naive but intelligent questions of everyone and press them to the wall. I could also audit courses, use the library, attend seminars and, in fact, give seminars.

When Jerry found out I was an artist, I had studied at the Boston Museum of Fine Arts School before earning my undergraduate degree, he was happy with the idea that I would paint murals on his walls in Building 20 at MIT, which I did.

Jerry and his wife, Maggie became my dear friends. Maggie was into natural healing, exercise and healthy food. She was the mother of their three children. Her slender form could be seen on public television where she did a program on fitness and health.

Jerry was a huge man, not only did he have a large frame, but he carried a lot of weight. He was warm and friendly, and often when he saw me he'd give me a big hug. For lunch he was likely to go out to the lunch cart and get a large pastrami sandwich. He seemed to live on coffee and cigarettes.

I was to study color vision. How do we perceive color? That was the question. He assigned me works by Helmholtz, the German scientist, to read, and I set to work.

At that time there were two competing theories of color vision, one was the color-opponency theory, which focused on the fact of complimentary colors and the other was the trichromatic theory, which focused on the fact of there being three primary colors out of which the others were composed.

How do we perceive color? All of the material I was reading assumed that color was a quality in the object perceived — indeed the philosophers called it a secondary quality, something that did not go to the essence of the object but which was nevertheless an attribute.

Popular knowledge has it that color is in the object. Who would doubt that the blueness is not in the sky? Our entire language is set up to express this reality: The sky is blue; the grass is green.

I began my reading and studying and learned that Newton himself had written a piece on perception in which he had separated white light into its component colors with a prism and had concluded that white light was made up of colored light, which when mixed together canceled each other out.

Indeed, from my studies as an artist, I had learned about primary colors, red, blue and yellow. They are primary because they cannot be made by mixing any other colors. All the other colors can be made by mixing different proportions of the primary colors. So purple is made by mixing red and blue. Green is made by mixing yellow and blue. Orange is made by mixing red and yellow.

And I knew the color wheel in which the complimentary color was opposite its complimentary mate. They were complimentary because when mixed together they produced gray. Who would doubt that all these colors were in the pigment and it was something about the pigment itself that caused this curious phenomenon. It was clear to me that the visual system incorporated both the color opponency and the trichromaticy in it functioning.

From Newton's work I learned that the short wavelengths of light produce the blues and the very long wavelengths produce the reds. The rest of the spectrum is spread out between the blue and the red in orderly fashion. Each color corresponds to a different wavelength of light. Indeed, it looked as though the wavelengths entering the eye are seen somehow as color and that it is the wavelength that carries and specifies the color information to the eye.

Before the discovery of light waves, philosophers had thought there was some active property of the object that was somehow transmitted to our eye. It was thought, and still is thought to a great extent, that all the information is in the world out there and our eyes are like a camera, which simply receives this information and records it in its cellular function.

Jerry and his friend, Humberto Maturana recorded the electrical impulses from neurons in various parts of the frog's optic tectum. It turned out that different cells in the frog's brain were specially constructed to receive and to respond to certain sets of stimuli in the outside world. Jerry, McCulloch, Maturana and Pitts had already published their seminal paper on vision, "What the Frog's Eye Tells the Frog's Brain," in which they revealed that the cells in the frog's optic tectum are specially tuned to different complex attributes in the environment: 1. Sustained contrast; 2. Net convexity; 3. Net dimming, and 4. Moving edge detection.

This changed the way the visual processing apparatus was understood at the time. Previous to this, the visual processing was thought to be made up of small concentric dots, like a mosaic, which is true to some extent at the very earliest stages of processing, but quickly becomes more complex as the processing continues to operate on the information it sends to the higher centers in the brain.

Jerry set up a hollow, metal hemisphere about the size of a large basketball cut in half and placed the frog so that its eye could see the inside of this hemisphere. He then passed different stimuli across the inside surface of the hemisphere. He found that certain cells fired wildly. On his amplifier you could hear tick, tick, tick sounds and you could see the oscilloscope jump, in the dimmed room in which the hushed and intent students were standing around watching.

I learned how to make electrodes. I made my own amplifier and my own recording set-up and I recorded from the brains of frogs. The electrodes were thinner than the finest thread and the amphibian is very resilient. The frogs were not hurt in any way and afterwards they recovered completely. In fact I made a place where the frogs that had been used in experiments could retire and live out their lives in a natural setting.

I felt I was in a privileged place; the very core of learning; the very cutting edge of human knowledge, here in this nondescript cellar room in Building 20, with the lights dimmed and the oscilloscope ticking, and little spotted, green frogs sitting there alert, and lively.

Hubel and Wiesel at Harvard were conducting experiments with cats and monkeys and recorded from visual cortex cells that were sensitive to the orientation of lines flashed across the screen. They found cells earlier in the processing network that responded to or were inhibited by various configurations of concentric circular fields. And so I could see that this visual system is much more than a camera. The visual system is impeccably designed, or rather, has designed itself through evolution, to respond selectively to certain occurrences in the outside world and to relay that response in a structured way to higher centers.

The retina is made up of rods and cones. There are three different kinds of cones. One type of cone has a spectral sensitivity that peaks in the long end of the spectrum at a wave length of about 564 nanometers, another type of cone whose sensitivity peaks in the mid range or about 534 nm and the third that peaks at 420nm. The sensitivity of the rods, which are more peripheral, is greater in very dim light and its sensitivity peaks in the short wave lengths at about 498nm. I saw that these three differentially sensitive receptors must be responsible for the fact of the three primary colors.

I learned that the photo-receptor is a microscopic structure looking sort of like a bottle brush that rises perpendicular to the plain of the retina and contains molecules of rhodopsin, which is a photosensitive pigment. When a photon hits a molecule of rhodopsin, the rhodopsin changes shape, and this change of shape is translated into a change of cellular membrane potential, and this change of potential initiates a tiny microscopic voltage change, which then runs along the axon of the cell to the retinal cells that make up the next level.

In humans there are generally five levels of retina cells and among these are a multitude of subtypes. Each level is highly specific in what it does. At the first level are the receptor cells, which simply transmit the fact that they were hit by a photon of light. Great numbers of these receptor cells feed onto each cell in the next layer. In fact, they feed on to more than one cell in the next layer forming geometric areas of photo sensitivity. They can feed in a excitatory way, which means that when they are firing rapidly they excite the next cell in line, or they can feed on in an inhibitory way, which means that when they are firing rapidly they inhibit the next cell in the chain.

There are: 1. horizontal cells, which link receptors to each other laterally and connect the bipolar cells to one another; 2. Bipolar cells, which synapse with the rods, cones and horizontal cells and can take on an entire scale of voltage potentials; 3. Amacrine cells, which connect the bipolar cells and the ganglion cells laterally and have to do with temporal processing and motion detection; 4. Ganglion cells, the axons of which comprise the so called optic neuronal tract and lead from the retina up to the lateral geniculate nuclei, the superior colliculus and the pretectal nuclei.

It occurred to me that horizontal processing might be the place where contrast enhancement takes place. Adjacent cells would have contrasting potentials at each moment in time. As the eye moves over the scene the potential of each receptor is continuously varying and this continuously varying voltage potential is compared with the continuously varying voltage potentials of neighboring cells in such a way as to identify and enhance a boundary. I wrote a short note on the subject in 1978.

The bipolar cells which can take on a positive or a negative voltage on a sliding scale caught my interest. Each bipolar receives from numerous receptor cells through the secondary cells. It occurred to me that the bipolar was a precise device to find a differential, that is, to take the ratio of, and, in that way, both compare and reflect the inputs from differently sensitive photo receptors. The resultant sliding potentials in the bipolar would be analogous to a spectrum of color. This could account for the opponency of complimentary colors.

I read in Helmholtz about complimentary colors. He did experiments with colored shadows and after images. If you look at a blue object on a white background intently for thirty seconds and then close your eyes, you'll see an image of an orange object on a black background. This is an afterimage. These images show clearly that the mechanism of contrasts is complimentary in terms of color so that the after-image of blue is its compliment, orange, the after-image of green is its compliment, red, and the compliment of yellow is purple. I thought this contrast mechanism must have something to do with the interplay of the horizontal contrast processes and the proto-color generating bipolars.

It seemed to me that the contrast mechanisms were what were generating these complimentary proto-colors and that the absence of a positive voltage was being seen as the presence of a negative voltage and vice versa, when contrasted with a light or dark background respectively. This seemed to me to indicate a mechanism whereby a voltage potential was in effect being reflected over a floating zero point as in the null point of the bipolar and at the same time a contrast between center and surround or back ground was being reversed by a rebound of a contrast mechanism.

It occurred to me that this type of comparative-contrast mechanism might be ubiquitous in the nervous system and provide a mechanism, at various levels, for taking ratios, that is for weighing differentials and that this ability to make comparisons is vital to neuronal activity and function.

I mused about the concentric on/off cells in the cat lateral geniculate found by Hubel and Wiesel at Harvard.

I thought about these matters a great deal as I ran, for I was still running miles and miles every day. I worked at M.I.T. and ran out across the athletic field and followed the Charles River upstream. In the spring I raced alongside the racing shells as they were rowed, like ancient Roman warships, up and down the river.

Everybody was talking about color as though it was a property of the light reflected off an object but the more I studied these incredibly intelligent visual systems, the more I began to wonder, "Does the eye just respond to reflectances of light as processed in the visual system? Does the spectral composition of the light actually have to enter the eye to produce the sensation of color?

It was then that Jerry took us all over to the Polaroid labs to see the experiments of Edwin Land. Land had made a patchwork of light and dark rectangles on a photographic slide. In fact, he had made two patchworks. He put one in each of two slide projectors. Through one slide he projected medium wavelength light, which looked green. Through the other he projected long wavelength light, which looked red.

Independently illuminated, the Mondrian patchwork simply looked like different shades of green or different shades of red. But when he showed them both together superimposed... Suddenly all the colors of the rainbow were there!

I was stunned! Here was the answer to my question.

The full spectrum of subjectively perceived color was present even though the only wavelengths of light that fell on the retina were green, which stimulated the mid-wavelength (around 534 nm) sensitive receptors and red, which stimulated the long-wavelength (around 564 nanometers) sensitive receptors. This meant that subjective color is generated by the comparisons of the states of two types of wavelength sensitive cone receptors. That is, the comparison of the states of two differentially sensitive cone receptors is all that is necessary, and is sufficient, to produce our subjective experience of color. The presence of the third or short wavelength sensitive receptor intensifies and clarifies the color by adding the blue dimension.

This is what I had been looking for. Color is created in the visual system. Of course it is! That is why we see three primary colors, because we have three types of receptors. By the comparison of voltages of the differentially sensitive receptors our nervous system constructs the full range of color.

Thus, the voltages of the receptors do not reflect the wavelength of light out there in some absolute way. The eye is not looking at the wavelengths out there, nor is it even extrapolating what the wavelengths must be from its comparative potentials. The eye is looking only at the comparisons between its own differentially sensitive receptors, which pick up a broad range of overlapping wavelength at different intensities.

The impinging light has a different effect on each type of receptor depending on the spectral sensitivity of the receptor, to be sure. But the actual color is created in and by the nervous system itself and the specific color created depends only on the comparative voltages of the relevant differentially sensitive receptors.

"But if we create color", I thought, "What is out there? Color is not out there." It is not as though there is one kind of color in a colored object or in the light and some kind of analog of that color in our minds; it's that there is no color in the objective outside external world at all. Color is totally created in our eye-brain system. Color is purely a subjective experience!

Well then what is out there? It looks as though what I see is out there. I see the blue sky, I see the colored balloons, I see the patchwork of color in the spectators' jackets and pants. It looks as though color is out there. But the truth is that color is a subjective experience. It is not out there at all. Color does not exist until it's created in our eye brain system. Well then what is out there?

We see the world we think we see. It is nothing like a camera recording what's out there. It's a highly intelligent and complex system creating our sensory experience.

I had already realized that we can never know what is out there directly and all we ever know is our interaction with what is out there. We can never stand outside of ourselves to see it objectively. We can never know what it is, outside of our perception of it. But now I could see in detail how this pertained to visual perceptions, particularly our perceptions of color.

All we know of the external world is our interaction with it. We can only know it by interacting with it and by experiencing that interaction through the medium of our own senses, subjectively.

We take on faith that what we produce in our sensory system has some relationship with whatever is out there.

We know only our interaction with the outside world and we know only our subjective experience of that interaction.

We theorize about photons, but even our idea of photons is a concept that we have created. We can never know what is out there directly. All we ever know is our subjective perception or conception of our interaction with it. I had seen this in a more global philosophical sense many year before, but now I was seeing it dramatically at the physiological level of the neurological processing that goes on in our out eye-brain.

Color is not out there any more than is sweet, sour, odor, touch, heat, cold or texture. This was beginning to give me that same feeling I got when I tried to think of the universe as having no outside. I saw so clearly, that this whole compelling reality, that we see, is not at all out there in the way that we perceive it. Something is out there, and we are subjectively perceiving our interaction with it. But what is out there we can never know directly. All we can ever know is our subjective experience, of our interaction with it, from our point of view.

CHAPTER FOUR: PERCEPTION

Bugs

As the day begins to heat up, the bugs that have hatched out in the new warmth swarm. We are running so fast, no bug can keep up with us as we whiz by. One little bug makes an attempt to land, but the wind we make as we run blows him or her away. No time for bugs today. For the first few minutes of the race hidden in my hooded sweatshirt, I'm not recognized as a woman. What will I do when the men around me realize? At what point should I reveal my gender? Will the men be angry and shoulder me out of the race? Will the crowds be hostile, since I'm doing something so far out of the accepted social norms—something no woman is supposed to do? Running in public is considered unlady-like and abnormal. And what will the police and the officials do when they find out? Will I be arrested?

I'm very well aware I'm doing something I'm not allowed to be doing. In my quiet way, I'm challenging the structures of social convention and going against the rules of sports; and I know it. My mind wanders and focused for a moment on a bug that seems to be lost, sort of like me.... A lone bug buzzing on a different flight pattern from her companions, like me. It's strange to think that bugs have perceptions. They have eyes and antennae with which they sense their environment.

What is perception and how do we perceive?

The bug eye samples the same bouncing photons as we do. But, when those photons fall on the eye of the bug, the bug creates quite a different image of the external world; equally valid and useful,

44

equally real to the bug; perhaps even equally beautiful. But quite a different view of so-called external reality than we have.

I had thought it over before. I had seen that our neural network, sensory organs and brain are interacting with the outside world in this highly structure and highly organized dynamic way, which has evolved in and by the very world it is sensing. I could see that it is in and by and through this highly structured, dynamic, intelligent organization that we construct and create our perceptual realities.

This was beginning to have some of that same feeling of paradox I had whenever I contemplated the nature of reality, the nature of this self-creating universe. Only in the case of perception, the paradox is that we can never know anything objectively or directly. We can only know our interaction with it and we can only know that interaction subjectively. The nature of that interaction is implicit in the structure of our nervous system.

Just as there is nowhere outside the universe from which to observe it, there is nowhere outside our perceptions from which to perceive.

We find ourselves with an intricate, intelligent eye-brain system, which interacts with the very cosmos which has evolved us.

The universe evolves complex living, perceiving systems with which it perceives itself.

I knew this was right, but it was so far away from how everyone else was thinking of the nervous system: as a machine or a computer. I could see that the nervous system is nothing like a machine or a computer.

Our subjective experience of color appears to be nothing like a voltage potential.

We can stick an electrode into a bunch of neurons and measure the voltage potentials. This is nothing like our subjective experience of color, taste, smell, hearing or touch. I had mused about this many years ago.

What are these delicate pinks, the oranges, the blues, the greens, the nuances and shades of color that we directly experience? Where are the subtle pastel pinks, apricots, oranges and lavenders of a misty sunrise, the magnificent purples, mauves and expansive oranges of a brilliant summer sunset, the vibrant reds, greens and oranges of a field of poppies? A subjective experience is a totally different order of being than electrical impulses in a neuron or in a system of neurons. This is the modern version of the mind-body problem.

Perception, that is, our subjective experience of perceiving, is an entirely different sort of phenomena than the firing of neurons, and yet, I had seen that it is exactly the same thing.

The nervous system is full of little blips of energy running around, voltage potentials, highly structured neurons, cells, ganglia, cortical regions and deep brain structures. To nature there is absolutely no gap at all between the electrical and biochemical activities of the brain and nervous system and our perceptions of what we consider the outside world. There is no problem for nature in going from varying voltage potentials to complex patterns in our cortex to our sensation of blue. So if we are making a problem out of it, it must be because we are not understanding what either mind or body is.

I remembered the thoughts I'd had years before in which I had realized that any universe that could evolve perception could not be entirely mechanical. Indeed my self-creating existence is not mechanical, because a mechanical system is one designed and created by something other than itself. And here All-That-Exists is creating itself in this most mysterious and miraculous way.

Neurons and neuronal systems simply take on different voltages. How can it be that different voltages are perceived by us as different colors. Our subjective experience of color seems to be an entirely different kind of thing, an immaterial thing. How can an externally measured voltage be subjectively experienced inwardly as a color? Yet it is. What is the translation between voltage and the subjective experience of color?

I could see that certain combinations of voltages in certain especially structured combinations of cells in various parts of the brain correspond exactly to our subjective experiences of color, faces, words, sounds, language and everything else. I could see clearly, for example, that the visual system is creating what I, whatever or whoever this "I" is, perceive as color. Through its structure and organization, the visual system takes the voltage changes occasioned by the impinging of photons on the photoreceptors, and then processes these signals through the retina to the ganglia cells, which carry the processed signals to higher centers, up into the layers of the visual cortex and, from there, into the associative areas and sensory of the brain.

I saw that information is actually being created in the visual system itself. I had already developed a different way of thinking about information. I saw that these higher level cells, in a sense, know something more than each single receptor cell knows. More than that, these higher levels "know" even more than the sum total of all the receptor cells, taken together, know.

For example, by viewing these specially constructed configurations of inputs from receptor cells and secondary cells, the bipolar cells can create an entire spectrum of contrast that can code for what we eventually perceive as color, within it, in the form of sliding voltage potentials that are transmitted to the next layer of cells, which further processes these signals and sends them on to the next level. How then does that voltage become translated into color; into that enigmatic, insubstantial, inward, subjective experience of color?

I went to Jerry with these insights. First, that color is not in the outside world; that color is created in the individual nervous system. And second, how could it be that these voltages, these complex organized systems of changing voltage potential can be perceived by us as color? They seemed to be two ontologically distinct things. One is a little bit of voltage on a cell membrane. The other is an entirely subjective experience of the color blue in the sky.

Jerry was delighted at my thinking and assigned Leibnitz for me to read.

Leibnitz is a philosopher, and lawyer by trade, who was a contemporary of Newton and who invented the calculus at the same time as Newton. He wrote on perception: If you think of the nervous system, (I'm paraphrasing him) you think of the perceptual machine as a big mill, with parts working against each other and you go inside the mill, you see all the parts working, the gears turning the levers going up and down. But nowhere, he said, do you find perception or anything to explain perception. By that he meant the subjective experience of perception, that is, what we subjectively see.

Perception is not explained by the mechanical workings of the mill and perception is not explained by the electrical activity of the nervous system. There is nothing to explain our subjectively experienced, immaterial, direct, qualitative, experience of perceiving what we perceive.

Exactly! This is what I had seen. It seemed to be an insurmountable obstacle. I had thought and thought and thought about this problem. Here is the nervous system, highly structured in time and space with the voltages and electric potentials running all around it, and we see a visual world full of color, motion, action and objects all out there appearing to be exactly as we see it, while all the time we are actually creating it.

Jerry used to say that we are sort of like the blind man with a stick. Only our stick is a very sophisticated and intelligent visual system. This blind man sitting in a tower would hear the shutter banging at a certain frequency and he'd know that the wind was blowing north by north east at twenty knots, that the fish would be running in the harbor, that the on-shore breeze would allow the boats to harvest the fish, that tonight's fish chowder would be plentiful and the men would be at home, and that therefore more babies would be conceived on this night than on the nights the men were out working overtime or drinking, and so forth.

The eye is an outpost of the brain. All that comes into our visual system is a smattering of photons picked up by the rhodopsin in our visual receptors. That is all we know, all that comes in, those photons. And out of that rain of photons, the mind brain constructs our entire visual experience.

What relation does our distinctive subjectively experienced sensory world have to these changing voltage potentials? How can a voltage potential be seen by us as a color, or a colored object? In looking for the answer of the mind-body problem I could see that we are viewing the mind and the body incorrectly.

There is no mind body gap in nature. Nature has no problem with voltage potential being subjectively experienced by us as the color purple, or green or red or as objects, or heaviness, or coldness or heaviness or soft or sweetness. Yet none of those qualities are out there in our environment, and none of these qualities are in the voltage potentials of nerve cells.

A mechanical system is essentially a dead system, which works according to the laws of applied force and linearity. You move this lever and it turns that wheel. I had seen that this mind-body problem is a delusion born of a misunderstanding of the fundamental nature of the universe and of life itself.

I saw clearly that we cannot account for subjective experience by the workings of our nervous system as long as we think of the nervous system as being a mechanistic system.

How then do we account for perception?

I thought about what Jerry has said, that the nervous system is the machine and the subjective experience is just the processes of that machine. I could see clearly that there was nothing other than the nervous system and its processes. There is no "ghost in the machine." I could see that there is nothing added to the nervous system outside of it, which, like an invisible soul, enters into the machine and perceives the TV screen. Mind is not one substance and body another. All there is is the brain and its workings, but this can't explain how our inner perceptions arise.

I had realized, however, that process alone is insufficient to account for subjective perception. Process, too, is an outside view of the workings of a machine. A grain mill has a process, but it has no subjective experience.

I had long ago realized that our perceptions and thoughts are an *inside view* of the processes of our nervous system. Process alone is insufficient to account for perception. There must also be this *self-reflexive, inside view* of process of itself.

But it is not just us looking at the inside of our nervous system. It is the insideness of the view of the processes of themselves that accounts for perception.

But what kind of machine process has a self-reflexive, inside view of its own workings? What is the inside view? And, what has the inside view? This insideness of view cannot be explained by the machine or its processes.

If body is all there is, then I reasoned, it must be a different kind of body than our material view of the universe has hither to allowed us to conceive because it also includes mind as its own inside perspective on its own processes.

Our subjective experience is the inside view that "we" have of the workings of our nervous system. The coordinated voltage potentials seen from the outside correspond exactly to our subjective experiences as viewed from the inside. Subjective experience is an inner perspective on the same sequence of events we see from the outside as coordinated voltage potentials in the nervous system.

The question no one was asking was, "What kind of system has an inside view of its own activity?" What wondrous kind of system is this, then, which has an inside view of itself? No one was talking about this. No one even seemed to see it except me. Everyone was thinking of the perceptual system as a complex machine. Indeed this was the entire focus of the Artificial Intelligence Program at MIT, affectionately known as "A.I."

But I could see that this inside view is something no machine can ever do; even the most sophisticated computer relies on a human with a mind to design, to build and to perceive it. A mechanical system, that is, one built by humans out of inanimate parts, never can have an inside view of itself, therefore, the nervous system is not a purely mechanical system, even though it may have its mechanical aspects.

O.K., so the nervous system has an inside view, but what inside the nervous system views?

What is it that actually perceives? Who is it, then, who sees?

I began to trace the nervous system — the visual system. I could trace the response in the photo-receptors up through the bipolars, the horizontal cells, the amacrines that detect motion, to the ganglion cells the project up to the lateral geniculate. I could see how the neurons were especially wired in order to create contrast and to detect motion. I could see the nervous impulses projecting upwards from the lateral geniculate to the layers of the visual cortex that, as Hubel and Wiesel at Harvard had shown, map these neural impulses onto coordinated columns of cells, each one sensitive to a different orientation of line and to different directions of motions.

Beyond that, the impulses go on up through the associative cortices and combine with stored information in complex recursive circuits through the basal ganglia, thalamus, and myriad other brain structures and thence on to the higher cortical areas.

I could see that more and more information is being generated in the system but I could never find any "who." I could never find any "one" who was looking at all this information. It was an eerie feeling, as if no one was at home. All this information was being generated and juxtaposed but no one was there to see it. It was a paradox.

I had seen that the sensory world we perceive is a creation of our own nervous system. The visual system creates color; the visual system creates its entire holographic three-dimensional world of objects and motions we experience. I knew that the nervous system doesn't just receive passively, it actively creates its own subjective experience of its own internal model of its interactions with whatever is out there.

But now I was seeing clearly, in detail, that the nervous system creates subjective experience. Furthermore, our subjective experiences *are* the processes of our brain self-reflexively, self-experiencing themselves, subjectively from the inside. I saw that subjective experience is not localized in only one place in the brain. There is not just one part of the brain that is capable of this inner self-viewing, and every other part is just a mechanical system with no innerness of self-perspective. Rather the brain as a whole works to create the totality of the subjective experience that it itself reflexively perceives. This curious self-reflexivity of inner viewing by means of which the brain is looking at itself, or to say it differently, the processes of the brain *are* the very subjective experiences that the brain experiences from the inside of itself.

This is incredible. The brain is looking at itself, subjectively from the inside out!

Further, I saw that this innerness of view cannot possibly arise from the juxtapositioning of purely mechanistic parts, because mechanistic parts are external and extended, by definition, and therefore are not capable of internal self-viewing.

I concluded that it must mean that all the parts of the nervous system must have in innerness of self-viewing in which their own processes are, to themselves, their own subjective experiences accessible only to them. This would mean that the retinal cells have an innerness of self-viewing that is accessible to themselves, and so would the lateral geniculate and so would the levels of cortical processing have their own type of innerness of self-viewing. These innerness of self-viewing compile as the systems compile in complexity so that new dimensions of self-reflexive subjectivity emerge at the cortical level.

What kind of system is capable of this subjective innerness of view of the processes of their own activities, in which those activities *are subjective experience,* to the system whose activities they are?

I saw that the fact of the existence of this innerness of self-viewing, and subjective self-experiencing, must be fundamental to natural existence. Furthermore I saw that this means that what we call the material universe cannot be the external, extended, massive reality that we have conjectured that we see.

Rather, I was looking for a monistic substance that is more fundamental than matter, energy and atoms that includes this innerness of perspective in its intrinsic nature. The fact that a material object—the brain, which looks like a pinkish gray conglomeration of cells from the outside—is having subjective experiences from the inside, forces us to change our entire conceptual models of the fundamental nature of physical reality.

To summarize, I saw clearly in detail that the brain does not contain something that sees the activities of the brain subjectively. Rather the dynamic activities and process of the entire brain, and, in particular, the cortex and higher levels are, to the brain itself, subjective experience. The brain is creating its own subjectively perceptual model of its own interaction with whatever is out there, through the dynamical structures and activities that comprise the brain.

There really is no one at home looking at all this activity. Rather, our subjective experiences are the reflexive, subjective, self-viewing of the processes of our brain, which identify themselves as us. No one is viewing all this activity. *The activity of the brain is our subjective perception, in which the brain's processes are a paradoxical self-viewing, subjectively, self-reflexive, self-identity-self viewing.*

In a sense then although we say that no one is home viewing all this, in truth, we can say, more profoundly, the brain *is* the home and the brain *is* the "one" who is both experiencing itself subjectively, and creating the activity that when seen from the outside, by something other than itself, looks like fluctuating patterns of voltage, in a mass of brain cells, but from the inside *is* the subjective experience itself.

This means most profoundly that the universe cannot be the strictly material, mechanistic, extended construct that we have imagined it to be. The fact that subjective perception can and does arise in a massive object, namely the brain, indicates that the universe is not as we have conceived it to be. This has profound consequence for physics and for our entire concept of reality as we will see.

CHAPTER FIVE: FORM AND WHOLENESS

Tree

The sounds of men breathing, the muffled beat of running shoes on pavement surround me. Now the men know and have accepted me as a fellow runner! We chat as we speed along. This is the way I want life to be — men and women sharing all aspects of life together.

I want to heal the splits and end this stupid war between the sexes once and for all. I want men to be able to have feelings and show feelings of tenderness. I want men to be able to participate in the miracle of the birth of their own children and to be able to spend time raising their kids.

I want women to be able to have independence, take initiative, be strong in body and mind. I want men and women to be free to be whoever they most truly are and to discover and develop their unique talents and abilities, whatever they are, and not have to fit into stereotypes and the rigid prescriptions of society.

I want to redefine the forms of social conventions to broaden and free self-expression and self-discovery for everyone no matter their gender, race, ethnicity, political persuasion, nationality or any other accident of birth. I want each unique and valuable individual to be free to develop their unique talents and abilities and to be able to live in freedom and safety.

On the left towers an enormous tree, an outrageous natural form, building itself out of the materials and energy of the air and soil. The tree reaches its arms to the sky, its roots buried deep within the nourishing soil, its buds swelling in the April sun expanding as the embryonic flowers, furled inside, grow. I watch this glorious self-building tree whirl by, marveling at this form, which has evolved over millions of years on earth.

How and why does anything in nature have the form it has?

My thoughts on living systems had brought me to ask what is form and how does it occur in living systems? What is this as-a-wholeness that seems to characterize self-forming systems?

Physics explains the world in terms of mass, energy, space and time. But these parameters are not enough to account for the developing form of things. In physics there is no principle to explain why or how anything has form.

Historically, in the mythologies of the world, it was the female divinity who brought forth form. And when the female was eliminated from Western mythology, this bringer of forms then disappeared both from religious and scientific thought.

I had seen that the intrinsic nature of living systems embodies this self-forming principle from within. The Female Divinity brings forth forms out of her own body/mind from within, and the systems remain, even in their individuality, part of the Divine Matrice. It is a totally different act of creation than the external designer/builder of the mechanical world.

This inner, autonomous, self-formative, self-building is a property of the egg cell, the primal living unit, from which all individual living forms, both male and female, arise.

But what causes form? I wondered.

Plato took forms as patterns or ideal templates, which had a metaphysical existence that informed the specific shapes of things. Aristotle took form to mean the actual entity itself, which he believed was formed according to its internal essence.

I conceived of form as an intrinsic dynamic self-activity through which the entity achieves and maintains its identity as itself.

Form, as a concept, applies to all natural systems. A system is a form. A form is ultimately a system. And living systems are a type of natural system that form themselves into various self-generating, self-maintaining dynamic organizational forms, from the materials and energy of their environment.

I realized that this self-formative power was not something residing in an already existing living system. It was not some elan vitale in the machine.

Rather, the very nature and existence of the system is that it is an expression of this formative principle from within. These natural forms are not the result of anything external to the systems. Rather they express a deep principle of the Matrice itself.

I had seen that the living system isn't just organizing itself into patterns. It is organizing itself into existence.

This self-organization is a type of self-formation in which the parts interact to form a whole.

The form of something is determined by its organizational structure. What we call form embodies the organizational structure. When we form clay into a sculpture we are imposing an organizational structure onto the clay. In this case it is not the clay forming itself into a sculpture. The form, that is, the organizational structure, is imposed from the outside. When computer designers write a program that defines a graph or shape or collection of dots they are imposing form externally. This has been the model in religion and science of a mechanistic world in which form is imposed from the outside on something other than the organizational structure that is formed.

Because systems engineers believed living systems were mechanical automatons, and that one could design and build a machine with the properties of life, they couldn't see that this intrinsic autonomous self-formative-self-activity of living systems, is an example of an intrinsically paradoxical, self-reflexive, self-formative principle in nature, which can not be designed into a machine or an electronic model. Indeed if one has to design it, it would not be autonomously self-forming.

No one seemed to be seeing this paradox.

I called systems that organize themselves into existence, Teleosystemic, from the Greek word, "Teleos," which means end seeking, or acting towards some end goal. Why? Because these self-building systems, as they build themselves, take actions that are towards the end goal of self-creating, or self-building an organization that at each moment in time transcends what it was before.

But what is this paradoxical, self-formative self-activity, I wondered — that activity by which the living system designs, builds and activates itself from within? It is not something that exists in or in addition to the system. Rather, this activity by which the living system designs and builds itself, is intrinsic to and the essence of the system itself.

Living systems do not design themselves anew in the present moment, as the mechanic designs a machine or as pattern-generating computer algorithms seem to design patterns. Rather, living systems have designed themselves over billions of years of evolution. Even the chemical systems out of which the living systems evolved had evolved for billions of years before they became what we would call living, that is, being enclosed in a membrane that separates it and selectively joins it with its environment and having the ability to continuously construct itself from the materials and energy of its environment.

When you look at a living system, you see that it is composed of internal organs, parts and processes, which act together to form the whole. Each part functions not only for its own benefit but also for the benefit of every other part. The stomach digests food, which feeds the liver, which in turn helps the stomach to digest food. The heart pumps blood to every cell in the body, which in turn provides the heart with food and oxygen so it can create and maintain itself, and so on. There is a circularity in which the activity and existence of each part is necessary to the activity and existence of every other part, which in is necessary for the existence and activity of the whole. *I called it a mutually integrated, reciprocity of cause and effect.*

Systems engineers were saying that this is what accounted for the ability of living systems to organize themselves, that is, that self-organization was explained by noting that each part in the system participates in the production and transformation of every other part.

Certainly there is a complexity of interrelationships among the parts and processes, each of which acts to affect and to regulate, and to be affected by and regulated by, and to aid in the continuous production and transformation of every other part. But is such an interrelations of parts enough to account for the emergence of a functional organism, or is it simply a description of what such a living system is already doing?

To systems designers, self-organization was the production of a set of patterns of interrelationships such that, the operation of the system produced the patterns of interrelationships among the parts.

The problem with this was that they assumed the existence of the system and its operation to begin with. They assumed the existence of the system, which then produced the patterns. They didn't see the paradox that until the living system acts to organize itself it doesn't exist. The system isn't just producing patterns of relationships among its parts. It is the patterns of relationships, which embody itself as an existant entity.

But how can it act to organize itself into these patterns of relationships until it exists as these patterns of relationships? Once the system exists, yes, it is observed to have this characteristic mutually reciprocally interrelationship of parts, but this does not explain how it can exist in the first place, how this mutually reciprocal interrelationship of parts can come about.

Nor does it explain how the mutual interrelation of parts can lead to a functional organism. The mutual interrelation of parts is assumed to be the same as a functional organism, but is it? And if so how? What about the universe allows parts to come together to function as wholes? This is true even at the molecular level. What allows atoms to come together to form molecules? It is an intrinsic self-formative ability of the matrice, a characteristic of the universe, which is so taken for granted that it is not seen.

What, then, is the relation of the internal parts to the whole?

In the case of a mechanical system, the designer/builder specifies the parts and then specifies their dynamic interrelationships in such a way to get the machine or computer to work as a whole functioning system. Each part is specified, and its relation with each other part is specified. Then the machine or computer is built according to plans.

In the living system there is no human designer/builder to specify the parts and their interactions. There is nothing else, no vital force, no little green men. Parts, processes, and their interactive interrelationships, are all there are and they organize themselves into the whole.

It seems an insolvable paradox. In a living organism, there exists a paradoxical reflexivity wherein the whole is both the cause and the result of the interactive interrelationships among all the parts, processes and activities, which make up the system.

There is a pile of molecules on the table, all the molecules of the living system. But it is not a living system. Those same molecules in a frog are a living system. The difference between the pile of molecules and the frog is the intrinsic, paradoxical, self-reflexive, self-acting-as-a-wholeness by which the organism creates itself into existence as a system of organized parts and processes.

How then does the living system act to form itself into a whole?

All the parts act together to mutually create themselves and every other part, but only as parts of the whole.

A living organism is a system of interacting parts. But is it the interactions of parts, which creates the system, or is it the system-as-a-whole that creates, and specifies, the interaction of parts?

How do the parts (know how to) organize themselves into this particular whole? Or do they? They are organized into the whole by the whole. But the whole doesn't exist apart from the organization of the parts. So, how can the whole act to organize the parts into itself until it exists as an organized whole? There is no independent "whole" that can act to form itself out of the parts. Therein lies the paradox.

The parts and their interactions cannot exist except as part of the whole organism. So to say that the whole is reducible to the parts and their interactions is a mistake. The parts and their interactions are necessary but not sufficient to account for the whole. But the whole is not anything added to the parts and their interactions.

What then is this "whole"?

When I describe the properties of a whole frog, for example; it breathes, it hops, it catches flies, these properties cannot be fully described in terms of the interrelated interactions of its parts, for example its eyes, its stomach, its legs, its nervous system, even though the properties of the whole depend on and are the result of the parts and their interrelated interactions.

Hopping is not a property of molecules, stomachs, or even of the processes or the relationships between hearts and livers. Hopping is a new property that the whole system has which cannot be reduced to a description of its parts and/or their processes or interactions, even though, the parts and their interrelated processes and interactions are all there is in the system.

I called this the *Principle of Irreducibility.*

What allows, or causes, the whole living system organism to form? It is a mystery, which we do not even see. This is the paradoxical self-formation of living systems that I had seen in the moss: this "acting as a whole."

This acting as a whole to create itself into existence as a whole entity is beyond linear cause and effect. It is, I realized, an example of a new concept, which I called The Law of Paradoxical Self-Formation of Whole Living Systems.

This "Law" goes beyond the individual living system to the very basic nature of the Matrice. The Universe is of such a nature that living systems spontaneously form. What about the Universe makes it possible for living systems to form themselves?

Everyone was trying to explain this ability of living systems to organize themselves by "process."

A process is simply an ongoing cycle of activity, which is organized, or which organizes itself in time and space. Mechanical processes are organized by the designer/builder. Living processes organize themselves.

But I could see that although the paradoxical self-formation of systems, is both a cause and result of the processes of living systems, it is not itself a process, because it is beyond linear cause and effect, it is in some sense teleological. The present anticipates the future. In the embryo, the notochord forms itself in order to become a backbone. Mechanical process, in contrast, occurs in time, the past flowing causally into the present into the future.

What then explains how a living system can form itself as a whole organized system? The parts, the forces of interaction between the parts, the interrelationships of the parts, even the self-activity of the living system are all necessary, but not sufficient, to explain how the whole forms itself as a whole entity.

Gregory Bateson and Humberto, both came up with the idea, based on McCulloch's work, that there is a Mind in Nature, which organizes living systems.

Gregory Bateson wrote a book entitled "Mind in Nature" in which he revived a pre-industrial age notion of nature having a mind. The ancient Athenians thought of God as a "Self-thinking Mind." Mary Baker Eddy conceived of Divine Mind as the creating and organizing force in nature. The Hindu culture regards Mind as being, not inside the head, but outside as the Ultimate Reality, behind the illusion of physical reality. Even Newton made the analogy that: Objects of physical reality are to the mind of God, as ideas are to the human mind.

I realized that the issue of mind had re-emerged because mechanical (human designed) systems always require a designer, with a mind, to design them. Paradoxical self-creation is not possible for a machine.

But systems thinkers were quick to say that this "mind," which was seen as the organizer was not a separate entity, like a soul inhabiting the machine; rather the mind, as they conceived it, was the process of the machine.

This solved the mind body split, it was thought.

But it seemed to me that it intensified the mind body split and still ignored the fundamental paradox.

Mind is the inner subjective experience of nervous system. Human mind is the inner subjective experience of human nervous system. This itself is something completely inexplicable by a mechanical or electronic model.

Mind is the internal view of the system of itself and its changes, as it interacts with whatever is out there. I had seen this from my work on perception.

Process is still an external view.

So process isn't mind.

Nor does process explain how the living system organizes itself. To be sure, the process we see, of a living system organizing itself, is a process. But to say that it is process that organizes process is a tautology, and to call this "mind" seemed to me to confuse the quality of subjective experience with the quality of self-organization without explaining either.

Because systems designers wanted to design machines that could think and that could create themselves, like living systems, they couldn't see that it is precisely these two phenomena, namely the ability to perceive itself from within, and the ability to paradoxically create itself into being that are intrinsic to living organisms that can never be mimicked by human made machines, including computers, no matter how complex, or how many servo loops.

I realized, that in order to explain and understand living systems, we need an entirely new shift in perspective. Living systems cannot be explained in terms of the old paradigms.

We need a new understanding of nature that says that the intrinsic self-activity of the living system, by which it acts to create itself as a whole, is a dynamic, paradoxical, continuous act of self-creation, self-organization and self-formation.

This law of self-formation is a result of the fundamental nature of the Matrice, which is intrinsically, paradoxically Self Creative. The Matrice creates itself as a whole, out of itself, in to itself. This paradoxical Self-Creating is prior to the subject/object split.

You can never explain life if you start with the model of human-made systems. Living systems design, build, and maintain themselves as parts of the Self Creating Matrice. There must be an understanding of nature, which starts with the paradoxical Self-Creation of the universe and conceives of life as an expression of the fundamental, paradoxical, self-creation of the Matrice. This is my entirely new way of viewing reality.

The Universal Self-Creating Matrice creates Itself into all the myriad living forms that we see and that we are.

In the Divine Act of Self-Creation there is no gap between Divinity and Reality. All-There-Is is The Divine Self-Creating Matrice. All existence is Divine as it is. Everything in Nature is the Divine Matrice paradoxically creating Itself, out of Itself, into Itself.

It is the manifestation of this intrinsic, self-formative ability of the Matrice, in which the organism acts as a whole to reflexively self-form itself out of the material and energy of its environment, and yet it cannot do so until it has already done so, which is the paradox, the mystery and the wonder I had seen so long ago in the moss. It is this paradoxical self-building of living systems that embodies the self-formative capacity of nature. This self-formative capacity of the intrinsic self-active, self-interactive Self-Creating Matice is fundamental to nature and to All-That-Exists.

Chapter Six: Evolution

Swamp

It's too long, too long to wait for spring here. But, the buds haven't given up. Their subtle swelling is a statement of their faith. Even late April flurries can't fool them now.

You can smell spring on the wind, wafting a scent of green from a thousand miles south of here.

The days are longer than the nights. The heat of the sun is awakening the trees. The sap is rising in their trunks and running out their tiny twigs, turning the grey browns of winter to soft reds, purples and olive greens.

The crowds thin out in this wooded, swampy place, away from houses. Last year's leaves lie in chaotic disarray under these bare woods, while next year's leaves furl inside of brown, shiny bud coats.

The air is full of the primitive pulsing of the spring peepers. I have seen these little tree frogs at night with a flashlight. It's not hard. They just sit there and watch you, enchanted by the light. These little tiny creatures make that high peeping sound that fills every bog and wet place in the spring. Thousands of little voices fill the night in a primeval rhythm that makes your heart rise up.

They peep in the daytime too, but if you move, sudden silence. They all stop their peeps, telling you that you are being watched. Tiny, fragile frogs with their little frog brains, sitting waist deep in water, singing the only note they know how to sing, having sung it for millions upon millions of years; singing it before mammals were even heard of; singing it for time spans that makes the entire span of human existence seem like a minute.

We Homo Sapiens are running upright, on dry land, with our

strange two-legged gait, and running shorts. Our legs and arms are moving rhythmically, oppositely, in perfect balance. We are pulling air in and out of our lungs. Our blood, like currents in a salty, ancient sea is coursing through our bodies.

We are part of this ancient life, which has come to us through billions of years of evolution, through the bodies of fishes and amphibians, and before that, in the lives of amoebas and coelenterates.

The sound of spring peepers is an affirmation of that ancient life, a celebration of ourselves, before we were human, as we evolved in quiet warm seas for billions of years, to emerge on to land, to live and to run today.

The tree frogs prefer the bogs, warmed by the sun, where they can peep their nocturnal songs and feel again life pulsing through their cold-blooded bodies and perform the spring mating ritual to the beats of a thousand tiny drums.

Yes, the sound of Peepers never fails to make my heart soar with the joy of life on earth, this rich and abundant planet, covered with living forms.

I think of how it must have been when the first living forms on earth made the first sounds that rose up from the warm moist living surface through the new fragile air. The earth is singing its first song to the huge, vast cosmos.

How did all of this evolve? How did we evolve in all this? What is this evolution?

Evolution means the process of development of systems from the simple to the complex, over time. It's always amazed me that there has been so much controversy around this idea of evolution as if one had to choose between God or evolution.

Life took billions of years to evolve a single cell. Then from those first cells evolved all other life forms. But did this imply a mindless, meaningless mechanistic process devoid of Divinity? I didn't think so.

The phyla are broad categories of living creatures. The simplest phyla, the protozoa or single celled animals, evolved around five billions years ago, judging from fossil remains.

Animals evolved as the hollow-bodied coelenterates like hydras, corals and jellyfish that at first were colonies of single-celled animals with specialized functions. Then the phyla of worms evolved, then the mollusks, like clams and snails, and the octopus. Next the phyla of animals in exoskeletons evolved, the echinoderms or spiny-skin creatures like starfish, the crustacea like lobsters; then the spiders and insects.

Finally four hundred million years ago primitive animals with an internal supporting rod appeared. From them came the cartilaginous fishes like sharks and skates. Then the bony fish with spinal cords enclosed in a vertebral column appeared—then the amphibians, the reptiles and the birds and finally the mammals. This revelation filled me with wonder.

Each evolutionary phylogenetic stage represents a step in the increased complexity of living systems.

I had seen from my work on living systems that a living system is a manifestation of the intrinsic, self-formative ability of the Matrice, in which the organism acts as a whole to reflexively self-form itself out of the material and energy of its environment, as a self-generating, reciprocally interrelating system of self-organizing parts and processes. Yet it doesn't exist, and so cannot act to organize itself, until it is organized by itself, (by the very parts and processes which comprise it.) Thus its existence is paradoxical, that is, the result precedes and is simultaneous with the cause.

Could evolution explain this paradox? I wondered. Each living thing is, after all, the result of billions of years of evolution. Each present life form extends back in time in an unbroken line of generation from the first living cells.

What is the cause of the interrelated interactions of the parts? This is where the complexity occurs, I realized.

The basic parts are the atoms and molecules, which make up the organism. These are organized or organize themselves into complex biochemical and biological processes and compounds, which ultimately are organized or organize themselves into the organs, which carry out the functions of the organism.

The organs of an organism accomplish the diverse functions of the whole in specialized ways. In the primitive life forms, the mouth was the stomach, the intestine, the excretory organ and the body cavity. As organisms evolved, the functions differentiated. Indeed this process of differentiation is crucial to evolution, both in terms of the complexity of the individual organism and also in terms of the diversity of the species.

We can see this clearly in embryonic development, where the prototype cell, as it divides and multiplies, at each generation becomes a group of more differentiated cells, which interact with each other in more and more complex ways, as the functions of the embryo become more and more defined and refined.

We see this same pattern in the evolution and differentiation of the species. And you see that in the most recently evolved species the internal functions have become more and more differentiated into more and more complex organs.

The increased complexity is the result of the increase in differentiation and multiplication of interrelated parts and processes.

Not only do the individuals of the emerging species become more complex, but the entire living fabric of the earth becomes more complex as more and more members of more and more diverse species interact.

It appears that life is one phenomenon with a multitude of different forms.

Why? How? I wondered.

How could life evolve in the first place?

When I was at the University of California in La Jolla in the 60's Harold Urey, the Nobel in thermodynamics, was there. He and others like Prigogene and Miller studied systems in which certain types of energy, added in certain ways, to the system, increased rather than decreased the order. These are called systems far from thermal equilibrium. The most notable of this type of system is of course the living system.

Urey and Miller had wondered if living systems could have formed from the chemical reactions that were taking place on the surface of a primal earth. So they put together, in a flask, some methane, water, nitrogen, carbon dioxide, and other compounds approximating the primal atmosphere of the earth. They then sent a spark of electricity through it like a lightning bolt, and lo and behold, amino acids, the building blocks of life, formed.

This meant that amino acids can, when energy is added, spontaneously form from a non-living solution of chemicals on the primitive earth. Of course, amino acids are not themselves living, but they form the universal building blocks of proteins, which are the structural components of living systems.

How can the actual living systems have arisen from these molecules? I wondered?

Then my biochemistry professor gave me a book published in 1964 by a Russian Scientist A.P. Oparin, entitled: Life: Its Nature, Origin and Development. In this remarkable book Oparin sets out a theory of how life could have evolved on earth from solutions of chemicals.

Oparin sketched the picture of the primitive earth as a hot, wet, lifeless planet surrounded by clouds of methane, ammonia, water vapor and carbon dioxide. On the planet were pools of hot liquid, rich with naturally occurring organic molecules. Carbon compounds, amino acids and other complex molecules simmered in these pools warmed by the sun.

More recent experiments have shown that you can take a flask full of water, insert gases that existed on the primitive earth and under the influence of ultraviolet radiation many of the molecules found in living systems will spontaneously form, including ribonucleic acids, the RNA templates for protein formation, Adenosine Tri-Phosphate, the universal energy carrier in living systems, amino acids, a host of complex hydrocarbon compounds.

In these seething chemical reactions, which were taking place, long chains of hydrocarbons and other complex substances formed. These chemical reactions were catalyzed by enzymes, which are proteins made of amino acids, and form stable cycles in which various products were continuously formed, including the substance that began the cycle. These processes depended on the continuous input of certain types of energy and materials, but once established maintained a dynamic continuity and stability.

Finally primitive, continuous cycles of fermentation, which formed the basis for early metabolism, reactions evolved, in which energy was transferred from molecule to molecule by the formation and breaking apart of hydrogen bonds.

Oparin hypothesized that in these pools, colloidal coacervate droplets formed, enclosing portions of these seething chemical solutions. Once the droplets formed, their membranes defined and inside and an outside.

Then the droplets could selectively concentrate certain molecules within themselves, out of the environment.

Inside the coacervate globules, enzymatic reactions formed stable, dynamic cycles. This may have gone on for billions of years.

Eventually the globule utilized the energy and materials generated in its internal chemical reactions to continuously structure itself. When this happened, the first simple pre-cellular, living chemical systems came into existence.

What struck me was that chemical reactions were themselves evolving.

In the seething mass of interacting chemical compounds in the primeval pools, more and more complex molecules and long dynamically stable cyclical sequences of complex chemical reactions were emerging. This meant that the process of evolution didn't begin with life, but was also a characteristic of certain chemical systems. How could this be?

This seeming drive to spontaneously become more complex, seemed to fly in the face of what I had been taught about chemical thermodynamics.

One of my ancestral relations was Josiah Willard Gibbs, an eminent American scientist, who studied thermodynamics at Yale around the turn of the century and invented the concept of Gibbs Free Energy, which is "useable" energy.

Systems of reacting chemicals proceed in such a way as to conserve energy, but to decrease the amount of useable energy. This loss of useable energy was explained in terms of the configurations of the initial and final states — the system tending to move in the direction from order to disorder, as well as from high potential energy to low potential energy.

The measure of disorder of a system is called "entropy" and Boltzman had given it a statistical meaning.

Chemical potential energy is a measure of the reactivity of the participants. The more reactive the reactants, the higher their potential energy of reaction and the lower their stability. The chemical reaction proceeds in a direction where the products are more stable, i.e. less reactive than the reactants.

The laws of thermodynamics apply to physical as well as chemical systems. In state-change situations, for example, when you heat a pan of water, the molecules become more statistically disordered, that is the kinetic energy between the molecules increases with the heat absorbed, and the molecules bounce faster and more frequently against each other leading to the vaporization of liquid to gas.

This can be thought of as an increase in the degrees of freedom of the molecules, or a decrease in the constraints that the molecules exert on each other in moving from the liquid form to the gaseous form.

But here, in Oparin's chemical solutions, photons of light energy were being added to the system but instead of becoming more disordered, as in the case of boiling water, the system was becoming more ordered. But that order wasn't the static order of ice freezing, it was the dynamic order of complex dynamic processes and forms. The only way this order can be maintained is by the continuous flow of energy through the system, unlike the case of ice where energy flowing into the system disrupts the order.

How could this be? I had wondered.

It was then that I had taken a course in Organic chemistry. There I had studied chemical reactions in which a stream of light was shown on chemical solutions of a mixture of simple hydrocarbons and chlorine, and long chains and complex cycles of carbon compounds formed.

Here, energy was being added to the system, but instead of becoming more disordered as in the case of boiling water, the molecules in the system were becoming more complex, more ordered.

"Why?" I wondered. " What is the difference between this situation and the case where heat is added to water and the molecules become more chaotic?"

Suddenly I realized. In the case of the hydrocarbon and chlorine, the energy of the photon was actually absorbed by the chlorine molecule itself, which then broke into two highly reactive unstable radicals. These radicals then reacted with the hydrocarbon, which split apart into activated configuration states.

In contrast, in the case of the water boiling, the energy, in the form of heat, was not absorbed by the molecule, but went into producing kinetic energy between the molecules, vibrating one molecule relative to another.

The difference is that in the case where complexity spontaneously occurs, it is preceded by a highly reactive activation state in which the incoming energy is absorbed by a reactant molecule itself.

But how could this lead to complexity?

In any given chemical solution of reacting molecules, the reaction tends to proceed in the direction that reduces the chemical potential energy of the system, like water running downhill.

Every molecule in the reacting system has a shape and a chemical reactivity that defines the way it interacts with the other molecules. Once the activated molecule is formed by the absorption of energy, it becomes very reactive, that is, it is highly unstable and acts to stabilize itself by reacting with other molecules.

The activated molecule can stabilize itself and reduce the chemical potential energy of the system by joining with other molecules. This is just what it does.

It is this joining together of simpler activated molecules to form a combined, and therefore more complex product, that results in the spontaneous emergence of systems of greater complexity.

But the fact of this ability to stabilize by joining with other molecules is built into the very structure and activity of each molecule in a specific way, reflected in its configuration.

Therefore it is the interplay, of the absorption of activation energy with the energy potentials inherent in the configurations of molecules that leads to the spontaneous formation of more complex products.

So when we add energy that is absorbed by the reacting molecules themselves, the reactants move against the entropy gradient and assume more complex configurations.

Is this increase in complexity against the laws of thermodynamics?

No. Because the reaction is following the energy gradient built into the configurations of the molecules themselves.

In Oparin's pools of seething chemical reactions, the energy of the sun is absorbed by a molecule, causing it to go into an activated state. In this activated state, the molecule reacts with other molecules, causing them to join together into more complex configurations in order to stabilize themselves. Therefore, more complex forms occur spontaneously in situations where useable activation energy is supplied and absorbed by the reactants themselves in contrast to when the energy goes to increasing the kinetic energy between the participants in the reactions.

Could this same formation of activation states, factored over the energy configurations of the participants, explain the formation of stable dynamic cycles of complex reactions?

In solutions of interacting complex organic molecules, cycles of reactions would emerge usually catalyzed by an amino acid, where one of the products of the reaction was one of the reactants.

This cycle could remain intact indefinitely as long as conditions remained favorable and the needed reactants were available. Indeed, in some cases these cycles could reproduce and evolve into other cyclical chains.

Again, I saw that it was the interplay of the activation energy acting to precipitate the activation state, which in turn activates the reactions, implicit in the configurations, properties, energetic characteristics of the interacting molecules, in a suitable medium that then acts in concert to form these dynamic cycles.

In long chains of reactions, the absorbed activation energy is, in effect, passed along like a hot potato from molecule to molecule. As each molecule absorbes the energy, it subsequently regains stability by joining with other (activated) molecules or atoms, and in so doing creates more complex forms and cycles.

If the activation energy keeps pouring in, as it did from the sun in Oparin's example, and is absorbed by molecules, which then assume activated configuration states, then more and more complex processes and structures form as each reactant seeks to re-stabilize itself by joining with other compounds.

This process can be accelerated by the presence of protein molecules that act as catalysts, which become activated and act to activate other molecules, the catalysts then returning to their initial state.

So the overall thrust is for the participants in the reactions to try to assume as stable a configuration as possible, as required by the laws of thermodynamics, but the fact of the activation energy having been absorbed, and producing a destabilizing activated state, means the participants in an evolving chemical solution have to go to greater lengths to stabilize themselves, and they do this by joining with other compounds, assuming more and more complex forms, and forming dynamically stable cyclical reaction in which one of the products is one of the reactants.

If the activation energy ceases to flow, then the compounds again seek the most stable configurations, which without the continued input of activation energy, is to break up into simple forms again. Indeed this is just what happens when a living system dies.

I called these systems of interacting parts "dynamic aggregate systems", in which the parts are interacting, to distinguish them from "whole systems", in which the whole acts as a unity itself.

I was interested in the evolution of dynamic aggregate systems into whole systems.

In the process of forming more complex products and cycles, the individual atoms lose their individuality. By joining together these dynamic conglomerates of interacting parts begin to function as parts of a whole system.

Was this a key to my Law of Self-Formation of systems? I wondered.

In effect, the complexity gradient is the inverse potential energy gradient, wherever the components can achieve a more stable configuration by joining into more complex forms or stable cycles. All this is in accord with known chemical theory.

But what is this chemical energy of the system?

The chemical energy of a system is a result of the energetic configurations of the interacting parts.

So the very existence of chemical potential energy presupposes the dynamic configurations of the parts, which is what I called form.

My Law of Paradoxical Self-Formation says that a living system acts as a whole to reflexively self-form itself out of the material and energy of its environment, yet it can't act to do so until it has done so. Or to say it differently, the parts act to form the whole, but the parts don't know what whole to form until the whole exists.

The Matrice is the Divine Creator of Itself. Evolution is the Divine Self Creatrix becoming Itself. Therefore evolution is itself a Divine act. All-that-Is is designed to evolve. Designed by what? Designed by the Divine Creator. But what is the Divine Creator? The Divine Creator is All-That-Exists. No external designer is necessary, or possible, since any external designer would have to be self-created by the Divine Self-Creating Matrice, and so would be part of it, not external to it. So evolution, far from being opposed to the Divine, is a fundamental expression of the Divine, the Divine being defined as that which creates and sustains all existence.

Chapter Seven: Complexity

Woods

The woods in April are at once subtle and stark. Stark in the brilliant noonday sun and the vast expanse of clear blue sky shining through the bare branches; leaving long purple swaths of shadow behind every tree, glinting off the smooth spring bark. Subtle as that same bark turns tiny bits of lavender and mossy greens into the delicate fabric of spring,

I watch the huge bodies of trees wheel by, the near trees sliding across the far trees. The arms and branches of trees, like spokes on wheels, are revolving slowly in a kaleidoscope of changing patterns and forms.

Birds sing their new spring songs; every day more feathery journeyers arrive from the south and busy themselves claiming nesting territories, males vying for females. A complex pattern of inter-related life forms continues to evolve on this magical planet.

What is complexity?

I'd wondered this in high school.

My junior year in chemistry class with Miss Travis, who became Mrs. Peabody half way through the year, I was enthralled with the magic, mystery and beauty of the elements and their different shapes and sizes and their ability to bond with each other to form new compounds. It amazed me that atoms exist at all. Who or what could have come up with such an invention as atoms made of protons and neutrons in the nucleus surrounded by clouds of electrons. How could this be? Why not just one huge empty void?

I asked my dad, who was a professor of chemistry, if he thought of everything as made of atoms. He said that although he knew that was so, he didn't think of it as he looked around the room. But, I did. I went around thinking of everything as made up of atoms and molecules.

I was amazed by the periodic table of the elements, which showed, in a big chart, the increasing complexity of the atomic structures of atoms, from hydrogen, the simplest, to the most complex of the lactinide series. These atoms were structured in terms of increasing numbers of protons and neutrons in the nucleii and increasing numbers of electron orbitals around the nucleii.

The inner-most electron shell could contain two electrons, the next shell eight electrons and the next shell thirty-two electrons. I noticed that these were every other power of two: 2, 8 and 32, that is, two raised to the first power is two; two raised to the third power is eight; two raised to the fifth power is thirty-two. I wondered why this was. I thought it might have something with sub-systems that could be in one of two possible states, like the flip of a coin, heads or tails.

I marveled that this increasing complexity compounded in a regular ways and that the structures of the atoms allowed them to join together to make molecules. How and why would something like this exist at all? Why and how would the Self-Creating Matrice form itself into such a thing?

The more I learned about science the more I marveled at the wonder of the Divine. Why and how would all this wonder and intricate delicacy exist in the first place? And why in the way it does?

I wondered what caused the increasing complexity of the elements and why, and how, and by what, the elemental atoms were formed, or formed themselves, so that they could interact with one another.

Do atoms, like life-forms, evolve?

To evolve means to develop from simple to complex.

What is does it mean to be complex? I wondered.

To be complex simply means there are more numerous and diverse interrelations and interactions among more numerous and/or diverse parts and processes in the system.

Nature is full of systems that spontaneously become more complex under certain conditions. How is this possible?

I had called this tendency to form more complex systems, Complexification. I developed a *Theory of Complexification that says that under the right conditions simple systems tend to interact to form more complex systems. This was my Fourth Law of Thermodynamics.*

There is no apriori reason why this should be. What about the universe makes it possible for systems to join together at all? And why should complex systems that are formed from the joining of pre-existing systems develop new sets of properties over and above the properties of the sub-systems?

What is it about the Universe that makes this possible?

Clearly, the key to developing complexity is the ability of systems to form continuing interactions.

Just as simple systems can compile to become a more complex system, these more complex systems act as whole systems that can, in turn, combine to form yet more complex systems. This layered compiling of systems results in nested systems of systems of systems that exhibit novel and emergent properties at each level of complexity.

The process through which interacting parts can unite to form a system that acts in a unitary fashion when taken as a whole intrigued me. I had seen that in the case of living systems this as-a-wholeness of the living organism is both formed by the interaction of parts and also acts to form the parts that interact to form the living organism in a paradoxically recursive manner. I had called this my *Law of the Paradoxical Self-Formation of Living Systems.*

Now, in observing the increasing levels of complexity in the elemental atoms, I was again seeing simple systems interacting to form more complex systems. But in non-living systems, as contrasted with living systems, I did not see the whole acting to form itself out of parts that it, itself, had formed as parts. For example, in the frog, the parts, like the heart lungs, brain, and legs are formed by the system that they are in turn forming.

So in non-living systems, *I considered my Fourth Law of Thermodynamics, simply that parts spontaneously come together to form new, more complex wholes when in a favorable environment.*

Later I began to define in what consists a favorable environment.

These concepts of interaction, formation, and complexification are all intimately related. I wondered if the more complex atoms themselves developed under appropriate conditions from simpler atoms.

Hydrogen is the simplest element, consisting of a positively charged proton surrounded by an electron in a given orbital shape. Hydrogen is ubiquitous in the universe. As hydrogen atoms move towards each other under the force of gravity, they begin to form aggregates, which in turn draw more hydrogen atoms towards them.

Gravity, then, exerts a primary ordering force, tending to concentrate atoms into one region, in opposition to the dispersive effects of the random bouncing of atoms against each other.

As more and more hydrogen atoms fall together the pressure on the internal atoms grows and the aggregate heats up. Gradually over eons of time when the pressure and heat in the cores of these aggregates reaches the ignition temperature of nuclear reactions, the star begins to "burn.'

In the seething hot plasma, the hydrogen atoms enter activated states, in which the tremendous threshold energy they have stored in their individual configurations is overcome. Two activated hydrogen atoms then join to form a helium atom, which is more stable.

Helium has two protons in its center and two electron orbitals around it. Reconfiguring as helium allows the activated hydrogen

81

atoms to reduce the potential energy of its system and in the process releases great quantities of electromagnetic radiation, which we experience as heat and light.

As this process continues in supernovas, populations of more and more complex elements emerge. In each case, as the complexity of the atom increases, more internal parts interact in more complex ways that give rise to more and more complex orbitals around larger and more complex nucleii.

What this means is that the elements themselves are evolving from simple to complex in environments where useable activation energy is absorbed by one or more of the interacting components. These energized atoms then form activated configurations that interact with one another. By joining together in new unitary systems, the activated atoms succeed in assuming more stable configurations. These more stable complex configurations reduce the net potential energy of the interacting, simpler elements and result in the formation of species of elements that are more complex. During this process there is a loss of individual identity of the parts, but a creation of a new mutual, more complex, more stable identity.

"Remarkable!" I thought, "That the very elements that evolve in stars, find themselves, eons later in suitable environments, ubiquitous throughout the universe, as parts of living systems. We are truly born of the stars in every atom of our being.

So living systems are not an anomaly. The evolution of living systems from non-living systems is an expression of the same fundamental principle that allows complexity to occur at all levels. This ability to form more and more complex systems is fundamental to the cosmos.

The cosmos doesn't have to exert a separate "formative" force externally. The Cosmos or Matrice is so structured that the interaction of its parts spontaneously self-forms more complex systems under appropriate conditions.

I called this the *Law of the Self-Evolution, or Self-Formation of more complex processes and systems from simpler processes and parts*. It is the way the matrice acts to create itself into more and more complex systems.

Evolution and complexification have to do with the emergence (of populations) of more complex systems, whether in the plasma of stars, the solutions of chemicals, or in the evolution of the living forms we see on earth today. *The Law of Evolution and the Law of Formation is implicit in the formative aspect of existence at every level.*

There is a drive, a tendency in Nature to do this, that is, to become more complex, when activation energy is available. This tendency to become more complex under appropriate conditions is, I believe, just as much a principle of nature, as the Second Law of Thermodynamics, which states that an isolated system left to its own devices will decrease its complexity.

This tendency for an isolated system to devolve into disorder, or decrease its complexity is described in the Laws of Thermodynamics, which as we saw in the essay on evolution, is called Entropy. But in order for complex systems to devolve into simpler systems the complex systems have to have evolved in complexity in the first place. Only after there are complex systems can they devolve. And of course complex systems do devolve into simpler systems and into component parts all the time so that cycles of evolving complexity and devolving simplicity characterize existence.

Everyone was saying that the first three laws of thermodynamics, that is, that energy is conserved, that entropy spontaneously increases, and that there is a statistical interpretation to the first two laws, were sufficient to explain the spontaneous increase in complexity of natural systems.

I could see that the first three laws of Thermodynamics were necessary but not sufficient to explain the emergence of complexity in the universe. Energy and Entropy, while necessary in a description of degrees of complexity, are not sufficient to explain how and why systems of interacting parts can arise in the first place.

To explain the spontaneous emergence of order, or complexity, we need to understand the importance of dynamic form, that is, of the energetic configurations of systems and their interactions.

In effect, the ability of interacting parts, at each level, to form more complex systems, depends on and arises from their characteristics as systems, in their own right, and on the properties that they, as systems, have, including their specific abilities to interact with other systems to form more complex forms when useable energy is available.

Remember that it is not the interaction of parts that causes the formation of wholes. The interaction of parts is a necessary but not sufficient factor in the formation of wholes.

Without the Principle of Complexification in the universe that allows and causes wholes to form from parts, the parts would bump into each other forever and never join to form wholes. *Indeed, the very existence of the structure and nature of the elements presupposes this ability of parts to join together to form wholes and so reflects the deep Principle of Complexification embodied in the very existence of the Cosmos.*

Without this intrinsic ability of systems to interact to form more complex systems, evolution and complexification would not be possible. Thus the possibility of evolution, that is, the development of complexity in systems, is not some accident. The evolution of complexity is based on a deep Principle of nature, as we have seen, my *Fourth Law of Thermodynamic: The Law of Spontaneous Emergence of Complexity in Energetic Systems of Interaction under certain conditions.*

Clearly Interaction is fundamental both to the emergence of complexity and to the evolution of the elements.

We explore the concept of interaction in another essay. Let it suffice to say here that an interaction is an "action between," in which the participants each act to change the other. When two participants interact they can do so briefly. This would be analogous to a one night stand. On the other hand, they can merge into a continuing interaction. This would be analogous to a marriage. When they merge they become imbedded in a dynamic system that that includes both. This combination, then begins to act as a unity.

When we consider the merging of two simple unitary systems into a new combined more complex unitary system, we need to include, not only the elements themselves, but also the trajectory of their interaction as they merge.

In a chemical reaction, for instance, molecules in solution break apart and join together again in various configurations. The strength and duration of an interaction is measured in terms of bond strength. The bond strength reflects the structure and activity of the participants.

Each bond between atoms has a certain bond strength that is calculated in terms of how difficult it is to break that bond. These bond strengths are described by their heats of formation, that is, the amount of energy that has to be applied to break the bond. These bond strengths also describe how likely it is that any two atoms will join together and how strongly they will bond. When there is a large bonding strength between them they tend to join. When there is a weak attraction or bond strength between them they are less likely to bond or to stay bonded.

These bond strengths, or heats of formation, can also be thought of in terms of a measure of their strengths of interaction. We have seen that interaction is the basis for the formation of more complex systems, not only in biology but, now we see, also in chemistry.

Not only are the bond strengths relevant in the interactions of atoms and molecules, but also the measure of disorder, that is entropy, is important in determining the course of chemical reactions. Here we are focusing on the energetic aspects of bonding.

I was seeing that even in non-living chemical systems parts form unities at their own level and then interact with one another to form new unities at the next level of complexity. Systems that act as wholes are comprised of continuing interactions of parts that join together to form the more inclusive system.

The ability to form Whole Systems is implicit in Complexification. It is not immediately obvious that a whole system, which is greater than the sum of its parts, should arise from a continuing interaction. This ability of systems to merge to create a new unitary system is not explicable by the laws of mechanics. The unitariness of the whole is not something that is explicable by pointing to the interactions of the parts. There is no apriori reason why systems that join together should develop new properties that transcend the simple sum of the parts.

When a piece of clay merges with another piece of the same type of clay, there is a larger lump of clay, but no new properties emerge. Why? Because there is no new dynamic systemic interaction of parts into a dynamic new system. The clay is simply an aggregate, not a system.

In contrast, when smaller systems form continuing interactions in which a larger whole system is formed, then new properties emerge. For example when two hydrogen atoms, which are unitary whole system at the level of the elements, interact with an oxygen atom, which is also a unitary whole system at the atomic level, to form a water molecule, water is formed with properties that are more than the sum of the properties of hydrogen and oxygen together.

When hydrogen gas, comprised of molecules consisting of two hydrogen atoms joined together is subjected to heat, the heat activates the hydrogen gas and causes it to split apart. If this is done in the presence of oxygen, then the activated hydrogen atoms will bond with the activated oxygen and burn to form water. In this case the orbital structure of the hydrogen atom contains an electron shell that can contain one electron when filled. The oxygen atom contains an outer electron shell that can potentially contain eight electrons when filled. When the oxygen atom shares two of its electron sites with two electrons, one from each of two hydrogen atoms, the oxygen atom and two hydrogen atoms become bonded through the sharing of these electron orbitals. In so bonding they merge their potential energies and create a more stable compound.

This bonding is purely a result of the dynamic structure of the atoms and their interactions. As we have seen, each atomic element has a different structure in terms of its electron shells and therefore it has different bonds that each can make with other atoms. The new unit that results at the molecular level is a consequence of the bonding capabilities of the parts. Therefore each atomic element exists in patterns of potential interactive abilities that become actualized in the bonding of atoms in different environmental atoms and molecules.

What we have then, in the case of atoms and molecules are two components: First the atoms themselves with their characteristic bonding capabilities, and second the bonding energies or bonding strengths among the various atoms and molecules that tends to bring them together. The bonding energies of course arise from the individual structure of the atoms and molecules that are interacting. In addition, the reaction often requires heat or a catalyst to overcome the threshold energy that otherwise prevents the atoms from joining.

So we can think of bonding energies as being their tendencies to interact in particular ways in particular environments. I think of these tendencies to interact as gradients of interaction.

What is a gradient of interaction?

An interaction, as we saw, is an action between. An action between is an action that is reciprocal and mutual, and in which each component causes a change in the other and is in turn changed by the other.

A gradient is a trajectory that a process follows.

A simple example of a gradient is a hill with a ball balanced on the top of it. The ball is attracted by the gravitational force of the earth and the earth is attracted by the gravitational force of the ball in a mutual interaction. At the top of the hill the ball has the potential to rolling to the bottom. This potential is expressed as its potential energy. When the ball actually rolls down the hill it follows its maximum gradient of descent. In rolling down the hill the potential energy that the ball had because of its position at the top of the hill is changed to the kinetic energy of motion.

The same process occurs in chemical reactions, only instead of gravitational energy that fuels the interaction in the case of the ball on the hill, it is the bonding energies of the particular atoms involved in the reaction that comprise the gradients of interaction.

A gradient of interaction can be thought of as the path of least resistance. The interacting systems act in such a way as to maximize their trajectories of descent as they move from the higher energy, less stable configuration, to the lower energy, more stable configuration. As we saw in the example of the ball rolling down the hill, the earth-hill-ball-system of interaction evolves, or develops in time, in such a way to minimize the internal potential energy of the system. To do that, the system changes in such a way so that motion of the ball follows its maximum gradient of interaction.

Although the system does not have a conscious intention, such as we experience, never the less we can say that the system evolves "in order to" minimize its internal potential energy by following its maximum gradient of interaction. We will look at this in more detail in the essay on Causality. *The marvel is that the Universal Self-Creating Matrice has designed itself in such a way that these gradients of interaction result in the self-formation of whole systems under appropriate conditions.*

CHAPTER EIGHT: HUMAN NATURE

People

Nostrils flared, legs muscles hot and strong, like wild horses freed from a corral we run, churning as if we are all part of one vast white creature with hundreds of legs. We are running side by side. People have come out to see us run by. Their cheering fills us with elation.

"What a celebration!"

Grouped alongside the road, standing in dried, spring mud, spectators clap gloved hands together, their pale winter faces stretching into smiles as they excitedly shout encouragement. Behind them, dark green, shaggy pine trees, bare, grey maples and brown oaks, cluster around the little New England cottages that line the road.

Far above, the quiet blue sky reflects the perfection of the day, looking on with detached awareness at the tiny human activity going on below. A minute stream of runners, like ants, moves along a road lined with other humans.

Isn't it funny? Here we are, a river of running people, rushing along a road where spectators stand as if on the banks of our human river; people watching people.

What strange and wonderful animals we are with our huge knobby heads and toothy smiles running on our hind legs. People are most amazing! There is no such thing as an ordinary person. Everyone is extraordinary and unique! Everyone is a valuable part of the whole of society.

What are human beings?

Two million years ago in the plains of Africa the first pre-human, stood up and walked on two of its four legs. In the ensuing two million years for some reason this species gradually evolved a larger and more complexly connected brain, particularly the cerebral cortex. As recently as one hundred thousand years ago the modern human evolved and migrated throughout the world.

We human are connected with all other living things on earth. We are part of nature. In our blood we carry the salty waters of primitive seas. With every breath we take we share in the holy communion of life on earth. We drink the sacred waters. Nature gives us food. Everything we receive through our economies is originally from nature.

We ourselves are nature. Our hearts beat, our stomachs digest, our brains think, our lungs breathe. Billions of highly coordinated chemical reactions are taking place in our cells every minute of which we are totally unaware. The very atoms of our existence were formed in the stars. The iron molecule at the core of our hemoglobin, which today carries the oxygen from our lungs into our blood stream, originated in a supernova explosion billions of years ago.

How did we get here?

In our studies of biology we learn that ontogeny recapitulates phylogeny, which means that the development of the human embryo touches on each of the main animal phyla as it develops from a one-celled creature to a human being.

The embryo goes from the one-cell stage of life to a multi-cell ball of undifferentiated cells like the sponges. Then this sphere folds in on itself to form a two-layered sac, the gastrula stage, like the hollow-bodied animals, coelenterates hydra and jellyfish, which are actually colonies of differentiated cells.

Then, the embryo forms itself into three cellular layers: the ectoderm, which will eventually become the skin and nervous system, the mesoderm, which will eventually become the muscles and bone, and the endoderm, which will eventually become the interior organs, following the path of evolution.

Bilateral symmetry and a head and tail arrangement as found in all animals after the flatworms. Finally, the notochord, the primitive spinal cord, signals the first appearance of the vertebrates, which is the equivalent of two billion years of evolution in about two months.

Finally the fish stage appears where the embryo develops gill slits as it, in some mysterious way, remembers the pathway of evolution by which it came to be human. The same quadrupedal arrangement of limbs persists throughout the families of vertebrates.

Written in our bodies is the unconscious lives we have led as all the phyla of life. We remember in our original metabolism the warm seas in which we lay pulsing with primeval currents of life. We remember, in our muscle fibers, the first muscles ever to evolve on earth, in the bodies of protozoa. We remember with our hearts, the first circulatory system, and with our lungs, the emergence of fish-like creatures onto land.

We all carry within us a road map of the entire history of the evolution of life on earth.

We are born out of and connected to the entire cosmos. We share the same deoxyribonucleic acid base molecules with every other living form on earth. We evolve in and out of nature. Does this mean we are not Divine?

I don't think so.

I believe we are all Divine, in the sense that we are part of, and an expression of, the ultimate Self-Creative Power of the Cosmos.

And we are at the same time Human.

How can this be?

What is it to be human?

How does the biological view of the origins of human beings fit with the view that humans are made in the image of the Creator, or as I've discovered, the Self-Creating Divine Cosmos?

The philosophers speak of "man" as born with grandiose

91

capacities, rights, and liberties before they are even potty trained. (The babies I mean, not the philosophers.)

But I could see that that's not the way it is at all!. Even philosophers arrive here as crumpled, helpless, infants, completely dependent on their mothers for survival. The mother nurses them. The father and mother hold them, clothe them, care for them, and love them.

Without this parental love the baby would die. The child grows to independence and autonomy through the continuing love and care and sensitivity of the family and the community. This is a far cry from the picture that Rousseau paints, of an independent, autonomous human being.

Each of us comes into this world through the body of a woman who forms the central core of the family. We are born into families. This is part of our essential nature, which has been overlooked by theoreticians.

Yet, our philosophical heritage, stemming from the Age of Enlightenment thinkers, Rousseau, Locke, Descartes and later philosophers, Hume and Kant, treated human nature as male nature and saw men as independent autonomous adults who somehow arrived full blown on the scene and contracted away some of their autonomy in a rational way to achieve the benefits of mutual society.

The experience of being born is part of what it is to be human, a part we share with all mammals. Children are born into families. Much of human social life revolves around the care and raising of the next generation.

The family forms the basic human social organization. So human beings are family creatures and so, social creatures. It's amazing how many people think of humans as solitary individuals. It is true we are all individuals, but we live in groups.

What is it to be a social creature?

Much has been written about the dog eat dog competition

between individuals in the fight for survival, a neo Darwin survival-of-the-fittest sociology, but I could see that to be social means to cooperate for mutual benefit.

Our very being and existence depends on others. Our highly intricate political and economic systems are made up of millions of people all cooperating; all coordinating their own individual lives with the lives of others in organized activity. Even competition occurs within a basically and overwhelmingly cooperative system.

There is no such thing as a totally independent autonomous person who needs no one else. And so the social contract theory has to be modified.

Our communities and governments are cooperative. Hundreds of thousands, indeed, millions of people live in our cities. Each person is living his or her own life, working, raising children, each in his or her house or apartment, all getting along. If we were not fundamentally social animals we couldn't begin to do this. Social cooperation is the matrix we live in. We take it for granted, like air and water.

The individual is important. It's the individual, who lives, who is born and who dies, who breathes and thinks and creates and loves. But we all have this dual nature. We are all social individuals. Although we are each unique individuals, we are born into a social matrix and much of the content of our minds comes from other minds, our entire language, the words with which we think, are passed down to us as part of our cultural inheritance.

This ability to pass knowledge and culture down from generation to generation is deeply human. Many of the thoughts that we think and concepts we hold come from people who lived thousands of years ago.

What is the basis of our ability to be social creatures? What is it that allows us to cooperate, to live and work together?

We cry at sad movies. We jam on the brakes to avoid hitting a pedestrian. Rescue teams go to any length to save people. There are story after story of ships lost at sea where men and the elderly gave up their places on the life rafts to women and young children. I don't think these are scattered accidents. This ability to stand in the shoes of others, to empathize, is intrinsic to human nature and is a much more basic and integral part of human nature than people have realized.

I think this built-in empathy is the basis of human society and of the innate morality that underlies society.

Empathy is the foundation of our intrinsic sense of fairness, which I think is fundamental to our sense of justice. I think these qualities are built into human beings but they have to be developed in children by the giving and receiving of love.

Love is that warm personal regard, that sense of valuing another which is essential to the healthy development of the child into the adult.

Empathy, like the ability for language, is an inborn capacity, which has to be developed. This is part of what parents do. They teach their children how to consider others. "Johnny, don't hit Sally. Suzy, don't take Jamey's toy. How would you feel if Billy hit you?

A sense of fair play is built into each human being. When that sense of fairness is abridged or transgressed it causes a sense of outrage.

When a child is abused, for example, she feels a sense of outrage. When a person is cheated he feels a sense of outrage. When we see other people hurt or victimized we feel a sense of outrage on their behalf. This sense of fair play underlies our whole system of justice.

In a healthy society the individual sense of fairness and empathy is intact. It is this sense of fair play, based on an intrinsic ability to empathize, that holds societies together. The good of the individual is thus precisely related to the good of society.

This concept that the good of the individual and the good of the whole are intrinsically related dates back to the classical Athenian democratic city-states. It makes sense when you think about it.

The good of the whole is dependent on the good of each individual and the good of each individual depends on the good of the whole. It's a balance. This is the essence of individual and societal health.

The Athenians had a word for it. They called it "Justice." The just man is the man who in modern terms is psychologically balanced. A just society is a society, which is functioning in a fair and balanced way. The individual and society are two sides of the same coin, inseparably linked.

My conviction is that the ability to empathize and love one another is the basis of society.

To treat others as you want to be treated and to love your neighbor as yourself is not some exhortation to do something that is intrinsically contrary to human nature. It is natural to love your neighbor. And these premises are the foundation of every legitimate religion and moral system.

Are humans basically evil?

The conclusion of Freud and other materialistic psychologists is that civilization is an unnatural state in which the fundamentally violent, rapacious, uncontrollably evil nature of man is being forced to conform to social mores, and that man periodically breaks through the confines of civilization and re-exerts his true nature, which he had temporarily sublimated to receive certain advantages of civil life. This is a popular and widely held view today. Indeed watching the evening news one is led to similar conclusions.

This is also the Judeo-Christian view of the nature of man. In the second chapter of Genesis God concludes that Man is evil from his youth. The entire edifice of the Medieval Church and the Reform Protestant Church too was built on the belief that man was naturally fallen, sinful and evil, and had been driven out of the Garden of Eden for his sins. Damnation and eternal punishment was assured without the intervention of the Church.

But I believe that people are fundamentally good.

95

What is it to be good? It doesn't mean to live by a rigid set of rules that define you as good. It means that we are already good, in our basic nature. To be good in the sense that God sees all things, including humans. Good in the sense that God rested on the seventh day in the first Chapter of Genesis and saw that creation was good. It means we are naturally good, just as we are naturally healthy. We come into the world absolutely good, perfect and healthy.

What we call evil is damage, distortion and disease.

Here we must say that much of what we have considered good and evil can be seen as the difference between a mentally, emotionally, spiritually and physically healthy human being, and a mentally, emotionally, spiritually or physically sick, dysfunctional, imbalanced or unhealthy individual, group or society.

Many of the Indo-European traditions, including the ancient Athenian culture, assumed the intrinsic goodness of human beings.

In Aristotle's Nicomachean Ethics, written in about 350 B.C.E, we find a description of the just man, which in modern psychological terms would be the healthy or balanced human being.

The just man is seen to be the good man. The ultimate good was seen to be happiness, which is an activity of the soul in accord with virtue. The just society was seen to be a balanced society composed of just human beings.

If we can see that we are fundamentally and naturally, good, empathetic creatures, with a keen sense of fair play and justice, that will change the way we understand ourselves, each other and our societies, in a crucial way, which will, I think, help to heal ourselves and our cultures.

We do not say that human beings are characterized by their ability to come down with cancer or diabetes or tuberculosis. Why then should we say that human beings are characterized by their ability to become mental, emotionally or spiritually sick or imbalanced?

If we begin with the premise that human beings are fundamentally good, then the task is not to suppress, repress, punish or sublimate basic human nature, but to unfold it, enhance it, refine it and express it.

This is exactly the opposite of what has been done for the past two thousand years in which man has been misunderstood as sinful and fallen.

The basic assumption that human beings are fundamentally good leads to an entirely different psychology, sociology and religion than the assumption that human beings are fundamentally evil.

If you believe that humans are fundamentally evil, then the purpose of psychological treatment is to reinforce the inner constraints, which are implanted by society to force the individual to restrain his or her basic nature, and to conform to the unnatural demands of society.

This belief is echoed in the feeling that there is something dark and dangerous about the unconscious. If one's subconscious desires are evil, one must constantly be on guard against one's own inner nature, lest it bust out and you are seized with an uncontrollable urge to rape, murder, steal or inflict other kinds of harm on one's self or others.

This belief that one's fundamental psychological make-up is inherently destructive leads to immense inner tension. Especially if one is taught that one's sexual feelings are evil and must be suppressed.

How confusing it is for people to feel that the delightful sensual awareness of life and of sexual desire is bad.

For Freud, sex was the driving force of the psyche. How debilitating then if this driving force is conceived of as dirty, bad, shameful and wrong. This wrong belief in one's inner nature becomes a direct cause of mental illness and psychological distress.

So many of society's ills are caused by wrong ideas and ideologies that are destructive and not healthy. So many of society's miscreants and criminals are individuals who are psychologically ill.

In contrast, when we realize that we are intrinsically good, then the purpose of psychology becomes to release the blocks and heal the damage, so that we can more perfectly be who we truly are. When we accept our sexuality as part of our God given nature, as a gift, as a pleasure and as a source of energy and meaning in our lives, then we are freed of the terrible conflict, which has caused so much psychological pain and led to so much bizarre sexual behavior, guilt and abuse.

When our sexuality is integrated into our personality in a healthy way, it takes its place as a part of the whole and it is appropriate and balanced. If we were sexually abused as children by people whose sexuality was full of guilt, fear, repression, and often distorted by previous victimization, then we can heal.

How? By accepting our sexuality as a good and beautiful aspect of ourselves in the present.

This is true of every aspect of our personality, as soon as we accept and love ourselves as we truly are, we begin the process of healing. Then psychology becomes the processes of helping us to heal through loving ourselves as we are. In the end, it is the love and compassion of the therapist which heals and which gives us the sense that we are understood, and loved unconditionally.

This is after all what Jesus did. He did not condemn. He never said that sexuality was bad. He loved women. He loved men. He loved all children. He especially loved the sick, the sinning, the poor and the cast-a-ways of life.

He healed by seeing the Divine in everyone no matter how distressing the disguise. He loved the sick as divinely whole. They felt this immense unconditional love and this is what healed or saved people.

So a psychology that heals has to be based on unconditional love.

This is what we all crave. This is what heals. This is the great gift we can give to ourselves and to each other. And this includes the love we have that expresses itself through our healthy, appropriate sexuality.

The assumption of humans as evil, not only affects the psyche of the individuals who accept that as the social norm, but it also affects the forms of government and religion in a society.

If our sociology is based on the premise that man is by nature evil, fallen bad, then the rape, pillage, destruction and war, which historically has ravaged human existence is the expression of man's true nature. If the task becomes to coerce human beings into the right behavior by force, or threat of force, then this would mean a police state is the natural state of human society. This view of human nature as evil and bad has been used to justify every totalitarian regime and oppressive theocracy that has ever existed.

The problem, of course, is then if all men are evil, so are the men who would coerce their brethren into "being good."

On the other hand a sociology which teaches that humans are fundamentally good, loving, empathetic, creative, sensitive, intelligent creatures and realizes that evil, violence, war, rape, pillage are aberrations of the true nature of human nature, which occur under certain conditions, will believe in democracy and freedom and will encourage individuals to actualize their best potentials.

Once we have the fundamental belief that humans are basically good and that evil is an aberration, the task becomes to identify those conditions that lead to the imbalance and harmful behavior of individual people and break down of society, whether these causes be genetic, physical, emotional, mental or spiritual.

Once sociology embraces the fact that the violence, war, overpopulation, substance abuse, slavery, oppression, poverty, crime, rape, robbery, and corruption that has plagued human history is not the healthy norm, but is a diseased condition, then great breakthroughs can be made in sociology that parallel the great breakthroughs in medicine that we have made.

If doctors had been content to say that diphtheria, plague, small pox, polio, cancer, aids, tuberculosis were just the natural fallen state of man, we never would have found cures or vaccines. Billions of people would still be dying and leading short diseased lives.

But once sociology clearly encompasses the idea that the dysfunctions of society are a different kind of disease, steps can be taken to heal these social diseases. A healthy new society will emerge populated with healthy human beings.

In addition, a re-setting of our religions to the understanding that human beings are fundamentally good, and that evil results from physical, spiritual, emotional, psychological or mental aberration, will provide a foundation for a great transformation, not only in the religions themselves, but also in the societies these religions inform.

What is the effect on religion of believing that humans are fundamentally evil? Religious belief in general holds that there is a supernatural deity who is the creator of the world. There are different names for this Being depending on the religion— God, Alla, Brahma, Yaweh, Eloheim and Jehova, for example.

The belief that humans are fundamentally evil introduces a schism into the fundamental relation of the individual with her or his God. The unconscious idea of God that individuals in a given society have, fundamentally affects their individual and social lives at every possible level.

What God, or Supreme Deity, would create, or cause, one of its creatures to be evil.... especially the creature most believed to be made in the very image of God?

Since the Supreme Deity is by definition Good, if humans are evil, this would mean that humans are not made in the image of God.

But to think that humans are not made in the image of God destroys the very core of one's intimacy with the Supreme Deity.

It is only when we understand our true nature as the very

expression of Divine essence, that we attain our full spirituality.

Therefore, humans cannot be, in their essence, evil. Rather humans express, in their very being, the essential, infinite goodness of the Creator.

A religion that holds that the fundamental nature of human beings is evil unconsciously embraces the idea that God is evil and this has devastating effects on the culture. If I and the father are one and I am evil we are led to the erroneous conclusion that the Father Supreme Deity is evil. And this false idea is then used to justify unspeakable evils.

Imagine the great transformation that will occur when we all fully realize that we are not fallen, sick, sinning, evil creatures, not "evil from our youth", but that we are all divine.

Actually what Jesus was teaching is that, in direct contradiction to the Old Testament, God is Love and God is Good. The essence of Christ's teaching is the healing power of love. This was in opposition to the Old Testament Jehovah who punished and condemned mankind and intentionally destroyed all life on earth in a terrible flood.

We need a new image of the Divine Creator, which is wholly good and totally healthy. Then when we realize that we are the Divine creating itself as us, out of Its infinite Love and perfection at every moment, we understand that we are fundamentally good and unconditionally loved.

As more and more people realize their own divinity, and the divinity of others, the world will become a more healthy, loving, conscious place.

When we come to see ourselves as fundamentally good, empathetic, loving creatures, our religions will reconnected with our deep spiritual life which in turn will be seen as a natural part of human nature.

There will be less emphasis on the supernatural and on mind-altered states and more emphasis on unfolding the natural divinity in all of us.

The focus will be on understanding our connection with all of Divine Nature, not in separating ourselves from it.

Perhaps one of the most important shifts we can make is in our understanding of health and disease. Once we come to see that our task is to create healthy individuals, healthy societies, healthy communities, healthy economies, healthy environments, healthy ecologies, healthy governments and healthy political institutions, our focus will be on creating balance, on healing human beings, and on helping the earth to heal.

Nature, from which we originate, and in which we have our being, will be seen to be Divine. Human nature will, thus be understood to be *both* human and divine. There is no split between nature, human and the divine. Humans are the Divine that is naturally becoming Itself.

It is the Divine Self-Creating Matrice, which expresses, in its own paradoxical self-creation, the supreme sacredness of existence. The Divine is not supernatural but is perfectly natural in its unfolding. We are all nature becoming itself as us. And so our very essence and nature is that we are the Divine Self Creating Miracle becoming Itself as us.

We are, in our most fundamental being, the Divine Mystery unfolding itself as us, viewing itself through our eyes, walking on itself with our feet, laughing to itself with our songs, loving itself with our love, being itself with our being.

CHAPTER NINE: CHILDREN

Water Station

We careen wildly around the next bend. Up ahead I see a cluster of people on the side of the road and some sort of table. Runners veer to the side, enter the cluster and leave with something white and small in their hand, which they alternately bring to their lips and toss their heads back or reach up and pour the contents over their hot heads. The street is littered with blurry white objects trampled underfoot. I squint to make out what is happening.

As I approach I see children, clutching orange slices in small pudgy, outstretched hands as they hold out their small offerings. I reach out and feel the sticky, pulpy fruit compressed in the small soft hand. For a moment I think the kid is coming along with the fruit. Then the child releases me and the fruit. I run on with the image of that sweet upturned face and those open, unguarded eyes etched in my memory.

Children — the most vulnerable, the most precious thing we have. Luminous eyes peering out at a world they never made and wondering at what they see. We were all children once, looking out at the world innocently, seeing whatever we saw there.

I remember giving birth to my son.

The August afternoon hung heavy. Long, warm shadows lay across yard. Thick and pale blue, the air itself seemed to just barely breath. Green, leathery leaves dangled like laundry hung out to dry, on sensuous, woody limbs of tall trees, by invisible, tiny housekeepers. Cicada bugs cut the hot, humid air with their shrill, broken buzz, like static in a broken electrical connection. Heat weighted every motion.

I had spent the afternoon lolling on the edge of the stream feeling the warmth of the smooth water-carved rocks and looking at my huge, round belly, which had a horizon, just like the earth, from where I lay. I'd plunged into the rushing, bubbling water and was treading water watching the ripples reflect the overhanging trees when I felt my internal muscles contract. As I emerged I felt the warm amniotic fluid flowing down my legs

My husband, his sharp blue eyes peering out of his tan bearded face, his long blond hair hanging in a single braid, like a Nordic Indian, helped me gather sterile thread and scissors and a blanket.

Friends were gathering in the rustic wooden farmhouse in Vermont, with its charming home-made windows and doors. Dan, our doctor friend, appeared with his warm smile and his case of medical supplies. This was to be a well supervised home birth with the local hospital on alert. I prepared a clean blanket, drank a little water and I waited.

I felt the muscles in my uterus close like a hot iron fist wrenching my intestines and I sat down abruptly. A few minutes later, I felt as though my entire insides were being inflated to the size of a large elephant.

The pain was intense.

The elephant subsided. A few minutes later it started to build. Again I was being inflated to the size of an elephant by something inside of me, which wasn't me and yet it was. I felt as though a red hot hatchet was chopping my insides. Imagine breaking every bone in your body. That was the first thirty seconds of this pain and then it multiplied by ten every second it crescendoed in a searing, gouging, wrenching ache that was so enormous that I thought it would blow my brain apart. And there was no escape. It was inside.

My abdomen inflated to the size of a house. Imagine how it would feel if your abdomen was blown up to the size of a house. I screamed. I sweated. So this is what women have been doing for centuries, for thousands of years alongside trails and in back alleys and closets, and in hospitals, unpaid, unappreciated, unnoticed, deprived of honor, glory, rights, and even citizenship, scorned by major religions. My estimation of women was increasing by leaps and bounds.

Every ligament in my abdomen felt as though it was on fire, being torn apart fiber by fiber.

"And they give medals for running marathons?" I gasped as I grabbed the strong comforting arm of my husband, Bill. We had been to Lamaze classes together and he kept saying, "Breathe, breathe!!"

"I'm already breathing!!!" I screamed, vaguely aware of the ironic humour of this exchange.

I let out a blood curdling warrior's battle cry of life. Where did anyone ever get the idea a woman is a delicate frail weak little thing? Women are blood, sweat, strength, power; the creative force of the universe

After four hours of this roller coaster ride of having my abdomen excruciatingly torn apart from the inside as it was inflated to the size of a house, stretching every ligament, breaking ever bone, grinding my insides into fire, I suddenly felt lonely. Was I everything was going as it should? Was it really supposed to be this painful?

I decided that this had gone on long enough.

"Call the hospital and tell then we're coming in," I said.

We clambered into the back of our friend's camper truck. With a roar and an acrid puff of exhaust fumes, the truck started up and took off to the hospital bouncing and swaying over the dirt roads.

On my hands and knees now, it was so much easier.

Five miles later, my husband yelled, "Stop! Stop! Pull over! Pull over! The baby's coming!" The truck stopped bouncing and it was suddenly quiet.

I felt the baby's warm, wet head between my legs. The final

powerful contractions brought him slithering out into the hands of the doctor. I felt the warm slippery after birth ease out.

Outside, the translucent indigo evening sky opened up as if someone had pulled the curtains back on the spectacular theater of night. Tiny stars glittered like sparkles thrown across the sky by a joyful child. Distant Whippoorwills and an owl sounded. An immense peach-colored moon slowly rose as the earth rolled in the peaceful unhurried way she does. The whole world seemed to stop. Peace filled the entire universe.

"A perfect baby boy!" everyone exclaimed. I rolled over onto my back and pulled the baby onto my tummy where he lay, umbilical cord still attached. He gazed with quiet eyes open, breathing softly. Calm peacefulness emanated from him. He had a spiritual presence, an ancient wisdom, as if he knew he were a Holy Being.

He looked around as if everything was just the way he expected it would be. In the soft dim light we were surrounded by the awe struck faces of my friends. He never cried. After he had been breathing for a while the doctor tied off the umbilical cord and cut it. I wrapped him in a soft blanket and held him in my arms. His tiny, embryonic head wobbled. After a while his blunt, baby nose nuzzled my breast, which was gushing with warm, sweet milk.

He began to nurse. He was strong and self-assured. I could feel that he had a powerful sense of self already. I was overwhelmed with love for this little being. Instinctively I knew to keep the baby right with me. It's so important in these first few moments and hours for the baby to be with the mother, to feel that security, the familiar smell and touch.

He had just made an immense journey assembling himself from the far reaches of the universe, reenacting four billion years of evolution, in nine months. His brand new nervous system could hardly make sense of all the patterns of light and dark and sound, and the feeling of cool air in his lungs, which had never breathed before.

He needed the reassurance of being with his mother. It's this reassurance, which will lay down the foundation of a basic security in his character.

I watched him slowly, slowly close his eyes as he drifted off to sleep. The baby needs to be like this, quietly with his mother, knowing he loved and wanted and cared for, feeling secure from the very beginning. Body contact and love is so vitally important in the first minutes, hours and days of his new life.

His birth was holy and this child was holy.

Every birth and every child and every mother is holy. And the father, who protects and provides for his family is holy. This holiness informed my mothering. I felt the Presence I had known in the sunlight filtering down through the chestnut tree in the back yard, the love I felt with my Nana, the Presence I'd found on the mountain, the Self-Creative miracle of the universe itself. DiMa, the Divine Self Creative One was here all around the baby and me. She hovered close by; she glowed in my baby's face, his little arms, legs and tiny toes.

Birth is the mystery of the Divine self-creative being manifesting here now as a man and woman coming together in love to form new life and a mother creating a baby with in her, from her blood and bone into a new being. What can be more miraculous than that!

When I looked down at my baby's smooth skin and saw his perfect little face and his long eyelashes I knew he was a gift from God entrusted to me and that this is the way I would honor him.

This is the key, I realized, to child rearing — to treat the baby as I would have wanted to be treated and to love him unconditionally.

The first decision I made was to keep him with me and not let him be taken to the nursery by well-intentioned nurses.

It was amazing to me that he knew so many things. He had known how to turn at the right moment to slip out of the birth canal. He knew how to nurse. I kept watching him amazed that he knew how to breathe. He would open his eyes and practice focusing on things. I imagined he saw moving patterns of colors without knowing what these patterns signified. Over the next months these patchworks of colors would begin to cling together as objects, still without names.

Babies are constantly practicing things, teaching themselves how to use their little bodies, how to made sense out of what they see, how to focus their eyes, how to fold and unfold their little hands. Later they practice sounds, clucking and cooing to themselves. What sounds like baby talk to the unaware ear, if you take the time to listen, is really the baby practicing all the sounds of all the languages in the world. Gradually they build up their repertoire of motions and sounds, coordinating more and more complex behaviors and practicing these behaviors over and over again. It's as if their brains need to practice these repetitions to build up the neural and neural muscular co-ordinations that will last a lifetime.

The behaviorist theory of child rearing was in vogue when I was an infant. This required that the child be conditioned not to cry. This ruthless conditioning was supposed to be accomplished by never picking up the child when it cried. This method also required that the child be conditioned to a regular schedule— one that fit the convenience of the parent, not the needs of the child. The child was to be fed every four hours. If it cried it was to be left alone in its room. Only when it wasn't crying was it to be picked up and only at the convenience of the parent. Crying on the part of the child was seen as a manipulation by which the child was trying to get its own way. Parental authority was mistakenly believed to be paramount.

Spanking was encouraged as a way to curb the naturally evil tendencies of the child. In some cultures beating or whipping was added to the list of punishments that was supposed to bring the child and the young adult into conformity with morally acceptable behavior. All this premised on the unspoken assumption imbedded in the culture and in the religious teachings that human beings and especially children were evil by nature and had to be punished to bring them into line with social expectations.

But when one is reasoning from false assumptions, one can never arrive at a truthful result. The assumption that human beings are evil from birth is wrong. In contrast, I start from the assumption that human beings are divine beings and are good from their birth and are fundamentally good. Starting from this assumption one raises ones children in a completely different way.

First, one treats ones children with respect and unconditional love, which means not shaming or blaming or judging. So when my baby cried, I understood that this precious little being had just made an immense journey and was in unfamiliar territory, overwhelmed with new sensations. He had needs that were completely valid and as his mother, it was my joy, privilege and obligation to tend to his needs.

If he cried it was because he had a valid need to be picked up and held, comforted and loved. I respected those natural needs and when he cried I picked him and held him and rocked him and comforted him and fed him if he was hungry. And, being comforted and fed, he quieted down.

Contrast this to the way I was treated as an infant. I was left to cry for hours. Being a small child I was hungry every two hours, but the behaviorist's theory demanded that I be fed only every four hours. So by the time I ate I was ravenous and terrified having been left to cry in the dark alone for four hours. I gulped the milk so fast I threw it up, and then was hungry again in an hour or so, where upon I'd cry in terror and hunger. I was labeled "a problem feeder." All this is because of erroneous and false beliefs and assumptions that give rise to erroneous theories that lead to mistaken actions that have disastrous effects.

What was once considered the proper way to raise children, namely the "spare the rod and spoil the child" theory, is now considered child abuse. Child abuse is more widespread than realized. Abuse can occur in subtle, as well as, brutal ways. Domineering, bullying mothers can produce men who hate women. Men who hate women can become abusive and domineering to women and to daughters, who, being abused, perhaps sexually abused, grow up damaged and often abuse their own children. Men who have been abused as children by fathers or other men can in turn grow up to be abusive. So the patterns are passed on from generation to generation.

These patterns, and the assumptions behind, them shape, not only the family, but also the society. When a religion or culture embodies a series of false beliefs it can become a cult. The more outlandish the beliefs of the cult, the stronger the neurotic bonds among the faithful, and the fiercer the defense against the outside groups who challenge those binding beliefs. The crueler the enforcement of the false beliefs and the more abuse is incorporated in the cult, the more damage is done to the individuals who are in the cult, and the more damage they do to others. Humans can be susceptible to what we call in popular vernacular, "brainwashing" by other humans and it begins with the abuse of children.

The reality is that children can be damaged. Damaged people often damage others, not because they are intrinsically evil, but because they have been damaged. Some damage is genetic and occurs before birth. Other damage is acquired. Once we understand that people are divine, and are, in fact, the Self Creating Mystery, and they are vulnerable and can be damaged and once damaged can hurt others, we come to understand people better. Genetically damaged and mentally ill people can wreck horrible damage on others. But this needs to be understood not as the evil nature of humans, but as a disease. Once we see it as a disease, the way we deal with it is quite different.

The love of the Divine Creator is not conditional.

How can we as parents be so arrogant as to set ourselves up as

God and condition our love in order to manipulate our children.

This is not to say that "permissive" child rearing, in which no limits of any kind are set, is the answer.

Of course limits need to be set. Of course unacceptable behavior is not tolerated. The point is that when your children know at a visceral level that you love and respect them, you don't need to punish. The child is born with exquisite sensitivity and an inborn desire to please. If you respect this, you will inspire, through the love of the child for you, the natural emergence, not only of "good" external behavior, but also, of the intrinsic sense of goodness, which informs behavior, and serves as the real basis for empathy and love.

Love facilitates, and makes possible, the integration of the psyche.

What are children after all?

Children have come from the Divine Self-Creation, through all the billions of years of evolution to the present, where they appear as newly created divine beings. They are human and they are divine. They are the Divine unfolding itself in this unique person right here now right before our eyes.

Since giving birth is a holy event, since conception itself is the divine self-creation, then raising the child, too, is a holy process.

The amazing thing is that when you treat your children with love, reverence and respect they grow up to treat you with love, reverence and respect.

So we need to start by abandoning the false beliefs and by embracing the truth of the sacredness of birth and the divine nature of the baby. Every person on earth is, after all, the Divine Self Creator becoming itself as that person. We are all the Divine becoming itself as us. And so every child, every father and every mother is the divine expressing the holy, sacred creativity of the Cosmos in love.

Chapter Ten: Power, Good and Evil

Industrial Buildings

The stoplight turns red, and green, and yellow, and red, and green again, as the runners pour through Framingham. The streets are packed with spectators cheering and applauding, smiling, yelling. Out of the corner of my eye, I catch a glimpse of a brick building outlined in tan. Little tan "X" designs run along the top, like embroidery. To the left, the railroad tracks continue to follow along with their array of black, metallic signals, sticking up like lollypops, fenced in by a cyclone fence. The surviving trees have been cut down. A little bit of apricot-colored grass is making a comeback between the tracks and the cyclone fence.

Beyond that is an industrial landscape, dominated by an ominous, dark factory building. The giant brick edifice looks out at the world, with blank, unseeing windows that gaze unseeingly at nothing. A towering smokestack is testament to a century of toxic, acid coal dust spewed into the once-pure and soft air.

The factory calls to mind nineteenth century capitalism, industrial exploitation and sweatshop labor conditions, where children and women worked unimaginable hours in insufferable conditions, drowning in the spiritual poverty of power.

The Medieval Christian Church recalls the Dark Ages, the stark images of the Inquisition, the brutality of repression, the power of totalitarian Theocracy — the dark underbelly of civilization collapsed.

Telephone poles with electric wires and telephone lines stand in somber testament, reminding us of crucifixes.... The horror of man's inhumanity to man is immortalized by the story of one of the most enlightened human beings ever to live, murdered in a sadistic, demonic manner that twisted human minds invented in pursuit of power.

You wonder if there isn't just a subtle, or not-so-subtle, threat in the choice of this symbol, "This is what will happen to you if you're truly a good human being who loves and heals and points out the hypocrisy of organized religion, and the bankruptcy and terror of corrupt power."

What a strange way for God to appear to man.

A sea, of parked cars, glitters in the bright sun, like an assembly of giant metallic insects that, like parasites, feed on oil sucked from the nipples of Mother Earth. Auto showrooms, auto body shops, used cars for sale, pennants flying, prices marking the fronts of cars: the entire scene has become automobiles and the buildings that house them, service them, sell them, and feed them.

There is a sense of desolation here. It gives me a bad feeling.

I look at the apricot colored-grass that appears again. Here She is again, with her self-weaving loom, weaving back the raveled seams of life. The dainty little apricot grass delicately builds its lacey stalk, unprotected, unnoticed and unappreciated. Can this God who created the apricot grass be the same God as the God of the Crucifixes? Can this gentle, healing, ever-present, self-creative power of the world, which never condemns, but patiently, patiently, with infinite care, weaves together the web of life that men rip asunder in their greed, plunder, fear and lust for power, be the same god as the as the god of the Inquisition?

"How quickly we got here!" the runners are exclaiming to each other. Here we are in Framingham already. We're flying along. The skyline is obliterated by billboards, and we look down to watch our footing over some railroad tracks that cross the road here. I'm cheered by the sight of people, happy people, celebrating spring.

Black metallic railroad signals rise up on the left and symbolize

113

industrial strength, the power of money, the creation of a stupendous industrial powerhouse. In contrast is the apricot grass. All the grass can do is to grow: it doesn't spew out toxic fumes; it doesn't commit violence or mayhem; it doesn't fight wars. It seems to have no power at all, except to patiently become itself, slowly, carefully, peacefully by the side of the road.

What is power?

Is power industrial power, military power, hierarchal power, the power to destroy, the power to coerce, to conquer, to oppress, to control, to enslave, to rule, to become wealthy? Is this what power is?

In physics, power is energy expended per unit time. Energy is the capacity to do work. Therefore, power is the capacity to do work exerted for a certain duration of time. And yet when you think of power, you think of institutionalized power or political power, church power, the power of organizations.

People have come to associate power with evil. One thinks of Hitler marching his armies across Europe killing millions of people, or Stalin murdering the people over whom he had power, and one thinks that this is power. History is the long woeful tale of people killing one another, of empires rising and falling, of wars, treachery, murder and violence.

How does this mesh with our innate humanity, with our humanness, with the way we think and feel, with the warm, soft, tender places in the human heart? Is power always corrupt?

Power in its most general sense is simply the ability to get things done. Therefore, power is neither good nor evil. Energy produced or expended in a unit time says nothing about the use to which that power is put. Power can be used for good or evil. Energy can be expended over time to produce good or evil. What is good? What is evil?

Good and evil are human concepts. Are good and evil absolute?

Are good and evil relative? Relative to what? When we think of evil, we think of something that is damaging or destructive. When we think of good, we think of something that benefits or enhances life, happiness, wholeness.

Classical Greek philosophers thought of good, the Supreme Good, as that towards which all things tend. The Supreme Good, was the Unmoved Mover, that which moves all things. And, that motion was thought to occur through the force of attraction, that is, through love.

Aristotle had a functional definition of good. He said that we can talk of good musicians, good doctors. A good musician is one who does what a musician does very well. Then what is a good man or a good woman? What is it that a human being does very well? What is it that's uniquely human, the good to which human beings tend, the something in and of itself, which is not the means to some greater end, but which is the end itself. Aristotle thought the purpose of human beings, or that which is uniquely human is their exercise of reason, that is, the exercise of logos or rationality.

Good, Aristotle said, is an activity of the soul, in accord with virtue, which he calls happiness, or eudaimonia. Happiness, Aristotle said, is the highest good of man, that which is chosen for its own sake, not for anything else. And so, he said, if we take man's function to be a certain kind of life, and activity, and conduct of the soul, which involves reason, then a good man is one in which this activity of soul is in accordance with virtue.

In other words, the good man or woman is the just man or woman, what we saw in the essay on human nature, is the psychologically balanced person who is healthy in mind, emotion, spirit and body. The soul, the psyche, is balanced psychologically and spiritually.

In terms of the good of a society, the proper aim of the statesperson, Aristotle said, is to produce the good of the State, that is, the just State, the balanced State.

What, then, is evil?

If a volcano erupts and destroys a village, it is tragic, but we don't say that the volcano is evil. Why not? Because the volcano is incapable of forming an intent or making choices. So evil has the element of intentionality. This is why only humans are capable of evil; because only humans have the elaborate cerebral equipment to make such intentionally malicious choices. But evil can also result from ignorance or wanton disregard. However, when we say someone does something evil, the element of intentionality is implied.

A just society is founded on just laws and on a healthy, natural morality that is based on empathy, and on the belief in the intrinsic goodness of human beings, as we saw.

The basis of justice is fairness, tempered with mercy, that is, with equity and equanimity. "What is fair?" is the key question. The human psyche yearns for fairness and equity. In a healthy society laws are founded on fairness, with the purpose of maximizing the good of the whole and the good of each. These goals are not contradictory, but are mutually re-enforcing.

If the perceived advantage of some conduces to the extreme disadvantage of others, this is not a healthy situation, and the society as a whole is damaged. Moreover, those who deprive others of opportunity cannot be truly happy or safe in such polarized societies. And those who are deprived are discontent and angry and contribute to the chaos and sickness of the society as a whole. This is why fairness is so fundamental to a healthy society.

The orbitofrontal cortex in human is thought to have a role in abstracting and learning the social norms for a given society. When the brains of psychopaths are examined at autopsy, damage to various brain areas is evident, including malformed areas in the amygdala that processes fear and other emotions. These same areas of the brain connect to the dopaminergic reward system, the malfunction of which is responsible for drug addiction. The physical malfunction of the brain leads to psychological malfunction, to emotional and psychological stress and trauma. Conversely, emotional stress and trauma can lead to actual physical changes in the brain that lead to its malfunction.

Are good and evil absolute or relative? Just as there is no absolute left and right, but rather, left and right depends on the orientation of the person making the determination, so good and evil seem to be relative in many cases.

When the Hebrew Tribes conquered Caanan, the land of milk and honey, and killed every man, woman and child, to them it seemed to be the ultimate good. It ended their years of wandering in the desert, and gave them a place that was bountiful in which to live. But to the Canaanites it was the epitome of evil. To the Hebrews it appeared that their tribal God, Jehovah, was powerful, good and worthy of worship. To the Canaanites that God seemed demonic.

We see here the relativity of good and evil. What is perceived to be evil by one side is perceived to be good by the other. We also see that the bounds of morality are circumscribed, that is, the Ten Commandments apply only to the in-group. Thou Shall Not Kill applies only to members of one's own group. In times of war the bounds of morality do not extend to the opposition.

Both sides agree that the killing of one of their own members is evil. Both sides agree that helping one of their own members is good. So the standard of morality is universal. What is relative is not the definition of good and evil. What is relative is the extent to which it is applied to others.

So if evil is the intentional harming of another and good is the prevention of the intentional harming of one person or group by another, if we step back and view the entire situation, we find that the perceived good of one is often the perceived evil of another. In this type of psychological stance, the world is divided into friends and enemies. To treat your friends well is thought to be good. To harm your friends is thought to be evil, and the person you harm becomes your enemy. Conversely, hurting your enemies is thought to be good and helping your enemies is thought to be evil.

So in this polarized view, one's power may be defined in two ways: First the power to hurt your enemies and second the power to help your friends. In terms of societies, power can be seen as the power of a society to protect and provide for itself and this is a power for good as seen by the members of that society. Power can also be seen as the society's ability to harm its enemies, that is, to protect itself from others who would hurt it and to gain advantage for itself by harming other societies or groups.

This worldview conceives of power as a zero sum game in which whatever one's person or group wins another person or group loses. And, in this psychological stance, the game is to gain for one's self at the expense of others. From your point of view what you gain results in good and what you take from others still results in good. Whereas from the opposing side, what you gain from them at their expense is seen as evil or bad. Of course by acting in this way, you gain many enemies, since everyone you hurt becomes your enemy. And so this type of behavior within a society destabilizes the society. This is why laws are made and enforced to keep people within a society from hurting one another. Just laws enforce mutually beneficial behaviors and prevent people from hurting one another.

Why is the zero-sum premise amoral?

The zero-sum premise is amoral because the basis of morality is empathy, that is, treating others as you want to be treated, and loving your neighbor. When someone thinks only of his or her own perceived benefit no matter how that hurts other's this is an amoral position because he or she is not treating others as he or she would want to be treated. It is not a loving behavior. Self-responsibility is distinct from unenlightened pursuit of perceived self-interest. Self-responsibility has to include responsibility not only for taking care of one's self, but also for not hurting others and for working towards the common good.

When zero-sum behaviors occur between societies, that is, when one society or group harms another in pursuit of its own perceived self-interest, this results in conflicts that can become wars. This is why intergroup and international institutions and laws are set up to extend the bounds of fairness, equity, law and morality to the whole world and to prevent this type of zero-sum behavior from destabilizing the globe. We look at this in more detail in the essay on war.

In a corrupt society, injustice prevails. People lie, cheat, steal and hurt each other, taking for themselves and leaving nothing for others. Greed, selfishness, coercion, oppression and violence prevail, and the bond of trust between human beings is broken. In a corrupt society, power is used to benefit the most ruthless, least moral, least empathetic and most selfish at the expense of those who are more gentle, loving, thoughtful, considerate, empathetic, creative and caring. This leads to breakdown of society.

This means that we need to re-evaluate the zero-sum premise and the dictum to act only in one's own perceived self-interest. In my opinion, an enlightened self-interest must prevail over an unenlightened self-interest. A win-win orientation must supersede a zero-sum stance.

What is enlightened self-interest? Enlightened self-interest looks at the big picture accurately and concludes correctly that we are all parts of larger groups and that most of our abilities, comforts, advantages and needs are met in the context of the sweep of human history that has given us the institutions through which we operate in the world. Even something as basic as language is not something that we have invented, but something that has been given to us. Life itself is a gift given to us by our parents and nourished by society. The food we eat is grown on farms we've never seen, by people we've never

119

met. The list goes on. The skills we have, the businesses we work all involve thousands and sometimes millions of people.

Our well-being is intrinsically linked with the well-being of the whole. Therefore the health of the whole is crucial to our own health. A person who operates from a foundation of enlightened self-interest understands this. Moreover, our innate human nature as empathetic beings conduces to the same conclusion as our rational enlightened self-interest. Those humans who lack this ability to empathize are not healthy, but rather are suffering psychological damage. Those people who are unenlightened are lacking the fundamental perspective of the rational evaluations that inform their personal choices. Psychologically damaged and unenlightened people cause problems for others and for society.

The two orientations are in direct contrast. The "zero-sum orientation" predicts an "I-win-you-loose" outcome and is based on selfish, unenlightened, perceived gain, which hurts others and involves no sense of empathy or community with the victim. The "whole-sum orientation," in contrast predicts an "I-win-you-win" outcome that is based on empathy, fairness, justice, balance and an enlightened understanding of what conduces to individual and societal health, balance and trust. The good of the individual and the good of society, as we saw, are two sides of the same coin and are mutually re-enforcing aspects of ones' personal and social life.

So, what is power? Power is simply and ability to get something done. There are many types of power: personal power, military power, political power, economic power, the power of persuasion, the power of knowledge, the power of physical force, the power of psychological force, the power that comes from occupying a position in a hierarchy or organization, the power of vision, the power of technology and so forth.

The question for us today as we deal with interpersonal and international and inter-group uses of power is: "How can we create situations in which enlightened self-interest and win-win outcomes prevail?" The answer to this question needs to inform the relevant power structures of our time—to create win-win, enlightened solutions that replace unenlightened zero-sum outcomes. This is what legal systems based in equity do. This is what negotiation and arbitration does. This is what a just criminal code does: it keeps people from hurting each other. This is what is needed at all levels.

We have looked at power in terms of good and evil. Let us now look at power in terms of the power to destroy and the power to create and ask which of these is more powerful?

Any fool can blow up a bridge or a building. The real power is the ability to create the bridge or the building, to design it, to build it and to maintain it. The same can be said of a city or a nation. Any fool can drop a bomb and destroy a city. This is the power to destroy. But to create a city or a nation takes millions of people all working together to build the city and the nation and to keep it functioning. This is the power to create.

The real power is the power to create— to create a nation, a society, houses, buildings, institutions and the continuous ongoing activity of people within the cities and towns and nations. This power to create is so pervasive and all-present we take it for granted.

Our human ability to create is fundamental to our natures. We are creative animals and we use our brains to invent, and our hands to create. Our cultures, societies and environments are expressions of our human creativity. And yet there are limits to our ability to create. We can cut down a tree; and this demonstrates our power, but we are powerless to create a tree. We can plant a seed and water it, but if we had to sit down and build a living tree from scratch it would be beyond our ability to do so. We can build houses and furniture from the trees we cut down, but we can't create a tree. The tree has an innate ability to create itself.

We as human animals share this self-creative ability with all

121

living creatures. And we have, in addition, the ability to create technologies and to build cities to invent airplanes and computers, to send rockets to distant planets — abilities that no other animal has.

So we see the self-building apricot colored grass growing by the roadside is not as powerless as it seems because it contains within it the power to create itself.

The grass is in fact the Divine Self-Creator creating itself as grass.

We are the Divine Self-Creative Miracle and Mystery creating Itself as us. This is the ultimate power, the power of the Divine Self-Creating Miracle to create itself as all that exists.

And what is the deep nature of this Ultimate Power to create?

The deep nature of the Divine Self-Creatrice is love — an immense, incomprehensible love out of which and into which all existence is continuously being born. And what is this love? Love is connection, love is relationship, and since all things are connected and all things are in relationship with one another, the love that expresses this universal relationship is all-present. The closer the relationship, the deeper the love; the deeper the love the closer the relationship.

Since all existence is connected in a universal relationship, love permeates all existence.

Since the Divine Self-Creating Miracle creates itself as all that exists, this means that we are all intimately connected as parts of the same Divine Self-Creating Miracle, whose nature is pure love. Thus, the greatest power we have as human beings is love. To love your neighbor, to love your families, to love everyone, to love life, to love yourself, to love the universe and to love the entire cosmos and to participate in the all-present unconditional love of the Divine Self-Creator, whose nature is perfect.

CHAPTER ELEVEN: RELATIVITY

Railroad Station

As we speed through Framingham I notice, on the left, a classic turn-of-the-century railroad station, built of pinkish stone blocks and trimmed with darker brown stone.

I think of my grandfather's generation and the building of railroads across America. I remember as a child how I'd looked out of the window at a passing train and I couldn't tell if it was moving or we were. I'd feel as though we were moving and then my eyes would seem to stretch out the scene. How surprised I'd be to discover that we were still standing unmoved and it was the other train that had been moving. I think of my many rides on the train from Boston to Rockport where I'd look out the window and think about Relativity Theory. Railroads had been used by Einstein to illustrate some of the basic concepts of the Theory of Special Relativity.

What is Relativity?

Galileo had written a treatise on Relativity long before Einstein. In Galileo's example it was an oxcart, not a railroad, but the same phenomena can be seen on a railroad car. Suppose you are standing on a moving train and you throw a ball straight up and catch it again. It appears to you that you are standing at the same place when you throw the ball and when you catch it and that the trajectory of the ball is a straight line up and a straight line down.

But to a person standing on the embankment it looks as though you threw the ball upwards at a different place than you caught the ball and that the path that the ball travels is a parabola.

How can the path that the ball follows, at the same time, be both a parabola and a straight line? How can you simultaneously be moving and not moving? How can the place you throw be the same and different from the place you catch?

The answer is that place, position, speed and travel path are not absolute quantities. Place, position, speed, and travel path are relative to specific frames of reference.

We see that to the person on the railroad, the distance, or space, between the event of throwing and the event of catching relative to the railroad train is zero. However, to the person on the embankment, the distance between the events of throwing and catching, relative to the observer on embankment is a matter of meters, or feet.

Since the speed of the train can be measured in a certain number of meters, or feet, traveled by the train in a certain time interval, say one second, then the number of meters, or feet, between the events of throwing and catching, as measured by the observer on the embankment, must be the speed of the train relative to the embankment, that is, the number of meters, or feet, the train travels in one second multiplied times the number of seconds that the clock ticks off between the events of throwing and catching.

Notice that here we assume that the clock on the train and the clock on the embankment tick out the same time intervals, or to say it differently, that there is one universal, time clock for all events. We will later see that this is not true. Never the less we see that from early times it was known that different reference frames give different results for the observation and measurements of events. This is Relativity in its early form.

When you are speeding along in a railroad car, everything seems to proceed as normal. You do not observe everyone hurled to the rear end of the car. Rather people walk and talk and even eat meals as though they are standing still, even though they are whizzing along the track. The same can be observed in a ship or an airplane or a rocket ship. The only time you feel a force is when the vehicle changes its velocity.

In physics, coordinate systems that are moving relative to each other at a uniform velocity are called inertial systems, and the Law of Relativity says that physical laws proceed in the same way in all inertial systems. To say it differently, there is no way of telling whether you are moving at a uniform velocity or standing still by doing experiments within your inertial system. This simple statement is the Principle of Relativity.

In 1865 James Clerk Maxwell wrote the famous equations that describe light as undulating expanding and collapsing electromagnetic waves. At the time it was assumed that, being waves, the electromagnetic waves would have to travel in some sort of elastic medium, which they called "ether." In 1887, two English physicists Michelson and Morley began an inquiry, into this question by trying to measure the speed of light relative to the ether. They reasoned that in the spring the earth would be traveling in one direction relative to the ether and in the fall the earth would be traveling in the other direction relative to the ether. By means of an interferometer they measured the light waves. They expected to see some displacement due to the earth's motion relative to the ether, but instead they found nothing.

Thorndike and Kennedy followed their experiment with another experiment that forever changed our understanding of the physical world and astounded the physicists of the time. They set out to measure the speed of light.

They reasoned that in the spring the earth would be traveling in one direction around the sun and in the fall the earth would be traveling in the other direction, so that the velocity of light from a distant star would, in the spring, be traveling towards the earth as the earth moved towards the star and so the velocity of the light would appear to be greater because the velocity of the light would add to the velocity of the earth. In the fall, the light from the same star would appear to be traveling with a velocity that would be measured to be less because the earth would be moving away from the source of light, that is, away from the star so the velocity of the earth relative to the star would subtract from the velocity of the light so the light would appear to be traveling slower.

This is the same reasoning you would use to figure out your speed if you are walking through the coach of a railroad car. If you are walking towards the rear of the train your speed and distance traveled, as measured by an observer on the embankment appears to be less as measured with respect to the embankment, but if you are walking in the direction that the train is moving your velocity adds to the velocity of the train and you appear to be walking faster, that is you cover more distance in the same amount of time, walking towards the front of the train than walking towards the back, when measured relative to the embankment.

To their utter disbelief, horror and amazement, physicists measured the speed of light to be exactly the same whether the earth was hurtling towards or away from the distant star light source.

This would be as if you are parked in a car on a road that runs parallel to a railroad track and you measure the speed of a train coming towards you to be fifty miles an hour. Now you drive towards the oncoming train at fifty miles an hour. You would expect to measure the train's relative speed coming towards you as the sum of your speed plus the speed of the train, that is, one hundred miles an hour. But to your shock no matter how fast you drive towards the train it always appears to be coming towards you at fifty miles an hour.

Bewildered, you turn around and race away from the train at fifty miles an hours. You would expect the relative velocity between you and the train to be zero, that is, at fifty miles an hours, you would expect that you and the train would be keeping pace with one another. Instead to your amazement when you measure the train coming at you from behind, you find that it is still coming towards you at fifty miles an hour. You step on the accelerator and speed away from the train at one hundred miles an hour. You expect that this would subtract from the speed of the train and that the train would now appear to be dropping behind you at a rate of fifty miles an hour. Instead you measure the train still coming towards you at fifty miles an hour. It would seem like a bad dream.

This is what happens with light. No matter how fast you travel towards, or how fast you travel away from, the light beam, it always appears to be coming at you with the same speed, which has been named "c" for the speed of light in a vacuum.

The physicists of the time began to theorize what this could mean. Lorentz, a Dutch physicist, developed equations that expressed what others, including the French physicist, Henri Poincare had speculated, that relate the measurements of space, or distance, and time in such a way that the speed of light is always measured to be the same no matter what the uniform motion of the non-accelerating, non-rotating frame of reference.

These equations express a ratio of the relative velocity between the two frames divided by the speed of light. Therefore a ratio of distance traveled, as seen by each observer, can be expressed as the relative velocity between two observers' frames multiplied times time elapsed, as measured on each observer's frame, divided by the constant speed of light.

Lorentz noted that there must be a local time that is particular to each reference frame, that is, clocks on different frames appear to run at different rates. When reference frames are co-moving, their clocks are in synchrony, but the greater the relative velocity between the two co-ordinate systems the slower each other's clocks appear to be running in comparison with the clocks on each of the reference frames.

Einstein used the example of the railroad car to explain the relativity of simultaneity. Events that appear to be simultaneous in one coordinate system to one uniformly moving observer appear not to be simultaneous in another coordinate system to another observer.

Consider a railroad car with an observer standing in the middle of the car equal distance from the rear and the front. Consider another observer standing on the embankment. At the exact moment the two observers are face to face, two lightning bolts hit the railroad car, one at the front end and one at the rear end, leaving charred marks on the ground and on the ends of the train.

Einstein said that the observer on the embankment would see both flashes at the same time, but that the observer on the railroad car would see the flash that hit the front of the car first, because in the time that it took the light to travel from the front of the car to the middle point of the railroad car, the train would have traveled forward and therefore the distance that the light had to travel would be less.

However, this didn't seem right to me. It seemed to me that this missed the whole point of the constant speed of light and the relativity of observation. Why?

Since to all uniformly moving observers, the speed of light is measured to be the same, in my analysis of the railroad car and lightning example, both the observer on the railroad car and the observer on the embankment will see the lightning flashes as being simultaneous. Why? Because even if the observer on the railroad car is traveling towards one of the flashes, as seen from the embankment, and away from the other flash, as seen from the embankment, the speed at which the light travels from the origin of the flash to the observer is always the same. For the observer on the railroad car the origin of the flashes are the front and rear of the car.

Since the lightning struck both ends of the railroad car at the time the observers were face to face, even though the observer on the railroad car subsequently moved a distance relative to the embankment, he did not move a distance relative to the front and rear of the railroad car. Therefore, the light traveled, relative to the railroad car, exactly one half of the total length of the railroad car, and so to the observer on the train, the two flashes appear to occur simultaneously.

Likewise, to the observer on the embankment, the light appears to travel from the points where the lightning struck the embankment when the two observers were face to face. Since the observer on the embankment is exactly halfway between where the two flashes hit the ground, he will see light from the two flashes traveling exactly the same distances relative to the embankment and so will see the flashes at the same time.

However, when the observer on the embankment tries to figure out when the observer on the train will see the flashes, he will see the person on the train traveling toward the lightning bolt that hit the ground at front of the train and away from the lightning bolt that hit the ground at the rear of the train. The observer on the embankment will then calculate that the distance from the observer to where the lightning bolt struck the ground will be shorter than the distance to the place where the lightning bolt hit the ground at the rear of the train, and so he will conclude that the person on the train will see the front lightning bolt first.

Conversely, the person on the train will look over at the person on the embankment and calculate that the person on the embankment will see the lightning bolt that hit the back of the train first because the distance from where the lightning bolt hit the rear of the train to the observer on the ground, as measured by the observer on the train, will be less than the distance the light had to travel from the lightning bolt that hit the front of the train, to the observer on the ground, as measured by the observer on the train. So the person on the train will conclude that the person on the embankment will see the bolt that hit the rear of the train before he sees the bolt that hit the front of the train.

Therefore simultaneity will be relative, but not in the way Einstein described. The important point is that there is no way of objectively determining absolutely or objectively whether the flashes were simultaneous or not.

In contrast, if the railroad car were a flatcar, and, instead of two flashes of light there are two rolls of thunder just as the two observers are face to face, the observer on the train would in fact hear the thunder that sounded to the front of the car first. Why? Because the sound waves in both cases travel relative to the air and the air is stationary relative to the ground but in relative motion with respect to the moving railroad car. The observer on the train is moving through the air towards the thunder that sounded to the front of the car, and the distance traveled by the sound will be less than the distance traveled by the sound through the air from the rear of the car, so the observer on the car will hear the thunder to the front of the car first. Light, as we saw, does not travel through a medium, and travels at the same measured speed no matter what the relative uniform speed of the observer, so the situation with light is entirely different.

Lorentz noted that the lengths of objects as measured by the different observers in different frames of reference appear to shrink, or contract, in the direction of their relative motion. There is no "real" shrinkage, or course. To the observer co-moving with the object, the object seems perfectly normal and doesn't appear to shrink at all. Each observer looks over at the other and observes the objects in the other's frame to shrink. When the frames are co-moving, the measured lengths of objects of both observers are the same. The greater the relative velocity between the two frames the greater the measured shrinkage in the direction of their relative velocity.

Thus, Lorentz gave the observer on one frame of reference a way to calculate what an observer on another reference frame must see.

Albert Einstein and his first wife, Mileva Maric Einstein, a brilliant physics student, worked on this problem and used the equations that Lorentz had created. What they did, however, was to give the equations a new interpretation. They saw that there was no need to assume an invisible, undetectable ether as a medium for the light waves and they saw that there was no absolute time anywhere, no "God's eye" objective absolute time in the universe, but rather that all there is is Lorentz's local time. Poincare had already made this observation as had Ernst Mach.

Mileva saw with particular clarity that these time and space measurements could never be absolute measures of some objective reality out there, but rather, each measurement is relative to each observer on different frames. The universe is not a monarchy with a king reading out an objective time. The universe is not an absolute space comprised of something like a stage with floors ceilings and walls. Rather the universe is a complete democracy in which one uniformly moving coordinate system as good as any other.

It is difficult for people to understand that the reality we measure is not an *objective* absolute reality out there, but that our measurements give us only our *relative* observations of the universe from our own unique perspectives.

So at this point everyone could see that the speed of light always travels with the same speed as measured by any uniformly moving observer and, as a result of Lorentz's equations, they surmised that the speed of light defines the largest velocity at which a material object can travel.

Although trajectories, distances, and time measurements are not absolute, but rather depend on the relative coordinate systems and on the relative motions of observers, remarkably, buried in the very core of this universe of relative relationships there is discovered an absolute: the speed of light in a vacuum. This seemed extraordinary to me.

What is so special about light?

What does the fact of this absolute say about the nature of the universe?

To me this question goes to the fundamental reality of the universe. It looked to me as though light defines and perhaps in some way creates what we measure as space and time.

I'd made an observation in 1962, as I studied physics at Tufts, that it is not that velocity is a secondary attribute, derived from the composition of space and time, but rather that velocity is prior to space and to time. *I concluded that space and time are derived from decomposing velocities and are simply our way of ordering events from our perspectives, relative to our coordinate systems.*

The speed of light, and more broadly electromagnetic radiation, defines a fundamental parameter in the universe that creates and limits the measures of space, time and velocity.

Moreover, electromagnetic radiation partakes of that fundamental character of the cosmos that I discovered on the mountain, namely self-creation. The electromagnetic wave is comprised of a collapsing electric flux that creates an expanding magnetic flux that, when it collapses, creates an expanding electric flux. *Thus light creates itself as a mutually self-inducing interaction of two fluxes that don't exist until mutually created by the other.* This is remarkable and speaks to the ultimate nature of all that exists as paradoxically self-creative. Maxwell's equations describe how these expanding and contracting electric and magnetic fluxes generate one another and move in a direction perpendicular to the expansion and contraction.

Because the speed of light is the same in all uniformly moving frames of reference, the measures of time and space are always conjoined by this limit. The measures of time and space have to adjust so that the ratio of distance to time that light measures out in all uniformly moving coordinate systems is always the same.

So in effect although time and space are distinct entities, their measure is always linked by the constant speed of light. In this way one can talk of spacetime as superseding space and time. Minkowski a Russian born physicist conceived of spacetime as a four-dimensional continuum comprised of three space coordinates and one time coordinate. Since the time coordinate is always linked to the space coordinates by the limiting speed of light, time can be measures in units of distance. To be exact, time can be measured in terms of the distance that light travels in the given time interval.

But as we just saw the length of the time interval between events depends on the relative speeds of the coordinate systems from which the measurements are being made. When we make these computations of the spacetime coordinates of the time and distance between events from all these various uniformly moving coordinate systems, it turns out that we can discover a combination of these measurements that is the same for all uniformly moving coordinate systems. This is a direct result of the Lorentz transformation equations that show how to transform measurements among uniformly moving coordinate systems.

This invariant function of the spacetime transformations among uniformly moving reference frames is called the spacetime interval. In Professors Wheeler's and Taylor's book on Relativity this four dimensional invariant is compared to the three dimensional invariant that describes the Pythagorean theorem, that the sum of the squares of the sides of every triangle, no matter what the individual dimensions and orientations, is equal to the square of the hypotenuse.

In the case of the spacetime interval the distance components have plus values and the time component has a minus value. The time component is written as the velocity of light multiplied times the time interval. Because the velocity of light is the distance light travels per second, when we multiple this by time measured in seconds, we are left with a quantities in the units of distance, to be exact this is the distance that light travels in the specified amount of time.

The invariant spacetime interval between events is then expressed as the square of the three dimensions of distance minus the square of the product of the velocity of light times the time interval as measured in each particular coordinate system. This comes directly from the Lorentz equations. It is called invariant because it is measured to be the same from every uniformly moving reference frame.

When we have a situation where two events occur in the same place on one coordinate system but at different times, we say that the events are separated in time but not space. When we see the same events from the point of view of an observer on a coordinate system that is in uniform motion relative to the first coordinate system we see that the events as measured relative to the second coordinate system are not only separated in time, but are also separated in space.

In the chapter on Causality we will explore how freely moving particles behave as they follow their spacetime trajectories.

We human have brains that are constructed to keep track of where we are and to navigate through a maze of physical objects. The hippocampus and entorhinal cortex in our brains have place cells that keep track of where we are at each moment relative to the innate three dimensional coordinate system that we impose on what we perceive as the physical world. So it seems natural to us to measure events in terms of their locations and the distance between them. But what is space out there?

It is the opinion of the author that there is no such thing as space out there. What exists we can only know through our interpretations and models of interactions with it. So what we are trying to do is to create better models. This is what Special and General Relativity do, and what quantum mechanics does, and what we are trying to do here.

We are also biological creatures with rhythms and metabolic processes that organize themselves and give us a sense of time. But what is time? If nothing happened, there would be no time. Time is simply the way we humans order events, just as space is the way we order the distances between events. Events are simply happenings that we refer to places on our reference frames and to times on our clocks.

To happen is to change. To change necessitates an interaction. So what we are measuring is not space and time or spacetime. What we are measuring are our perspectives on interactions.

I'm looking for a meta-theory can replace space, time and spacetime as most fundamental. This is what I'm doing when I propose Activity and Interactivity as my new fundamentals and I link these abilities back to the paradoxically, reflexively self-creating cosmos. The reason I'm doing this is to propose a new conceptual basis for, or beyond, the current scientific paradigms.

My new fundamentals I take as Action and Interaction. The universe is not a big stage on which the theater of events happen, as in Newtonian physics, nor is the universe a succession of stages of varying dimensionality as Relativity and String theory hold. Dimensionality, the author believes, is not the proper explicand. Rather, if we take Action and Interaction as our fundamentals we can build a model that more accurately accounts for our interactions with all the phenomena, which we can only know as our interaction with whatever is out there, from our side of the interaction.

Moreover once we see that this fundamental action is the self-creative-self-activity of the Self Creating Matrice, itself, then our model can be viewed from an entirely different perspective. Because this paradoxical, primal self-creativity is prior to space and time and prior to spacetime, our models need to reflect this underlying reality.

CHAPTER TWELVE: INTERACTION

Pond

Water ripples its smooth, shiny skin opening up on both sides of the road. My mind flows out along its calm surface. The water responds to the wind, furrowing its surface and reflecting the sky. As we run, the pond slips in and out behind the slender birch trees and wooded areas.

To the right, a vast expanse of lake opens up, holding within it cool fish with unblinking eyes, and reflecting from its ruffled belly, the sun in dancing wavelets.

Along its banks stretches a grassy shoulder. I'm delighted to find grass to run on. I move over to the shoulder and run along the grass, feeling its soft, familiar springiness under my hot feet. The sight of some blue-green, smooth bark, on slender trees, growing up in a cluster, makes my heart leap up. Far hills are covered with pines showing dark green along the skyline. The pond is lengthening into a long estuary snaking along beside us.

What is it about sun dancing on water that never fails to fill me with a rising sense of joy? The lake is coming almost to the road, now, as though to say hello. "Hello, Lake," I murmur.

In nature, everything is continuously interacting with every other thing. And what is this interaction? The wind is actually touching the surface of the water, and the water meticulously responds to every tiny nuance of the wind. This star in some obscure corner of the galaxy is really our sun. The photons of light billowing from the thermonuclear fire of the sun are really bouncing on the surface of the water here on earth. This flood and rush of photons, infinitely abundant, takes eight minutes to get from the surface of the sun to our earth. Here they come, sparking on the surface of the water, some of them caught up by the photoreceptors of our eyes, triggering long, complex biological inter-reactions in our neural systems, and ending up as the subjective experience of light and color and motion, creating this joy that burns within me.

I see in nature this same interconnections that in human societies give rise to our sense of empathy and human love.

This is an expanded consciousness, I think, which reveals the truth. The truth is that everything is interrelated. When we let ourselves know and feel this universal interconnectedness, we experience it as the feeling of love. The more intimate the interaction, the more intense the feeling of love. When I look into the eyes of my beloved, I feel an upwelling sense of joy. I feel the universal connection that joins us with all that is.

And so it becomes a mutual thing. The exquisite reflexivity of the surface of the water, faithfully reflecting the blueness of the sky and the sparkle of the sun, tirelessly responding to every caress of the wind. This, it seems to me, expresses the quality of the entire universe, of all of nature, this reflexivity.

Since all of nature, each thing, is a manifold of the One, the one Whole, the wind is the Oneness becoming itself as wind, the water is the Oneness becoming itself as water, the sun, uncountable numbers of photons, the earth, each are the Self-Creating-Oneness becoming itself as sun, photons and the earth. All the diverse parts of the Oneness interact with each other in the context of this universal Oneness, which takes the form of the reciprocal interactions, through which form is born.

And we humans, seeing it with our eye-brain, feel love and joy, knowing that we are part of the Oneness. We are the Oneness looking at the different forms of Itself, each intricate design interrelating perfectly with each other part of itself.

What I see with my eye-brain is my own subjective interaction with whatever's out there. How the water responds to the caress of the wind is a result of the subjective nature of the water in its interaction with the wind. So each thing knows, in a sense, in its own unique way, its interaction with each other thing, and so, eventually, with the whole. I think this subjectivity of interaction is fundamental to the nature of Nature. This is something science hasn't even begun to contemplate.

Only very recently has the idea of the observer, and the relativity of observation begun to filter in to science.

All an observer can ever observe is her interaction with whatever's out there. There's no way to get "outside" of that which is observing. This is true in any interaction — the interactants can only know their own subjective perspective of the interaction. Each thing interacts from its own point of view, and responds to the interaction in its particular way.

It is the interaction of the wind and the water that makes the ripples. It is the interaction of the photons in the receptors of the eye, which, through incredibly long and complex interactive processing that becomes our subjective experience.

When I was first studying physics at Tufts University in 1962, as I read the chapter on elementary particles, it struck me that these smallest entities are not particles at all. When two subatomic entities collide at very high speeds it is observed that yet smaller particles spin off from the collision. But it seemed to me that these so-called particles were rather, bits of configured activity, and that, depending on the nature of the colliding particles and their speeds, the structures of these configured activities would vary depending on the interaction.

We detect these bits of self-activity through interacting with them and this interaction changes and defines these bits of self-activity from our point of view..

So I called them "interactons," rather than particles because they seemed to me to be bits of dynamic activity that depend on the nature of the collision, that is, of the interaction. When the interactions are different they produce different interactons. When the interactions are the same they produce the same type of interactons. I became interested in creating a fundamental theory of physics in which the fundamentals are not space, time, spacetime, mass, energy and particles as is currently thought. I wanted to express physics in terms of action and interaction.

It is interaction that defines reality. If we were to take all the so-called particles away and leave all the interactions, we would detect no difference in the physical world, I hypothesized. Physics has been brought face-to-face with the reality that each participant in the interaction knows the interaction only in its own particular way, from its own particular perspective.

The Heisenberg uncertainty principle is an example of how inseparable is the interaction of observer and the observed. Each time the observer interacts with that which she or he is observing, that which she or he is observing changes in response to its interaction with the observer.

When you measure the speed and the position of these tiny bits of wave-particles, you find that as soon as you attempt to pin down their velocities, you no longer have a clear idea what exactly their positions are. The closer you hone in on their positions, the less grip you have on their velocities.

Quantum dynamics and the Heisenburg Uncertainty Principle hold that in any interaction only one half of the measured parameters can be determined accurately by each of the interactants. This is a fundamental nature of reality. And I could see that the reason is that in an interaction each participant in effect "views" the interaction from its own standpoint and therefore can "know" only one half of the quantities and qualities of the interaction.

This is just one example of the general universal principle that whenever there's an observation, the observer and the observed interact, and the fact of that interaction affects the observed as well as the observer, so there's a relationality here, but what really happens is an interrelationship, an interaction, an action that goes between, a relationship that includes both. Each participant in this interaction responds from its particular perspective, in its particular way.

If I were describing the fundamental principles of nature I would include: 1. The paradoxical self-creativity of the cosmos; 2. The fundamental dynamism of self-activity or action; 3. The fundamental wholeness and unity of the cosmos; 4. The interconnection and interaction of all its parts; 5. The reciprocity of interaction; 6. The relativity of observation, such that every observation involves reciprocally an observer and an observed; and 7. As we will see, in later chapters, a subjectivity of perspective that is fundamental and ubiquitous throughout nature. This is quite a different picture of reality, I thought, as I reflected on these matters, from the mechanical view of nature historically presented by science.

No one has been able to figure out how to integrate quantum physics and relativity theory. But it seemed to me that what is fundamental to both relativity theory and quantum physics is the observer, and the reciprocal interaction between the observed and the observer, such that each interactant is the observer from its point of view and each interactant is the observed from the point of view of that with which it is interacting.

Every interaction can be analyzed in terms of a two-by-two interactions. Even in complex interactions those interactions can be thought of in terms of over lapping pairs of interactants. So interaction is fundamental.

How does this relate with Relativity? The concept of the observer's participation and viewpoint is, in my opinion, the key to a synthesis between quantum dynamics and relativity theory. Only when there is an interaction, do the interactants, in some sense, localize. This localization is always observed relative to particular coordinate systems. This accounts for the apparent transitions between continuous fields and discrete events. The fields do not have an external physical reality nor are they really continuous, because the probabilities of physical interactions are limited by the smallest unit of interaction — the quantum of action. This is not a particle, but is rather a quantum of possible interaction. This is exemplified by the non-divisibility of the quantum, of mutually self-creating electrodynamic fluxes that is called the photon.

In 1900, Max Planck hypothesized that light, that is, electromagnetic energy, can be emitted only as quantized units. He wrote this as a mathematical equation in which the Energy of the emission is equal to a constant, known as Planck's constant, times the wavelength of the emission. These units are called quanta of action.

You would never see a half a photon. The photon has a fundamental unity of action that is indivisible, in the sense that if it were divided it would disappear altogether.

In the Theory of Special Relativity, the observer measures events from his or her uniformly moving coordinate system. We saw how these measurements of space and time vary depending on the coordinate system of the observer. In the Special Theory of Relativity we were talking about the interrelationships between the observations of observers on uniform motion relative to one another. In the General Theory of Relativity we consider cases where the coordinate systems are in various non-uniform motions with respect to one another.

In the General Theory, which is based on Riemann's geometric analysis of gravitational fields, there is a symmetry between an accelerating coordinate system and a gravitational field. Einstein was a brilliant teacher and could express difficult and complex concepts as simple analogies. He compared a gravitational field to an accelerating elevator. When the elevator is in free-fall the passengers float about in a gravitation-less environment as if they were high above the earth in space, so to speak. It is as if gravity had been turned off inside the elevator.

On the other hand if you have an elevator out in space, where the passengers would be floating around, and then you accelerate that elevator, with a constantly increasing speed, the passengers would think that there was a gravitational field pulling them toward the rear end of the elevator.

A gravitational field then is equivalent to a constantly accelerating coordinate system. It is as if a gravitational field is a constantly accelerating coordinate system that is standing still.

As in the Special Theory of Relativity, where the trajectory of an object depends on to what reference frame the motion is referred, in the General Theory of Relativity whether you are seeing an accelerating object or whether you are measuring a stationary gravitational field depends on the reference frame of the observer.

We feel the same thing on a plane that is taking off and we are pushed back into our seats. But when the plane reaches altitude people move about the cabin without being pushed, or pulled, to the rear of the plane. There is an equivalence between a gravitational field and a constantly accelerating coordinate system.

Riemann, a German physicist, developed a theory of gravitation that was taken over by Einstein to describe gravitation as a geometric construct in which, rather than a force acting at a distance, gravity was conceptualized as a physically real structure of space-time that has an immediate, local effect on a massive object. That is, the interactions of masses were seen to be explained by their interactions, not with each other at a distance, but by their interactions with an invisible gravitational four-dimensional field that not only fills all of space, but actually comprises and gives physical form to space-time.

One of the stranger consequences of General Relativity is known as the twin paradox. In this example two twins are born on earth. One of them takes a spaceship ride for years out into space then turns around and returns to earth only to find that time on the rocket has passed much slower than time on earth and that he is consequently much younger than his twin.

This is because we observe that clocks on a reference frame that is moving relative to us appear to be running slower, that is, less time is passing. But remember, in the case of uniformly moving coordinate systems for an observer on the other reference frame, our clocks appear to be running slower, so the relativity is reciprocal. In the twin paradox, however, the slowing of time isn't reciprocal We can really tell which clock moved away and then came back again because when we bring the clocks, or calendars, back together again we can compare the clocks and calendars and see in which reference system the clocks were running slower, that is less time passed.

How is possible?

What is the difference between the case of relative reciprocity, in the case of uniformly moving reference frames, and non-reciprocity in the reference frame that undergoes acceleration?

If all there were in the universe were two coordinate systems and they moved apart and then together at accelerating speeds we could not tell which one or if both were accelerating and de-accelerating unless we are able to find on one or the other some expenditure of energy that would indicate that some force had been applied, that is some interaction that caused the change in the state or motion of one or the other. But to what would this change of state, or motion, be in relation?

In the case of the rocket ship we observe that energy has been converted to a change in motion of the rocket ship. On the other hand the earth has not experienced any additional energy input that has changed its state during the duration of the rocketship flight. We can determine which coordinate system experienced the acceleration. The situation of not reciprocally relative.

The acceleration of the rocket ship, then, occurs not only with respect to the earth but also relative to its interaction with the entire universe. There is a change in the earth-rocket-universe configuration such that the rocket ship, not the earth, is determined to have been the frame that changed its velocity with respect to the whole system. In this sense, although velocity is entirely reciprocally relative, with respect to uniformly moving coordinate systems, evidently, acceleration is not entirely reciprocally relative. That is to say we can make a determination as to which of the reference frames changed velocity relative to the configuration of the system in which it is imbedded, and relative to the expenditure of energy necessary to change the velocity of one or the other reference frames.

Whenever we have an interaction, that is an action-between, each interactant changes the state of the other in a mutual manner. In electromagnetic radiation we saw how the action of the electric flux changes the action of the magnetic flux and the action of the magnetic flux changes the action of the electric flux, in a mutually self-creating manner.

In a collision between two massive objects the momentum, of one object changes the momentum of the other in a reciprocal manner that Newton described by saying that for each action there is an equal and opposite reaction. Momentum is defined as the mass of an object multiplied by its velocity. This momentum has a value and a direction. In Relativity Theory that momentum takes into account the differential evaluations of mass and velocity on different coordinate systems.

In the case of electric and magnetic field we see that the measurements of these forces and fields depends very much on the state and motion of the measurer. Consider the case of a stationary source of an electric field. To an observer who is stationary relative to this electric field source there exists only an electric field. To an observer who moves in that electric field there immediately springs into real physical existence, in addition to the electric field, a magnetic field that acts at right angles to the electric field.

This magnetic field has real measurably physical effects for the moving observer, but for the stationary observer the magnetic field has no physical existence at all. So does the magnetic field exist or not? There is no absolute way of telling whether the magnetic field physically exists or not because for an observer on one coordinate system it does not exist and for an observer on another coordinate system the magnetic field does exist.

A field expresses what the force would be on a particular type of entity if that entity were there. Force is always reciprocal in that it is the action between, or interaction between, entities. So the presence of the interacting entities actually creates the interaction that we measure as force.

What, I wondered, is a force? When we see an interaction, we see a change in state. We then conceptually invoke a "force" that is, an invisible cause, to explain what causes the changes in state that the participants in the interaction undergo. But all we really see and measure is the change in state, whether it is a change in position or velocity, as in physics, or whether it is a change in chemical composition, as in chemical reactions. So in some sense, force, although it is conceived of as an ubiquitous causal agent, doesn't really exist.

So why not just speak in terms of interaction rather than invoke an invisible, metaphysical agent named "force" to explain what causes things to change? We simply say we observe a change and that change comes from interaction. Whether we conceive of the interaction being between two massive objects at a distance or whether we think of the interaction being between a massive object and a global space-time continuum, the fact of interaction remains.

There are interactions, for example, the collision of pool balls, in which momentum is conserved when we evaluate the momentum of the entire system, but in which the momentum of each part changes.

In the case of these collisions there is an interaction between the parts that changes the states of each part, but the parts do not continue to interact in such a way that they create an enduring system of interacting parts.

And yet interaction is essential for the creation and maintenance of more complex systems, as we saw in the essay on Complexity. DeBroglie commented that when particles approach one another and begin to interact they begin to pool their potential energies. This means that they cease to act as entirely independent entities, begin to lose some of their individuality and become parts in the ensemble of the interacting parts that comprise the newly forming system. This occurs naturally and spontaneously. The degree of wholeness of the forming system depends on the degree and nature of interactions of the parts.

We see that interaction characterizes chemical reactions. Whenever we have a chemical reaction we see that the molecular bonds between atoms break and re-form, creating new molecular systems that have different properties. For example, when hydrogen gas and oxygen gas combine to make water, entirely different properties emerge.

I called systems that organize themselves into existence, Teleosystemic, from the Greek word, "Teleos," which means end seeking, or acting towards some end goal, because these self-building systems, as they build themselves, take actions that are towards the end goal of self-creating, or self-building an organization that at each moment in time transcends what it was before.

In living systems, the interactions are orders of magnitude more complex than in purely physical interactions, or in chemical reactions. In living systems there are multiple levels of nested interactions, from the atomic level to the molecular level, to dynamic sequences of enduring and repeating biochemical reactions, to the level of the various organelles and cells, to the level of tissues and organs, to the level of biological systems to the level of the organism acting as a whole.

Everywhere we look in nature we see interactions, some of which are brief and others of which endure as complex systems. So there are different types and qualities of interaction. Understanding these various types of interaction helps us to understand how nature operates at multiple levels to self-create itself with what appears to be such precise self-formative intelligence.

This self-formative intelligence, as mentioned, I call Tellic or Intellic, and may or may not involve some sort of subjective innerness or subjective point of view or subjective experience. This self-formative intelligence of these Teleosystemic systems is something that has not been properly appreciated, but is characteristic of the Self-Creating Matrice of All that Exists, which is Nature in its largest sense.

Roughly speaking these different types of interaction can be classified with respect to their complexity and durability, from the briefest encounter to the most enduring, and from the simplest mutually self-creating electromagnetic fluxes to complex living systems to the most complex system of all— the entire self-creating matrice itself.

Analyzing phenomena in terms of events, which are interactions that cause mutual changes, and in terms of systems that are comprised of various levels of complexity and durability of interactions, can be a useful tool to bring about a synthesis in the different sciences, including the human sciences, like psychology and physiology, sociology, and anthropology, in which interactions among people, groups, nations and empires can shed light on the inter-relationships among all the different levels of behavior of systems from the subatomic to the human.

In a marriage for example we see two individuals in some sense remaining individuals and yet creating through their interactions a merging of identities that creates a new identity both collectively as a couple and also gives each partner new dimensions of their own behaviors and capabilities and activities that neither has alone. So in some sense the marriage confines the individuals, but in other sense the marriage gives each partner freedom to become more of who they are capable of being.

We see the same thing in any collection or group of people who cooperate together to work for a common purpose or end goal. The group can accomplish much more that any individual alone, and more than the sum of the individuals taken separately. This can be a constructive cooperation as in a business or in a political organization.

On the other hand we see destructive interactions between and among people, perhaps the worst of which is war, in which the interactions between competing groups results in massive death, dislocation, human tragedy and chaos.

History, like physics or biology can be analyzed in terms of interaction. We see the building up of empires, the creation of democracies, the evolution of human societies and the devolution of human societies as the sequences of interactions among people.

Psychology too, can be seen in terms of the interactions of an individual with other individuals, with groups of individuals and with societies. These interactions can be on multiple levels and have various effects on the person's behavior. From the point of view of neuroscience, the interactions between the organs of a person's brain and body can be analyzed in terms of chemical aberrations, and mal-adaptions, for example the tendency to Parkinson's Disease can be seen as an aberration of levels of dopamine in the substantia nigra, and in the interactions of the basal ganglia with the motor cortex.

So thinking in terms of interactions at all types and levels of systemic complexity clarifies our analysis in many areas of enquiry, and builds up a physics and a biology based on the comprehension of the fundamental self-creating self-activity of nature, which will open the way for a much deeper understanding of nature, and more accurate scientific models.

Chapter Thirteen: Democracy in America

Town Hall

Sweaty arms and sinewy legs flash. White shorts and shirts move in unison….. a sweet, musky smell of hot bodies running.

My body is singing, laughing to itself. I cavort up on the grassy bank. I want to keep running forever, the rhythms of our bodies running together, our legs moving together, dark and warm from the inside; our arms swinging in harmony. The other runners press around me. We are alive together. We are covering each mile in a bit under seven minutes well on a sub three hour marathon, even though I'm holding back, reserving energy, knowing that if I fail to finish I'll set women back forever…. The huge weight of responsibility weighs on me.

I look up. A sycamore tree, like some strange white apparition flecked with silver and gold, raises its bare limbs to the luminous blue sky. Held to the earth by sinewy tentacles buried deep in the dirt, the huge, silent tree weaves its stark silvery trunk and its sensuous white arms into the sky. We are approaching a town.

Natick center is jammed with cheering people. Police keep the crowds back. Waves of applause and cheering crescendo as I run by. These people are my family, and these runners are my brothers. Jerry Nason, a reporter from Winchester, has spotted me and is calling on ahead. A local radio station is broadcasting my progress along the route. Spectators and runners alike are celebrating life together.

I glance up and see the Natick Town Hall.

The Marathon is the most democratic sport. Any spectator can train and enter and become a participant with the elite runners. And someday the runners may be spectators. But all of us together—runners, spectators, volunteers, staff and organizers are making the marathon a celebration of the human spirit.

The Town Hall stands at the center of all these New England towns. Why? Because the people who created our country established self-governing governments through which we govern themselves. These Town Halls are centers of government where the people meet to make the decisions that lead to their common well-being.

I believe passionately in democracy and freedom, in self-government, and the expansion of human rights, civil rights and democratic institutions to every person on this earth. The United Nations Declaration of Universal Human Rights is the banner, the conceptual basis that informs our domestic and global politics for the next millennium and beyond.

In some sense, our democracy began with the landing of the Pilgrims in what would become Massachusetts and the writing of the Mayflower Compact. The brave people on board the Mayflower were about to create a settlement in a wilderness where there was no king or governor to tell them what to do, no church to usher them along their worldly trials, no one to call to repair the roads, no roads in fact, no houses, no government, no jails, no social security office, no hospitals, no police, no government at all. They were on their own.

How were they going to provide some kind of social order to enable them to live peacefully together and to make decisions? Were they going to do what the majority of groups had done from time immemorial? Was there going to be one strong man who dominated and bossed everyone else around? Were they going to have a dictator based on who was strongest or who had armed men he could order around and thus control everyone else to his own advantage, as so many societies in the world do?

William Brewster, who drafted the Mayflower Compact believed that decisions should be made, not by force, not by one man, not even by an elite committee, but by the vote of everyone. All decisions affecting the community were to be decided by gathering together, discussing the issues and then taking a vote. We can hope that the men in the council listened to their good wives, who were not part of these councils. It is well to note Native American women participated in the Native American councils and indeed the Council of Mothers chose the Tribal Chiefs. Who after all, would know their sons better than the mothers?

These first European settlers were making a radical break with the Old World: they prized freedom and democracy over hierarchal power. This was part of the American Dream— the dream of freedom from coercion, the dream of individual rights, opportunities and responsibilities, a balance of self-reliance and helping one another in a commitment to community.

In 1776 the Declaration of Independence declared: We hold these truths to be self-evident, that all men are created equal, that they are endowed by their Creator with certain unalienable Rights, that among these are Life, Liberty and the pursuit of Happiness.

Later in 1787, after the Revolutionary War, our Constitution was adopted and signed. We created a government that, instead of imposing an unwanted tyranny, guarantees our individual rights and our liberty. This is a major evolution of political thought and practice. This idea of democratic self-governance and the guarantee of individual rights and freedom is giant step forward in human and social evolution. The idea that a government actually can be an instrument for guaranteeing freedom and individual rights for all was utterly astonishing and completely new; it was an that idea that was diametrically opposed to the tyrannical rule that characterizes most of history.

A tyrannical rule occurs when a conquering group or an endogenous elite uses force to impose a government on an oppressed people who are, in effect, captive to the coercive government that governs, by force of arms.

In contrast, the American Constitution sets out a governmental structure based on the following proposition:

"We the people, in order to form a more perfect union, establish justice, insure domestic tranquility, provide for the common defense, promote general welfare, secure the blessings of liberty to ourselves and our posterity do ordain and establish this Constitution for the United States of America."

These words are, in my opinion, some of the most important and inspiring words ever written, and should be memorized by every single person in the world as a personal and collective goal of humankind.

To form a more perfect union means we can all get along, no matter who we are, where we come from, what our economic status is, what our race, ethnicity or country of origin. Our government, because it insures the rights and safety of every single person, forms the framework within which this openness can occur. Through our Democratic government we insure that no one person or group can gain ascendency over another, that all have equal rights before the law and we are all equally valuable in the eyes of the Creator. This is the truly race-blind, gender-blind, ethnicity-blind society that we are working towards.

To establish justice means to create a legislative system and judicial system in which fairness, the good of the individual and the common good are the governing principles.

In a democratic legislative system, the people impose laws on themselves for their individual and common good. We make the laws through which we govern ourselves. This is diametrically opposed to the tyrannical case in which an elite group, a conquering nation, or a religious organization makes laws that benefit itself at the expense of the people. The laws we make in a democracy are for the purpose of preventing the harming of one person by another, not for the purpose of imposing undue burdens or giving unfair advantage.

A democratic judicial system demands that there be an impartial judge who rules on the law and an impartial jury, chosen from the community, that decides questions of fact based on evidence. It means that all people have the right to a trial by jury and no one can be imprisoned without probable cause and a speedy trial. It means that every person has the right to be represented by an attorney of law. It means that corruption is speedily ferreted out and eliminated. Corruption occurs when a person in a position of public trust acts for his own benefit or for the benefit of someone who is paying him against the common good.

To insure domestic tranquility means that we recognize that there are people who will try to harm others if not controlled and so it provides a means for us to protect ourselves from those who would harm us, by creating a system of police and security officials who are working, not for a tyrannical government as we have seen so many times in history, but rather are working for us, the peace-loving, law-abiding people who want to be free to lead our lives in safety.

To provide for the common defense means we create an army, navy, air force and, in general, a military establishment that can prevent other nations from harming us. This means that we work together to defend ourselves from foreign attack, since history teaches us that when foreign governments seek their own advantage at the expense of other nations war occurs. Providing for our common defense also includes the establishment of international courts of law and legislative bodies through which nations can cooperate and resolve conflicts and disputes through other means that through the traditional warfare.

To promote the general welfare means that we recognize that although we are a nation of individuals, our individual wellbeing is intimately connected with the well-being of every other individual. It means that we need, not only to care for ourselves but also to care for others. It means that we need to cooperate to establish the means through which we as a nation can provide for each and every person what they cannot provide for themselves in terms of basic human needs, food, clothing, housing, health care in a manner that supports the dignity of each and every individual.

It means that we recognize that some people are from time to time, or perhaps permanently disabled, sick, psychologically unbalanced, mental ill or physically impaired and that we have a duty as a society to make sure these people are cared for.

It means that we operate on a philosophy of enlightened self-interest in which we recognize that "There but for the grace of the Creator go I." It means loving one's neighbor as one's self. So we have social insurance to which we all contribute knowing that we, ourselves, may someday need help, and more importantly, because we know that we are all connected in such a way that the individual well-being depends on the well-being of all. It is called empathy and doing what is right. It means treating others as we ourselves want to be treated.

To secure the blessings of liberty to ourselves and our posterity means that we constitute our own government through which we guarantee to ourselves certain inalienable rights for ourselves, for each other, and for our descendants.

Our guaranteed civil rights are contained our Bill of Rights and include: freedom of speech, freedom of the press, freedom to assemble, freedom of religion, the right to petition the government for the redress of grievances, the right to bear arms for the establishment of a militia, freedom from unreasonable searches and seizures, the requirement of probable cause for the issuing of warrants, the requirement of a Grand Jury indictment in matters of a capital crime, freedom from being tried for the same crime twice, freedom from being compelled to testify against one's self, protection from being deprived of life, liberty or property except by due process of law, freedom from confiscation of private property for public use without just compensation, the right of an accused to a speedy trial, the right to be advised as to the charges, the right to be confronted by the witnesses, the right to council, the right to a trial by jury, freedom from the levying of excessive bail or fines, and freedom from cruel and unusual punishment. These rights are fundamental to democracy.

Later, more rights were added, like the emancipation of former slaves, the right of former slaves to vote, the right of women to vote, and the right of all citizens who are eighteen or older to vote, for example.

Gradually over the centuries the democratic norm has spread to include more and more classes of people and more and more nations, until today the majority of countries in the world have some kind of democratic political system and the United Nations provides a democratic forum for the world's nations.

Democracy is based on universal moral, ethical and religious teachings.

There are two fundamental precepts that are the foundation of every ethical, moral, and legitimate religious exhortation and these are: To treat others as you yourself want to be treated and to love your neighbors. There is another precept that is more difficult: to love your so-called enemies. This may seem contradictory and counter intuitive but there is great wisdom in this because often when enemies are loved they become friends.

We see people who hate and fear their neighbors and who routinely do to others as they would object to being done to themselves. So what do we do?

The rules of the game are that people must treat others as they themselves would like to be treated and conversely people must not treat others in ways in which they themselves would not like to be treated. People need to be taught these rules from childhood. All legitimate legal systems are ultimately based on these rules and on the concept of fairness, which is dear to the human heart.

Human beings empathize with one another. A healthy human being feels what others are feeling. We cry at sad movies; we jam on the brakes to avoid hitting a pedestrian; we rescue those in distress even at risk to our own lives. This is empathy. The ability to empathize is innate, but it also must also be taught and learned as a social norm.

A legitimate legal system is a code of laws based on preventing people from hurting each other. This includes both the criminal code and the tort, civil and common law. Matters of conflict and law are adjudicated in a fair manner by impartial judiciary or board of arbitrators.

The legal system deals with the most egregious cases of transgression of the fundamental precept to treat others as you yourself would want to be treated and to refrain from hurting others. In addition, for lesser transgressions we recognize that some people lack the emotional, spiritual or mental capacity to refrain from harming others, especially when it gives themselves a perceived short-term advantage. The cases that fall short of criminal or civil prosecution can be referred to counseling services where people are re-taught the fundamental precepts, therapy treatment or halfway houses or other forms of removing people who harm others from society, even while treating them kindly and allowing them some supervised freedoms outside the criminal justice system.

It is natural to love your neighbor for we are social and community animals. As we become more enlightened our sense of community expands until we embrace the entire world in the reach of our love and care. There is absolutely no reason why people cannot live in harmony with one another and in harmony with the earth. Our task is set up socio-economic-political systems that allow this harmony, and indeed, that demands that this happens. The closest we've come so far is democratic self-governance and so we need to build on the strengths of democracy.

There are numerous ways in which democratic political systems can be structured for example the Parliamentary and Presidential systems are both democracies but have different advantages and disadvantages.

Political refers to the ways in which power is distributed in a society. A political system is the organized, structured ways in which power is distributed in a society. In the United States, governing power is divided into three main branches: The Legislative, Judicial and Executive, each of which has jurisdiction and power over areas specified in our Constitution.

The Founding Fathers knew that power corrupts and that absolute power corrupts absolutely. So they divided the power in ways in which various branches of government balance one another, so that no one structure can obtain all the power. This sometime makes for frustratingly slow and messy decision-making, but it also protects us from unilateral decisions that could be disastrous.

The author believes that democracy is the most natural form of government. When we look at nature we find millions of interrelated self-governing systems in which feedback from that which is regulated controls the regulator that regulates the system. These feedback systems maintain balance naturally because the governor is governed by the system that is governed, just as in a democracy where the people who are governed control the government that regulates them.

Even more explicitly, when we look at how our own nervous system makes decisions we see that it is like a Town Meeting or a democratic assembly in which the yes votes and the no votes are tallied. For example, a neuron in the brain makes a decision to fire, that is, to send an electrical impulse down its axon or not based on its ability to tally or sum the inputs into it from other neurons. This receiving neuron is like a Town Meeting in which all the other neurons that feed into the receiving neuron act to either activate or to inhibit the receiving neuron. The dendritic arbor of the receiving neuron is the branching structure of the receiving neuron that receives and processes impulses from hundreds and thousands of other neurons.

This dendritic arbor functions like a Town Meeting in which every incoming nerve votes yes or no on the question of whether the receiving neuron should fire or not fire. If the incoming neuron is inhibitory it votes no. If the incoming neuron is excitatory it votes yes. The total of all the yes and no votes is added together and this vote is tallied to determine whether the neuron sends a message to the next neuron or not. So the Town Meeting has a fundamental biological correlate in the structure of nervous activity in our brains.

Government is the means of regulating a society. To govern means to regulate. Government expresses, and embodies, the political institutions that hold the power to regulate a society.

Generally speaking there are two main structures of Governing Authority:

1. Top Down Hierarchies, which include: Plutocracy, Monarchy, Oligarchy, Totalitarianism, Dictatorship, Theocracy, Dictatorship or Hereditary Aristocracy.

2. Bottom up Power structures that comprise the various forms of Democracy.

In the Top Down forms of governance the power resides with a small group at the top that controls everyone else through a top-down political structure that is usually oppressive and often outright brutal. In some cases the top down government is political and leaves matters of religion to other institutions. In the case of Religious Theocracies the hierarchal top down control is absolute over every aspect of life, including the very thoughts of every individual and the relationship of the individual with his or her Creator. Often the hierarchal top down political system also controls a top down economic system.

In some cases there can be a benevolent Monarch or Dictator, but because power corrupts and absolute power corrupts absolutely, this is extremely rare. All too often, even well intentioned Dictators become increasingly brutal and oppressive. The abuses of King John led the Nobles in England to write the Magna Charta through which they restrained the abusive power of the King. This was far short of an inclusive democracy, but it was a beginning of the idea that the power of the top down hierarchy needed to be and could be limited.

Bottom Up Structures include various forms of Democracy.

In a democracy the power resides with the governed, who either participate directly in the governing body itself, or who elect representatives to a governing body, which makes the decisions and legislations that affect the political, economic and social context of society. True Democracies are characterized by equitable distribution of the means of livelihood, broad and inclusive political power, human and civil rights, and fair courts of justice. A democratic government serves to protect the rights and freedoms of every individual and to prevent one person or group from intimidating or marginalizing any other group. A democratic government functions to serve the well-being and over-all good of the whole of society, and of each and every individual.

Democracy stands alone as the alternative to top-down political power and democracy is the hope of humankind.

Yet to be able to self-govern, people need to acquire certain skills and attitudes that make self-governance possible. In the United States we have a collection of semi-autonomous states that have united to form something much stronger than a federation. The United States is a unitary nation made up of levels of governance that proceed from local precincts, to towns and cities, to counties to states, to regions, to the nation as a whole. Each of these levels of democratic governments give people multiple levels of control over their lives and over the laws and decisions of their communities.

Americans know how to spontaneously form associations and groups to work together to get things done. Traditionally if a bridge needed to be built, people rolled up their sleeves and pitched in together to build the bridge. There was no king or magistrate to call in to build the bridge. If people wanted to do something they had to do it themselves. This tradition continues to this day.

This ability to work together is crucial to a democracy.

So too is this attitude of tolerance, inclusiveness and acceptance, indeed this attitude of embracing and valuing diversity is fundamental to democracy. United States is perhaps the most diverse nation in the world, and yet we are also the most free. How do we do this?

We have no hereditary class structure. We have public education for everyone, where from the earliest age we teach tolerance and celebration of diversity. We have a fundamental law that says that although we are all unique, different individuals, we are equal before the law. So we embrace individual rights and freedoms and differences and at the same time we insure liberty and justice for all. We may sometimes fall short of this in practice, but we keep trying to perfect the realization of this concept.

Whereas in other countries we see rigid class structures and ethnic and secular wars in which thousands of people are denied basic civil rights and engage in murderous wars and conflicts, here in United States we learn to live together and we learn to love one another and to care for each and every person in our country.

How do we do this? The key is that everyone and each group has real power within the system, so that those who have grievances do not have to go outside the system to try to achieve some power and freedom. The system is large enough and flexible enough to evolve. A large part of this evolution of social and political power involves and depends on an evolution of individual consciousness as well. This evolution of individual and social consciousness can sometimes be messy, cantankerous, and at times violent, but it is alive, vibrant and life-affirming.

In a healthy society people have standards of individual integrity and empathy for others. Empathy is, after all, the basis of morality. When people believe they are their brother's keeper, and they try to live by these precepts of love and community, they act to create healthy societies and in so doing they feel a personal sense of belonging, satisfaction and fundamental human value and meaning in their lives.

If, as I believe, the real purpose of a society, and therefore of a political system, and hence of a government, is the health and well-being and balance of the whole, and of each member of society, then the only legitimate purpose of government is to regulate society to maximize the common good and at the same time to maximize the good of each and every person in that society.

Is that a contradiction?

No because the good of society and the good of the individual, as we saw, are two sides of the same coin. To have a healthy society it is necessary to have healthy individuals and to have healthy individuals it is necessary to have a healthy society. Therefore the proper function of government is to regulate to achieve a healthy society made up of healthy individuals. This includes mental, physical, spiritual, emotional and economic health. Since in a Democracy the ultimate power resides with the governed, democracy is the best way to achieve a healthy society made up of healthy individuals.

Now that we see what the proper function of government is we see what corruption is. A corrupt society is a sick society, where society is out of balance. The more corrupt and tyrannical the society and the government, the worse is the health and well-being of the people who make up that society. A corrupt society is characterized by a vast polarity of wealth and poverty, lack of education, and a failure of society to function for the common good. In a corrupt society people are not free. Freedom is necessary for the human spirit to be healthy. This dream of freedom is what motivated people to create America and still motivates people to come to America. Freedom is the central core of the American Dream.

What exactly is the American Dream?

It seems to me that there are two American dreams and one Nightmare. Each alternative is based on a different motivation among the people who came to America and whose descendants now live here. The first American Dream is based on the intentions of those who came here to gain religious and political freedom, to make homes, to settle, to raise families, to work hard, to make a community, to worship the Creator directly as they saw fit or not to worship at all. They were not interested in "getting rich" per se. They only wanted to have a prosperous, peaceful life, free of tyranny and persecution.

And then there is the second American Dream, a dream of economic success. America is a place where even the poorest person can become rich if he or she works hard and creates something of value. This is because there is no rigid class structure here that categorically denies certain classes of people opportunity. Although, this was not true for women, Native Americans and African Americans, and more needs to be done. Steps have been made, and continue to be made, to rectify this injustice. In this dream the dreamer actually creates a successful, thriving business that produces something of real human value and does well.

The third alternative is just a continuation of the nightmare of mercantile colonialism in which the goal is not just to create a successful business, but to exploit. In this nightmare businesses or huge corporations exploit workers and decimate the environment in the quest for ever more money. In this nightmare corrupt financial interests cheat investors out of their life savings and cause economic hardship for millions worldwide while piling up ever more wealth for themselves in ways that create no human value.

We must continue to work to prevent this exploitation of the environment and of people. In the past, this exploitive nightmare included sweatshops, slavery and indentured servitude. Today this nightmare includes corruption on Wall Street, human trafficking, vast global corporations moving to countries where labor and environment can be exploited, unfair business practices, discrimination, illegal trade in persons, arms and substances and religious extremism and so forth. This is not the American Dream, but is a global nightmare that has been going on around the world for millennia.

The first American Dream supports a broad middle class, an equitable distribution of wealth, education for all, equality of opportunity, an egalitarian commitment that includes preservation of the environment and respect for the dignity and worth of each individual. In this vision, justice and equity prevail. This leads to a healthy economic situation and a healthy society in which autonomous people cooperate for mutual benefit. This is the real American dream.

The second American dream supports healthy businesses and productive labor that leads to affluence and success and yet is fair to workers and employees who also prosper.

In contrast, the Third Dream is the exploitive nightmare that is not American at all, but is simply a continuation of Colonialism. In this second vision a wealthy and privileged elite hold all the political power and wealth, while the many are reduced to poverty. In this nightmare, empathy is replaced with a social Darwinism, dog eat dog, I am not my brother's keeper, I'll get mine the hell with everyone else attitude that is destructive to society and lethal to the human soul.

Which way will America go? Will we create a nation based the real American Dream of caring, empathy, love, equity, fairness, diversity, freedom, individual rights and responsibilities, where government and business function to create a healthy society made up of healthy individuals as in the American Dream? Or will we succumb to the Colonialist Nightmare of poverty, ignorance, oppression for the many and wealth for the very few, where we lose our precious civil rights, our freedom and society breaks down into anarchy followed by dictatorship?

In a democracy there is the problem that people through ignorance, or through believing the lies of those who would manipulate them choose the wrong leaders or the wrong policies. Sometimes erroneous decisions are made in dis-regulating financial institutions and this leads to financial meltdowns that affect the entire world. Various organizations, including church hierarchies, have had long histories of corrupting and subverting nations. This leads to tragedy and disaster and compromises the very basis and existence of democracy. Wherever there is power there is corruption, and, if unchecked, corruption can undermine democracy and lead to anarchy or dictatorship.

Ultimately, it is the American character itself, which has led to the success of democracy in America and will determine the fate of democracy and the fate of America. It is our commitment to preserve this innate sense of justice, equity, trust, honesty, fairness, goodness and empathy on which successful democracy rests. If this fails, our democracy fails. If this remains intact our democracy flourishes.

CHAPTER FOURTEEN: WAR

The National Guard

The river of runners flows on through Natick. Crowds line the streets. I catch a glimpse of an imposing church structure on the left, with three doors. I'm thoroughly warmed up as we pass the ten-mile mark. We are flying along Route 135, a two-lane road, with one lane going each way.

Up ahead on the right stands what looks like a miniature castle. The roof-line, looks like the turrets of a castle, where in days gone by, archers might have stood, shooting through the open spaces and hiding behind the walls on each side.

"MASSACHUSETTS NATIONAL GUARD," I read on the front of the building as we stream by. A big, beautiful elm tree, bare in April, and yet with the buds swelling, stands in front of the building. The National Guard protects us from violence and yet it brings to mind all the wars that the human race has ever fought. The entire history of human civilization seems to be the history of war and conquest.

When I was in college I wrote a paper called "The Causes and Cures of War," My thesis was that war is a social sickness, a disease, and that it can be cured. My professor gave me an "A+", but wrote in the margin that he didn't agree with me. He believed, as do many, perhaps most, people that war is an innate part of human existence, something written in our DNA, a behavior and tradition that at best is glorious, where men prove themselves in battle and where power is gained or lost on the world's stage.

War, historically, is considered a useful institution for acquiring territory, slaves, booty, women, raw material, power and a conquered population of people who can be forced to do the work and pay taxes to support the victors. On the other side, war is seen to be necessary to protect one's own group, clan, tribe, state or country from the predations of other groups, clans, tribes, states or nations who would conquer and despoil if they could.

War has characterized human history from time immemorial. Empires rise and fall, followed by periods of chaos, followed by new empires that rise and fall. This cycles seem as natural as the cycles of forests burning off, new growth starting, weeds, then brush, then trees again.

Clearly untrammeled population growth is one cause of war. Economic decline is another cause of war. As resources become scarce, or economies decline, people become increasingly desperate. Soon the morality of society breakdowns, stealing, dishonesty, greed and corruption becomes the norm. The bonds of empathy dissolve as, "Every man for himself," becomes the clarion call of survival. This leads to mental, emotional, physical stress that impels people to increasing levels of crime and violence and produces a generation of stressed children.

When under stress, or under the influence of mind-altering drugs, gangs of young men take to roaming the streets preying on others. Without proper police protection the civilian population begins to disintegrate. Soon we have a situation where, as governments fail, terrorist groups and organized criminal syndicates run rampant. Many of the people in these gangs are mentally ill, either genetically, or through the stress of living in violent or dysfunctional environments, or from the use of drugs or all of the above. We saw this in the 2000's in the Middle East, a situation where terrorists armed themselves and took over territory, taking women by force and holding captive populations in abject oppressive situations that bred more stress and more crime and more violence. This situation was a re-enactment of the primitive response to overpopulation, mental illness, drug abuse and economic and social chaos.

So is this a natural part of human nature?

The answer is yes and no.

In a healthy balanced society, where corruption, crime and violence is minimized and people enjoy economic stability, personal safety, and mental, emotional and physical health, war doesn't occur naturally.

However, just as a person exposed to toxic chemicals will develop disease, so people living in toxic physical, mental, emotional, social or economic environments can experience the stresses that ultimate lead to a mental, emotional and psychologically diseased state that leads to violence and war.

Within the bounds of a given group or society, certain human norms of behavior hold. In order to establish a functional civil society, certain behaviors are expected and certain behaviors cannot be tolerated. This is what we mean by "peace." Violence can't be tolerated, and so civil societies evolve laws that prohibit rape, murder, assault, battery, mayhem and other acts of violence. Since not all people possess the inner constraints and fundamental health and sense of morality to conform to these norms, police, judicial and legal systems have evolved to enforce these laws.

In civil societies there must be non-violent ways of settling the inevitable conflicts that continuously arise in the affairs of interacting human being. So we have the civil judiciary, tort law and courts of arbitration that have developed from the king's courts and the ecclesiastical courts of the past. We now have trial by jury, a great improvement over trial by fire, or trial by water, or no trial at all. So societies have evolved mechanisms for creating peaceful civil social environments.

Developments in neuroscience and mental health have allowed us to understand much of the psychological basis for creating healthy societies and have underscored the importance of including mental health as one of the basic components of health and happiness. Many of those who commit violence crimes are suffering from mental illness, either genetically encoded, or environmentally caused, or both. Indeed in most cases of schizophrenia there is a genetic susceptibility, but an environmental trigger. This makes it all the more urgent that we create benign environments in the home and in the community that do not trigger mental illness.

Indeed, even for perfectly normal people, stress can lead to aberrations in perceptions, thoughts, emotions and behaviors. Post-Traumatic Stress Syndrome is a dramatic example of this and is more common that realized. When people become economically stressed they can begin to exhibit signs of psychological stress and aberrant behaviors. When people lose their homes or worse when they are hungry or starving they become desperate and the bonds of morality and empathy that are intact in a secure society break down. It is well known that in times of economic collapse, for example in the Great Depression, the crime rate soars. It was no accident that economic collapse was followed by rising crime rates and social breakdown followed by World War II. This, I theorize, is the etiology of war as the end-stage of a diseased a society.

It is not always easy to separate out what is a disease of society from what is a social norm because in diseased societies, disease becomes the aberrant social norm. People growing up in dysfunctional societies, just like people growing up in dysfunctional families, learn dysfunction as the norm. Dueling among men was once considered a social norm, for example and is now considered a criminal activity. In an unhealthy society, vast polarization of wealth and poverty leads to oppression, social breakdown and, if not remedied, eventually to war.

Although, as we saw, historically, war has been considered as a way to gain territory, riches, resources and power, I maintain war is an indication of endemic corruption within and between societies that hold aberrant norms.

War has also been considered a way of forming an empire within which uniform laws can be enforced and regional and sectarian fighting halted. That is to say, when confronted with the incessant squabbling and the petty wars of chieftains or of neighboring princedoms, which result in constant raids, attacks, and inter-tribal, or interstate violence, the forceful merging of these warring factions by a superior force that compels a uniform legal system, taxes, and builds roads, schools, aqueducts, or in a later age railroads, can create an empire, within which the small wars stop and a kind of peace is imposed by force, as we saw during the early and middle stages of the Roman Republic and the Roman Empire.

Eventually this superior force breaks down, due to internal corruption, or in the case of the Roman Empire, the actions of the Christian Church, which sought worldly power by subverting the civil government into a Theocracy through which the Church hierarchy came to rule the Holy Roman Empire absolutely.

When the empire fragments, the petty wars between rival sectarian groups, chieftains, princes, dictators or kings begins again. We saw this with the advent of the Dark Ages in Europe.

All too often governments have represented, not the people who are governed, but have been the mechanisms through which a conquering nation or group subdues and oppresses a conquered society. As for example when Genghis Khan conquered China, he imposed what can only be described as a sadistic nightmare on the Chinese people. His government functioned to coerce and to oppress the conquered Chinese. Anyone who fought back was tortured and murdered. Millions of Chinese people have perished over the centuries in the hands of oppressive governments, which have engaged in outright slaughter of the Chinese people.

When the Japanese invaded China as recently as 1937 this resulted again in the mass slaughter of the Chinese. Even after their own revolution under Mao Tse Tung, millions of Chinese people were murdered in the Great Purge and millions more died in the famines that followed. China has overpopulated its own resource base again and again.

Biologically, nature's solution to over-population has always been war, famine and disease. That is to say, when a people over grow their resource base, war, famine and disease is the way nature re-establishes balance. Unfortunately various groups and governments and religions have pursued a policy of maximum breeding in an attempt to out breed other groups and gain power. Unfortunately the masses of children produced in these cruel programs grow up in poverty.

If man, who owns a farm that can provide for a family of four, has five wives and forty-five children he has condemned his family to poverty, lack of education, and to disease. The same is true of every group that has engaged in a population war, the plan backfires and results in disease, famine, poverty and war.

This brings us back to the causes and cures of war. When a nation over-grows its resource base it may at first attempt to colonize other countries by shipping excess people out of the country. When that fails, the over-populated nation, comprised of millions of highly stressed, desperate people without adequate food, clothing and shelter are ripe for war.

These stressed conditions lead to internal corruption as people try to grab for themselves whatever they can get. The bonds of morality and empathy go out the window. The government then mobilizes for war, through which they intend to use the frantic population as soldiers and to take by force the resources of other nations.

The solution of course is not war or slaughter but is birth control, which is used in a humane manner to gradually bring populations back into harmony with the resource base. At the same time, new technologies must be developed to reduce pollution and to provide unconventional sources of food and energy.

But over-population is not always the cause of war. Territory, booty, women, slaves, an oppressed and impoverished population of workers, property, taxes and political and economic power have always been considered the spoils of war. Indeed, as was the custom, the conquerors and their descendants became the ruling class, the titled nobility, the aristocracy and the conquered races devolved into peasants and commoners. We see multiple examples of how governments have been used to impose the rule of the conquerors on subjects, which practice is diametrically opposed to democratic governance.

Often those who are best at slaughter are actually mentally deranged, lacking human empathy, unable to feel love, sometimes, in addition, suffering from paranoia, schizophrenia, or other serious mental illnesses. Their greed and lust after power often indicates emotional and mental imbalances that do not equip them to create a government that ensures freedom, and pursues the common good. Thus the custom of war, while benefitting the victors, usually compromises societies and oppresses civilian populations.

Tribal, sectarian, state and national rivalries are often a cause of war, where competing groups vie for power. This power includes territory, resources, technologies, populations, land and property, procreating rights, and a general slew of economic and political benefits. Where these rivalries continue, wars periodically emerge.

As we saw, the bonds of morality, empathy, civil conduct and laws that bind and regulate intercourse within a group, state or nation do not pertain to outsiders. So that wars occur as a cause and as a result of the frictions between the regions of in-groups where the bonds of civil conduct are broken and there is no effective legal recourse.

My point is that where there is no effective legal recourse, and where the bonds of morality and law do not exist, there arises great stress at both the social and individual levels. We know that children raised in violent homes suffer a variety of emotional, psychological, physical and spiritual illnesses as a result of the stress. The same is true of people who grow up in violent, or corrupt societies, in places of extreme economic poverty, or in war zones where they are subject to unbearable stresses.

These stresses cause the appearance of emotional traumas that can lead eventually to war. When the stresses are caused by a sadistic oppressive endogenous or exogenous regime, this triggers a revolutionary war. When the stresses are caused by border friction with a competing group that inflicts death and destruction, this triggers wars of retribution. When the stresses are caused by economic collapse or overpopulation of a resource base, this causes an aggressive war of conquest in pursuit of the resources that are controlled or owned by another group or nation.

War, then can be understood as a social disease, the end result of corruption that tears a society apart and pits one group, state or nation against another.

When people live together in a way where they treat others as they would want to be treated, that is, in an honorable, respectful, honest way, this builds friendship and trust, and even love, and reduces stress. When people treat each other with disrespect, lack of integrity — cheating, stealing, corrupting and exploiting each other — this breeds hatred and stress. So the task becomes to find ways to build trust, and to cooperate to find mutually beneficial solutions to problems and conflicts. In this way the likelihood of war is reduced.

War is, I maintain, a breakdown of human morality, a sickness of the human mind and soul. Normal, healthy human beings are born with the capacity to empathize. Just as the capacity to learn language is inborn, so is the capacity to empathize. But just as the specific language needs to be learned, so the practice of empathy needs to be learned. Human beings love

173

fairness. A healthy person treats other fairly and demands that he or she be treated fairly. Fairness is the basis of equity and justice in all legitimate legal systems.

So the solution is to create the structures within which empathy and fairness can be expanded to include everyone, and within which one's bonds of friendship, love and community can extend to everyone else. Parallel with this. it becomes necessary to keep those who would bully, cheat, steal, or harm others from doing so. The unfortunate reality is that we need to get those who harm others to the proper treatment when possible, or keep them out of society where treatment is not possible.

Margaret Mead said that war is an institution, and until a better method of resolving conflict is invented wars will continue. So our task is to build intra-national and international mechanisms through which fairness and equity can be achieved, where conflicts can be resolved, and where the stresses that cause war can be minimized.

Internationally, this means we need to encourage the creation of institutions that provide discussion and problem-solving forums, dispute-resolving mechanisms, international enforcement capabilities and a body of international law and international courts of justice for imposing standards of fairness globally. We need to heal past traumas and to actively engage in reconciliation forums where prior enemies can reconcile and if not be friends, at least learn to live in peace with one another.

We need to find ways of sharing resources and of inventing new technologies that create entirely new supplies of resources. We also need to engage in family planning and in voluntary, benign methods of keeping populations to sustainable levels. In this way fights over scarce resources can be avoided and prosperity can be shared in an equitable fashion. We need courts of international law that can rule on the equitability of resource distribution and an enforcing international police force and international guard whose function is not to take sides, but is to prevent violent conflict.

We need to institute a new way of dealing with international conflicts.

As an analogy, if two gangs, one from New York and one from Philadelphia are locked in a gang war, the police from New York and Philadelphia would not take sides and fight each other in support of their favorite gangs. Rather the police, with the help of the National Guard, would act to stop the conflict, without taking sides. The perpetrators would then proceed to court for an adjudication.

Just as the police break up a fight without taking sides, so the International Police are charged with breaking up and preventing wars, without taking sides. The international police force, which is now comprised of United Nations Peacekeeping force and various combines of nations, should act to stop the bloodshed. The warring parties should then proceed to the International Court of Justice for an adjudication of the conflict.

For example, in the civil war that wracked Syria in the early twenty-first century, instead of cooperating to stop the conflict, Russia and Iran backed the Assad government and NATO and the West backed the rebels. This has been the traditional way of fighting wars, but all it does is to prolong and expand the conflict.

Into the void left by the collapse of the Assad government came murderous extremist Islamic groups, particularly the so-called Islamic State, or Daesh, which intensified the chaos and confused the warring factions.

What should have happened is Russia, United States, Europe and the other Middle Eastern States should have cooperated and worked together — not to take sides — but to stop the violent conflict. Once the conflict is stopped, the matter can be negotiated in an international tribunal or heard before and International Court of Law and Arbitration.

After the conflict ceases there would be international financial and on-the-ground aid to repair the damage, to create an inclusive governing authority that would be able to provide the services and stabilities that governments provide, until the Syrian people can elect their representative government.

Where violent conflict has occurred, just as when a terrible disease has occurred, a period of healing and rehabilitation is needed. The warring factions need either to split into independent regions as happened in Eastern Europe during the 1990's, or the warring factions need to reconcile and to learn to tolerate one another and to get along, perhaps eventually to become friends again, as has happened in Europe after the end of WWII. The Marshall Plan was instrumental in allowing this emotional, political and economic healing in Europe, and a similar plan is necessary in the Middle East and any other region that has been wracked with war.

In many parts of the world democracy has been unknown for millennia, so it takes time and an entire program of learning how to create democratic institutions in order to establish viable democracies and peaceful, functional societies. This often takes several generations.

In conclusion, it is well to look at what we mean by peace. Clearly the opposite of hate and war is love and peace. So our global task is to replace hate and war with love and peace, but this cannot be done naively, just by telling people this is what they need to do. It is necessary to understand what a real peace is and how to create it.

By peace, I mean a state of society where people are free become the best they can be, where opportunities are open to all, where people are educated, healthy and feel secure, where there is broad distribution of inclusive political power and a broad distribution of purchasing power, where the economy is flourishing and democratic governance maximizes the good of the whole and the good of each and every individual. Peace includes full human and civil rights for all, guaranteed by the government that not only insures individual rights and liberty, but also pursues the common good, while creating a framework that prevents individuals from harming on another. This is the basic formula for peace.

Peace doesn't not mean no conflict. Peace means that conflicts can be resolved through non-violent mechanisms that are fair and open to all. Peace is not a static state achieved by complete oppression and lack of freedom. Such a state of oppression is not peace but is a type of frozen warfare. Peace is a dynamic state, where free enterprise allows each and every person to create his or her own business and to pursue the career for which she or he is best suited. Peace entails the evolution of new technologies that create new resources, stable and equitable economic and political structures, research and development in science, engineering, mathematics, literature, art, music and all the domains of human creativity.

Peace also demands a strong defense system and the capacity of fighting wars. This sounds ironical, but until there is an international force strong enough to prevent wars and to ensure the survival of democracy, democratic nations must be able to defend themselves and one another against the forces of totalitarian regimes or religions that would conquer and enslave them taking their resources and overrunning their populations. Just as it is necessary for the healthy body to maintain a strong immune defense system so it is necessary for a nation to maintain a strong defense against corruption and crime from within and conquest from without.

Peace, then is a dynamic state of social health.

It is naïve to think that unilateral disarmament will somehow lead to peace. This would be just as misguided as if the body decided to retire its immune system and make peace with all viruses. Nature is not sentimental. Nature keeps its balance in ways that often appear ruthlessly cruel, and war is one of those ways. Therefore the way to avoid war is to maintain a balance in which war is not necessary. The maintenance of that balance requires a strong system of defense.

177

Nature balances itself through balancing opposing forces and so one needs to make sure that one's power is intact and that one uses that power for good, and to oppose what we call evil. That is, if we consider good to be a state of world health and balance where everyone can flourish, in freedom and peace, this is the state to which we must dedicate our force.

The alternative to Empire is the voluntary establishment of collections of democratic nations that form units of economic and political stability in which power is broadly distributed through mechanisms that guarantee human and civil rights.

Historically, nations where there is a polarization of wealth and political power ultimate fail, whereas, nations where there is a broad distribution of economic success and political power succeed and flourish.

This government of the people for the people and by the people really has to be of the people for the people and by the people, where people collectively and individually work to establish self-government in which power and money is pooled for the benefit of the whole. This type of democratic governance is ultimately inclusive, that is, everyone is included, no one is marginalized or left out and everyone enjoys individual freedom, safety, human and political rights. This means people are not discriminated for or against because of belonging to a certain group. Laws are made that protect people from violence and crime. Governments are established that are committed to the well-being of each and every person.

When democratic nations join together in unions of democratic states, they create larger institutions to which they voluntarily submit the settlement of disputes. Then the likelihood of war is minimized. Other states and nations are encouraged to become more democratic and are aided in creating democratic institutions, which respect human rights, while conducing to the general well-being.

Since economic decline and failure is a major cause of corruption, crime and war, learning how to create and to maintain healthy flourishing economies is paramount. To this end healthy, open, fair financial systems and graduated tax formulae are crucial, to insure the integrity of economic transactions and to counter balance the tendency for capital to concentrate, as we see in the Chapter on Economics. (See also *The Art of Inflation, Money Games,* and the *Art of Economics,* by the author.)

We see now, in the world, a concerted effort to invent conflict-resolving methods, as evidenced by the United Nations, the International Court of Justice and the various international treaties, arbitration boards and organizations in promotion of trade and dispute settlement. Our efforts to create effective international conflict-resolving institutions need to be accelerated.

When there is nothing economically to be gained by wars, wars will cease. That is to say, we need to create a world where livelihood is generally available for everyone and where both political and economic rights and responsibilities are broadly and inclusively shared.

Chapter Fifteen: Women

Wellesley College

Like charging charioteers, we gallop up the broad hill towards Wellesley College. The earthy, sweet, spicy smell of rotting pine needles teases our nostrils. Tall, rough-barked pine trees brandish their long hairy arms at the sky. An expanse of soft, grass-covered hills opens up, cradling in their folds, a wet blue pond. We can hear women screeching and yelling and laughing up ahead. It sounds like a day at the beach. We stampede on, enlivened by the sound.

Cresting the hill, we see before us scores of young women, smiling, laughing, their hair blowing in the wind. Some of them are standing in two lines facing each other. They make an arched tunnel by raising their arms and meeting the hands of the women opposite them. One of my brother runners confides in me, "This is the best part of the race."

We duck down and run through the tunnel. I glance up and see their laughing faces. They are screaming, "It's a woman! A woman is running!"

As a teenager I had rebelled at the role the society forced women to play. When I grew up in the 50's and 60's women had very little autonomy. Women's opportunities were few and women's lives were circumscribed narrowly. A woman's role was to marry, keep house, cook, clean, obey her husband, and produce and raise children. She had almost no political or economic power and lived a life of subjugation, giving up her individuality and her dreams to serve the needs and wants of her husband and children.

I had watched in dismay as my mother and her suburban women

friends drank increasing amounts of wine and downed tranquilizers to numb the pain of their unfulfilled lives. I vowed that if being a woman meant being like that I would not be a woman. I'd run away and live in a cabin somewhere in the wilderness.

I chafed at the stereotypical boxes that men and women were supposed to cram themselves into and longed for a society where each and every individual is free to become all that he or she can become in her or his own unique way. I believe that we all come here as unique and wonderful individuals with gifts to give and potentials to fill.

Each and every person is different and it is time that we forget the stereotypes, and celebrate the differences, knowing that we are all part of the same human race living on the same planet. The importance and sanctity of the individual is, after all, what our country is all about. We have created a government through which we govern ourselves and protect and by means of which we guarantee the freedom, safety and human and civil rights of each and every individual.

At the time I was growing up, in the 50's and 60's, in a suburb of Boston Massachusetts, there was no women's movement, nor was there a running movement. Hardly anyone ran, and for a grown woman to run was thought to be improper, abnormal and very far outside the social norm. "How are you ever going to find a husband if you're off in the woods running with the dogs?" my mother would chide me.

I loved men and wanted children, but I didn't want to play the social role that a woman played. I wanted an equal partner and I wanted to be free to develop my mind and body as I saw fit. I loved science and was curious about everything. I wanted to study physics, biology, chemistry and mathematics, subjects thought to be unnecessary for a woman, and unfeminine. I wanted children, but that's not all I wanted.

I disliked cooking, sewing, ironing, decorating, entertaining my husband's boss, cleaning and housework that would be my fate as a woman, confined to my husband's house. I wanted children, but not the way I saw most people raising them. I wanted having children to be fun and I wanted my future husband to share in the childrearing and house tending on an equal basis where we both earn money working, and we both share parenting, but at that time this was inconceivable and unheard of. The roles were strictly segregated in terms of gender.

At that time, women had only been allowed to vote for some forty years. For centuries in many places around the world, women were not allowed to go to school and this is still true in some countries. When I was growing up women were not allowed in most professions and it was difficult or impossible for a woman to go to law school or medical school. The Ivy League colleges were male only. A woman could not even get a credit card without her husband's permission.

It was difficult for a woman to start, own or operate a business, and women in corporate or political organizations were almost nonexistent. Women were seen as objects of ridicule, sex objects, home appliances, or objects of seduction and romance. There were very few women in science. Women were expected to be the support systems for men, to be passive and obedient, to watch from the sidelines as men did everything. Even the illustrations in children's reading books showed Dick actively climbing a tree, throwing a ball or making something, while Jane, in a little skirt, looked on.

I was born into a society that I couldn't live in. Either I would have to find some other way and place to live or I would have to change society. But how does one person change society?

When in 1964 I first saw the Boston Marathon I fell in love with it and something deep inside me decided that I would run that race. At that time there were no other major city marathons that I knew of.

Boston was the only marathon I'd ever heard of. The marathon expresses something deeply human that had almost been lost in modern society.

My decision was made internally and seemed entirely irrational. It was like falling in love. That I followed my heart, even though against all social norms and in the face of considerable social pressure. I set out to do something very far outside what was socially acceptable. In retrospect seems remarkable. When I started I didn't know that I would be making a social statement. It never crossed my mind that there were no women running.

I trained for two years to run the Boston Marathon. When finally in February 1966 I wrote for my application from San Diego California, where I was then living, I was shocked to receive a curt reply from Will Cloney, the Race Director of the Boston Athletic Association, that women were not "physiologically" capable of running a marathon and that they couldn't take the medical liability, and that furthermore, the Boston Marathon was a men's division race and women weren't qualified or allowed to run.

The longest race for women sanctioned by the Amateur Athletic Union—the organization that controls all amateur athletic events in the country— was one and a half miles. At the time I was running forty miles at a stretch.

Women themselves did not know they could run marathons because they were never allowed to try. This is the tragedy of prejudice and discrimination: How can you know you can do something if you're never allowed to do it? Here again was that mind-binding, infuriating, cage into which women were put. Since you belong to a certain class of persons you cannot be who you are; you can't follow your dreams; you can't fulfill your purpose or your destiny; you must submit to this indignity and prejudice. I was angry and sad.

Suddenly, I saw my chance! I saw a chink in the armor of

prejudice and false belief. I knew that if I could run the Boston Marathon and run it well I could demolish this false belief about women and this would throw into question all the other false beliefs that had been used to keep women subjugated for untold centuries.

So I took a three thousand mile bus trip from San Diego to Boston and arrived the day before the race. My parents thought I'd gone mad. My Dad thought I was delusional. But I convinced my mother to drive me to the start in Hopkinton.

"Mom," I said, "this will help to set women free."

This resonated with her. She was a talented, intelligent woman who resented having given up her dreams of being a journalist to be a housewife.

She dropped me off on the outskirts of Hopkinton. I was dressed in my brother's Bermuda shorts, a tank top bathing suit and a dark blue hooded sweatshirt.

I knew I was doing something I wasn't supposed to be doing. I thought I might be arrested. I knew if the officials saw me they'd stop me. What the reaction of the other runners and the crowds would be I did not know.

My biggest fear was that I would be stopped and prevented from demonstrating what I'd come to demonstrate. After warming up by running laps in an alley behind some buildings for some forty-five minutes, I crouched in a clump of bushes as close to the start as I could.

There was a loud bang. The men started running. I waited until about half the pack passed then I jumped in.

This was a crucial moment because if the men were hostile they could have easily shouldered me out. I was alone and unprotected.

To my great relief and joy, when the men realized I was a woman they were friendly and supportive. They wanted to share their love of running with the men in their lives. This illustrates how important it is, for those who are being discriminated against, not to buy into the stereotypes that limit them, but to challenge the false beliefs through which they are being imprisoned and are imprisoning themselves.

It also shows that the supposed enemy is not an enemy at all, but if treated in a fair and friendly way turns out to be a friend. Then both sides can work together to build a better world. I wanted to end the stupid war between the sexes and show that men and women can share all of life's joys and promise.

The crowds cheered and clapped. The Police, whom I'd feared, shouted "At a go girly!!" Reporters called on ahead that history is in the making. A local radio station was broadcasting my progress.

When I reached Wellesley College, at about the half way mark, the women were cheering and crying. One woman with a bunch of children called out, "Ave Maria, Ave Maria!" There were tears streaming down her face. Tears came to my eyes at the contact.

All of us knew that things would never again be the same for women. We all knew at that moment that we would never go back into that confining cage that had been imprisoning us.

In 1996, Diana Chapman Walsh president of Wellesley College, wrote about her experience standing watching the Boston Marathon, as a student at Wellesley College in 1966: "As I had done every spring since I arrived on campus, I went out to cheer the runners. But there was something different about that Marathon Day— like a spark down a wire, the word spread to all of us lining the route that a woman was running the course. For a while, the 'screech tunnel' fell silent. We scanned face after face in breathless anticipation until just ahead of her, through the excited crowd, a ripple of recognition shot through the lines and we cheered as we never had before. We let out a roar that day, sensing that this woman had done more than just break the gender barrier in a famous race... but we didn't know just how long and hard a struggle it would be for the women who would follow Bobbi Gibb."

When I reached Boston in a time of three hours twenty-one

minutes and forty seconds, in the top third of the finishers, the Governor of Massachusetts, Governor John Volpe, himself came down to shake my hand.

My feat was front-page headlines and word went out around the world that a woman had done the impossible and run the Boston Marathon. This was a pivotal event in changing the social consciousness about women and in bringing attention to running as a way of life for everyone and helped to galvanize both the second wave of the Women's Movement and the running movement.

In 1966 I was the sole runner in the yet to be sanctioned Women's Division of the Boston Marathon. In 1967 there were two of us in the Women's Division and I finished about an hour ahead of the second woman, Kathryn Switzer. In 1968 there were five women in the Women's Division and again I finished first. In 1969 I didn't not return, as I was finishing college and applying to medical school. Sara Mae Berman finished first among increasing number of women in 1969, 1970 and 1971. Finally, thanks to the petition brought by Nina Kuscsik, the Amateur Athletic Union finally sanctioned Women's Division marathons and Nina Kuscsik was the women's winner in 1972, in the first AAU sanctioned Women's Division Boston Marathon.

What else have women done, always disguised as men, or living or working through men? What ideas and insights have women had that have been claimed by their male partners? Maria Maric Einstein, a co-inventor of the Theory of Relativity, has never been given credit. Her husband Albert took all the glory. What happened to the woman mathematician at Barnard College, whose name has been buried, who did Albert Einstein's mathematics for him?

And what about Rosalind Franklin, who discovered the double helical structure of DNA, through her X-ray crystallography, that was credited to Watson and Crick who expanded and refined her discovery?

Rene Decartes, the famous seventeenth century French philosopher, scientist and mathematician wrote of Princess Elizabeth, the daughter of Emperor Ferdinand, "She has the only mind I have ever found to whom both metaphysics and mathematics are easy." Did she collaborate with Descartes? What happened to her genius?

And there was Camille Claudet, the woman who carved Rodin's greatest sculptures. And Nanerl Mozart, Wolfgang's sister who was also a prodigy and musically gifted; did she write some of Mozart's music? What happened to her gifts? And, of course, Anna Bach, Johann Sabastian Bach's first wife, who was also musically gifted. Did she contribute some of Bach's work? And recently there has been considerable research devoted to discovering the real identity of Shakespeare and growing evidence that his plays were written by a woman, a cousin of Queen Elizabeth. My own theory is that Queen Elizabeth herself drafted Shakespeare's plays, which were then edited and produced by Shakespeare's Stage Company at the Old Globe Theatre. And so it goes.....

Even women who were notable in their day like Margaret Mead and Eleanor Roosevelt are erased by the male hierarchy, which controls the recording and perpetuation of history, still in male terms. Queen Elizabeth I is harder to erase, but often her brilliant reign is characterized as a rather silly Queen who relied on male advisors who really ran things.

The fact is that intelligence, talent and giftedness is distributed equally between the sexes. So what is happening to half the human race? What is this belittling and erasure of women?

The amount of violence against women in this country is astronomical. And it pales by comparison to the violence committed against women in many other parts of the world. Something like every eighteen seconds, some wife or girlfriend, is physically beaten or hurt by a boyfriend or husband. Eighteen seconds? This is an outrage. And in India, women are burned alive by husbands who want to marry again and get another dowry. Of course in fairness it must be said that oppressed women sometimes poison their abusive husbands. How tragic for everyone.

In Africa and parts of the Middle East, the religious customs force young girls to have their genitals mutilated in a most sadistic and cruel way that interferes with their ability to ever enjoy sex. For centuries in China, women's feet were bound, crippling them for life. And on and on...

What is the root of this misogyny, this monstrous treatment of women? Is it the same as the cause of war, where men massacre and brutalize each other? Does it have something to do with the fact that men don't give birth? Is it because for centuries women have been considered one of the spoils of war, owned, like a slave, as property?

Freud wrote at length about penis envy, but I don't think I've ever read anything about birth envy, or womb envy, which I think is by far and away the more psychologically important element in understanding our social customs and individual psychologies.

Violence, I think, springs, not from strength or power, but from a feeling of fear, weakness, impotence, frustration, and a pervasive sense of lack of self-worth or lack of value.

We have talked about the social role of women, but let's look more closely at what it really means to be female. When we strip everything else away, what is to be female?

Biologically, sex and gender are for the purpose of the reproduction of the individuals of a species.

At the most basic level, in very primitive organisms, reproduction is accomplished asexually. When a one-celled organism reaches a certain size, it divides. That is, primitive organisms multiple by dividing. The mother cell divides into two daughter cells that have exactly the same genetic make-up as the mother cell. All there are are mothers and daughters. There are no fathers or sons at this early stage of evolution.

My biology teacher, Dr. Payne, used to tell us that the purpose of the male is genetic diversity. He would say this with a twinkle in his eye, himself being the father of four wonderful children, and the husband of a lovely wife, who was quite a person in her own right.

Sexuality means that the genetic material of one individual combines with the genetic material of another individual, and the resultant hybrid chromosome pair is more vigorous and more stable than if the genetic material came only from the mother.

The introduction of a strand of DNA from the father leads to more diverse and viable offspring. Some animals, like the earthworm, are both male and female, and when they mate, they conjugate, and they each impregnate the other.

In mammals, birds, amphibians, snakes, fish and in most of the higher animals, there is a male and a female of each species, which of course is obvious, but until you think of it, you don't realize how really wonderful and amazing this is.

So to be female is to be one of these two differentiations of the species. In humans, the woman is the man with the womb and a small penis for a clitoris. The woman is literally the womb-man. Or you could say the man is the woman without the womb and with a penis, or an enlarged clitoris. We all carry attributes of both genders. The woman carries two X chromosomes in her DNA and the man carries one X chromosome and one smaller Y chromosome.

To be female is to be the one who produces the egg. The egg is a highly complex structure. The egg a complete cell that has the power to develop into an embryo. In the mammal, of course, the fertilization and the development of the embryo is within the body of the female. This obvious fact that we all take for granted is really incredible when you think about it.

The female body is complex, with all the intricate groundwork for creating a new individual of the species. The situation is not at all symmetric as between the male and the female. To speak of equality is not to speak of identity, but is rather to speak of equal worth. The male has nowhere near such elaborate biological equipment, or the psychological adaptation of behavior that goes along with this incredible complexity of gestation, birth, nurturing and caring for the young.

The mother cat knows how to keep her kittens clean, how to nurse them, how to carry them from place to place, how to make a safe nest, how to devote herself to them in such a way that they thrive. So females, female humans, women, whether or not they have children, come equipped with all these capabilities, biological, psychological, behavioral, perhaps even spiritual, emotional attributes, qualities which are necessary for the bearing and raising of children.

In many bird species the father provides for and protects the mother while she incubates the eggs and the offspring while young. The male penguin has the major work of incubating the egg.

It is now realized that men have all these nurturing and protective capacities, too; the ability to love, cherish, protect and care for. The ability to parent, I think, is fundamentally, in the male psyche as well as the female. We see this, not only in birds and mammals but also in some species of fish, where the father is an equal participant in the caring for, feeding and protecting the young.

Men and women are identical genetically except for the difference of the X and Y chromosome. Women and men are much more similar than the cultural mores and training would have us believe. And there is a naturally powerful attraction between the sexes that insures the perpetuation of the species.

There is no argument that men and women are different, but what seems to be in hot contention is, which of these differences is truly a biological difference, and which are socially imposed through false beliefs? Underlying this question is the question of power; whether or not a person will be denied the opportunity to become all that she can be because she she's a woman.

My experience in the Boston Marathon in 1966 was a microcosm of this larger problem.

What, then, is it to be a woman in a given society or culture?

Freud had not the remotest idea of what women are all about. He finally threw up his hands in despair and said, "Alas for women! What do they want?" as though women were some sort of alien creature, so far removed from men as to be completely incomprehensible.

Any woman has no difficulty in telling you exactly what women want. Women want to be free to develop their gifts and potentials to the fullest. Women want to have power and control over their own lives and well-being. Women want to be free to develop friendships, to live in a community, to love and be loved, to have a mate, to have a healthy, loving relationship with that mate, to pursue their spiritual development, to heal, to lead healthy lives, to have children, if they choose, to be respected and treated with consideration, to be free of fear, to be safe in their persons and homes, to be free, to go where they choose without fear of violence, to be free to start a business or engage in the work they chose. Women want to be able to attend school and gain a viable education, to have access to health care, safe food, clean water, pure air, and they want the same thing for their children. Women want the same freedoms and opportunities as men enjoy. Women want to be able to shoulder the same responsibilities, to be respected and to be valued as unique individuals, with full civil, human and legal rights and to follow their dreams. This is what all people want, men and women and girls and boys, alike.

This is the goal of America to create for the first time in the history of the human race a truly gender blind, race blind, ethnicity blind, religion blind society where all people are free to become all they can be without discrimination or prejudice and without putting themselves or others into stereotypical categories. America stands for and protects the freedom and dignity worth and value of each and every unique individual. We are evolving as a human species towards a time and a state of consciousness where women and men love and value each other as unique, special individuals and share all of life's possibilities and opportunities equally.

Chapter Sixteen: Economics

Town

We run through Wellesley Town Center. Cheering people pack the sidewalks. Out of the corner of my eye I watch the storefronts, and the glass windows of shops reel by. These town commercial centers stretch from sea to sea, one after another, defining the face of America.

Every American town has this array of commercial districts, with cement or brick facades— a drugstore, cafe, restaurant, laundromat, variety store, shoe store, maybe a book or record store, an ice cream parlor, a hardware store. Up on the second floor you will see stenciled, in black or gold letters, the sign for a lawyer's office or doctor's office. Around in back is the bus station.

I used to wonder how people made a living in all these little places. And when I'd pass through a city, I'd wonder how this huge conglomerate of people, buildings and business combined to make an economy.

The economy seemed to me a mysterious, vast thing, which I did not understand.

What is an economic system?

I knew that I had to get a job to get money and that without money I couldn't live. People with money paid me money for doing something they wanted, say, for being a camp counselor. I did it so I could make enough money to do what I wanted, namely take a trip across America, but beyond that I didn't know much. I knew if I finished college I could get a better job, but I had very little idea of how the whole thing worked as a system. It seemed very impersonal

193

and often cruel. The economic system sometimes seemed like a voracious devouring monster with its head on Wall Street and its thorny tail wrapped around Appalachia.

I picked up a few books on economics, but they were all so abstract, full of dubious equations and removed from everyday experience that I had no way of telling if they were true or not, or what they meant in real terms for real people. So I decided to figure out for myself what an economic system is.

I started with basics. If I begin by thinking about this drug store, I see that it has people working in it who get paid for doing some service. It's in a building that architects were paid for designing and carpenters for building, and decorators for decorating. The big drug companies do research in labs, which employ highly educated, inventive people. Drugs are developed and patented, employing patent attorneys. Drugs are manufactured and bottled in plastic bottles, which are made from hydrocarbon residues, which is pumped from the ground by oil companies, made into plastic by people in plastics companies. The metal covers are made from ore, which is mined by people, hauled to the smelting plants on trains run by people. The store is built of lumber chopped down as trees by lumbermen, hauled to mills, sawed into planks by people, or from cement dug from earthen clay deposits. The trees grow on the earth watered by rain, shined on by the sun. The ore comes from the ground as minerals deposited when the earth cooled from a molten mass of interstellar debris.

It becomes quickly apparent that each one thing in an economy is connected to each other thing. It also becomes apparent that people are involved in every step of the way. We also see that the materials and energy that originate in nature are acted upon by people in certain ways.

So I decided to take these as my fundamental premises:

1. An economy is a system,

2. Which involves or is built up by people,

3. Using materials and energy,

4. Which derive ultimately from nature. but

5. Which are transformed by people, multiple times in multiple processes to other forms of materials and energy,

6. By means of techniques or technologies,

7. That are created by the human mind,

8. To provide livelihood for all who comprise the economy.

Then I decided to look in detail at what each of my basic premises means.

What does it mean to say that "an economy is a system?" I'd seen from my work on natural systems that a system is the coordinated activity of parts and processes such that the whole of the functional dynamic organization has new levels of properties beyond the sum of the parts and processes individually.

"Comprised of people," means that the economic system is a coordinated effort among people, for example, to build a ship involves the coordinated efforts of hundreds of people and is based on techniques that are learned and passed down through the generations. Shipbuilding is an organized activity to accomplish some end goal, that is, for some purpose. People operating together in coordinated activities are capable of doing more than the individuals separately.

"Using materials and energy," means that people take all kind of material, like metal, plastic, ore, oil, wood, lumber, that are made up of atoms and molecules and all kind of energy like combustion, nuclear fission, perhaps someday nuclear fusion, electricity, hydroelectricity, steam power, horse power, metabolism, wind power, geothermal power, tidal and wave power, photovoltaic power and the like and combine these things together.

"Which derive ultimately from nature," means that all the

material and energy we use in an economy is given to us in its most basic form by nature. The gasoline we burn in combustion engines is given to us as naturally occurring oil in the ground. The wind that turns wind generators is given to us by nature. The lumber with which we build is given to us as trees and so forth.

This is one of the fundamental principles of all economies:

The Givens of Nature are the fundamental material and energetic foundation of all economies. All the resources in an economy ultimately derive from nature. We ourselves derive from nature.

"Transformed by people, multiple times in multiple processes to other forms of materials and energy" means that people act on the Givens of Nature to create derivative forms of material and energy. For example, the energetic gravitational pull of the earth operating on a flowing waterfall can be transformed by turbines and electromagnetic generation into electrical energy. The energy contained in the chemical hydrocarbon bonds in oil can be transformed into heat energy and the like.

"By mean of techniques or technologies," means that the givens of nature can be transformed into other forms of material and energy only through certain techniques that are discovered, invented and passed on to others. For example oil was not a resource to the Bedouin Tribes. It was only when the technology of cracking petroleum was invented that oil became a resource in the economy.

The techniques through which the Givens of Nature are transformed into other products and services are discovered and invented by the human mind.

Therefore the Second Fundamental Principle is that the human mind and human energy operate on the Givens of Nature to create the goods and services that comprise the economy. That is to say, the human mind and human ingenuity discover ways of using the givens of nature, through which the givens of nature become the Natural Resources that are transformed into useful and necessary items in the economy.

The techniques through which we turn the givens of nature into useful or desirable items are what we call our *technologies*.

Thus we see that nothing in nature is a resource until the human mind discovers a way of using it. Conversely everything is a potential economic resource once the human mind discovers the techniques through which natural resources become the economic resources, that is, the goods and services produced and consumed in that particular economy. This is a corollary to the Second Fundamental Principle.

For example, in a herding economy the natural resources may have been the wild goats and the shrubs on which they feed. Once tamed and captured these goats provide food and materials for tents, clothing, sacks, and many useful items. The technologies of goat husbandry are passed from generation to generation.

"To provide livelihood for all who comprise the economy," means that an economy is the interrelated ways in which we all provide livings for ourselves.

This brings us back to where we started, namely: *The fundamental purpose of an economy is to provide for the well-being and livelihood of everyone who participates in that economy.*

Once we understand this basic premise then we can begin to structure economic systems that provide for the common good, and for individual livelihoods. We see that the aggrandizement of wealth of the few at the expense of the many is not a legitimate end to which an economy should function.

Moreover we will see that the providing of the livelihood and well-being of human beings through the production of value in human terms is the proper end of an economy. Specifically, the proper end of an economy is the production of healthy, balance, happy human beings, who in turn create healthy, functional societies. This goes without saying, though it should be emphasized, that in order to have healthy economies and societies there must be healthy natural environments, not only because all the natural sources of our economies are ultimately from nature, but also because we ourselves are

197

part of nature, dependent on nature for the air we breathe, the water we drink and the food we eat and even for the skyscrapers we build and the rockets we send out into space.

So to review, our three principles are:

A. The Givens of Nature are the fundamental material and energetic foundation of all economies.

B. The human mind is the fundamental transformational resource of any economy.

C. The fundamental purpose of an economy is to provide for the well-being and livelihood of everyone who participates in that economy.

How are these principles actually accomplished in an economic system?

The answer is these fundamental principles are implemented in the economy through businesses.

The fundamental unit of the economy is the business.

What is a business?

In its broadest sense, a business is an organized activity in pursuit of livelihood.

Giant international oil conglomerates are businesses, the tiny mom and pop variety store on the corner is a business. Each person is his or her own business, in so far as he or she has skills and capabilities or energy that can be used to provide a livelihood.

Businesses link the process of creating goods and services to the processes of consumption of those goods and services. In a healthy economy, those who create the goods and services are also those who consume the goods and services. As we shall see, in an unhealthy economy there is a disconnect between those who create the goods and services and those who consume them.

The process of creating goods and services is the supply side of the economy and the process of consuming those goods and services is the demand side of an economy.

The Market is where the supply side meets the demand side. The

Market is where the items and services produced are bought and sold.

For example if Mary knits a sweater as a gift for her niece this is not a business. However if Mary knits a sweater to sell, then this is a business. She buys yarn, she puts in her time she knits the sweater and takes it to market. The market may be a local bazar or maybe a shop where she sells on consignment. If she owns the shop where she sells her knitted produce then this is a larger business.

To be successful a shop has to make a profit, that is, the net income must exceed the net outgo. This is true in all biological systems as well. A living organism cannot spend more energy than it takes in or it will die. If you burn more calories than you take in you lose weight and eventually die.

If Mary expands her business she may hire other knitters. She may go one step further and buy a sheep farm and hire people to produce yarn for her. Each of the people employed by her are their own businesses in the sense that they are engaging in an activity based on their skills and energy in pursuit of livelihood.

Moreover, each business is based on one or more technologies. A technology is simply a technique of doing something. The technology of sheep shearing involves clipping machines, for example. The technology of knitting requires yarn, knitting needles and a learned skill.

A market, then, is simply how the seller and buyer transact the exchange. It can be a material transaction as in a store, where the customer walks out with an actual object, like a sweater, or it can be a virtual transaction involving non-tangible goods and services like the stock market. These non-tangible assets can be translated into tangible assets and also into contracts that represent tangible assets.

A share in a corporation, for example, can be bought and sold in a computerized market, but it can also be represented by a piece of paper. The share can also be thought of as a proportionate part of in the net assets of the corporation that issues the share or stock.

The value of that share may rise or fall, just as the value of Mary's sheep and Mary's sweaters can rise and fall.

This concept of value is a fundamental aspect of the market.

What is value?

Value is how much something is worth. But value isn't just a static number. The value of something can change. The value of something is triply relativistic. Value is relative to the person valuing. Value is relative to the conditions and context in which the value judgment is being made. The value of one thing is relative to the value of other things.

For example a glass of water to a man in the desert may be of life-saving high value, but that same glass of water to a man in a flood may be of no value. The value of a pink negligee to a new bride may be high, but to a lumberjack the negligee is of no value at all unless he wants to make a gift to his girlfriend or wife.

We could measure the value of one thing in terms of the value of something else. For example to Paul, the fisherman, the value of a bushel of apples may be two fish. To Mary who wants to make an apple pie the value of a bushel of apples may be one sweater.

Money is a brilliant invention because it allows the value of one thing at one place and time to be carried to the value of another thing at another place and time. And it allows value to be stored in a form that doesn't deteriorate. For example if Paul sells his fish on the docks for ten dollars and then travels to the country, and trades his ten dollars for a bushel of apples, money has been the medium, or intermediate, in the exchange.

By using money as a medium of exchange we can account all goods and services in terms of the value of money. We can say ten dollars is worth one bushel of apples and one fish. Or we can say one bushel of apples or one fish is worth one dollar. When we account value in terms of money we standardize our measure of value and make our accounting and our comparisons of value much easier.

In monetary terms, the price of something is the number of dollars or coins in money that expresses the relative monetary value of the good or service.

In a market economy the price of a good or service is set by the ratio of supply to demand. Supply is how much of the good or service is available at a given time on the market. Demand is how much, how many people want and need something. But Demand is more than this... Demand also depends on how much money people have to spend and how that purchasing power is distributed in the purchasing market. This later fact is vital to understand.

The Market Value of a good or service is then determined by the ratio of how much of that good or service is available on the market to how many people want that good or service, how much money they have to spend and how that purchasing power is distributed.

For example, in a community of one hundred people everyone wants and needs shoes. If shoes can be produced for three dollars a pair, and everyone has five dollars to spend on shoes, the price will be five dollars a pair and the number of shoes produced for the market will be one hundred. And the economy will include everyone and thrive.

But if in that same community ninety-nine people have one dollar to spend on shoes and one person has four-hundred and one dollars to spend on shoes, then the supply side of the market will organize to produce one pair of gold-plated shoes for four-hundred and one dollars, and ninety-nine people will have no shoes. In this latter situation the economy is out of balance and will deteriorate into a polarized situation of impoverishment, as ninety-nine percent of the people have little or no livelihood, and one percent of the population has obscene wealth.

This situation is unsustainable and leads to revolution and war and societal break down as history has shown. This is why it is vital to insure a broad distribution of purchasing power and a large middle class and to dampen the extreme ends of the scale. The question at hand is how best to achieve a broad thriving middle class and a broad distribution of wealth that supports a thriving economy. We will look at this below.

I measure demand in terms of Market Pressure, which I account as dollar-persons. Ninety-nine people, with one dollar each, exert ninety-nine person-dollars of market pressure. Ninety-nine dollar-persons is not enough to cover the expense of making the shoes, since it costs three dollars to make a pair of shoes. Business cannot organized to produce shoes at one dollar a pair..

One person with four hundred and one dollars exerts four-hundred and one person-dollars of market pressure. A business can organize to produce one pair of shoes for four-hundred and one dollars. So we see how the distribution of purchasing power in the economy fundamentally affects what gets produced and who buys it.

Fundamentally this is what is wrong with supply-side, free-market, trickle down, right-wing economic theory. We see how the inequity in purchasing power operates to make a free market system fail. A truly free market requires that purchasing power be more or less equally and broadly distributed in the market. Where this fails there can be no free market.

The market is anything but free to those with little or no money. It is not hard to see why the ultra-wealthy would promote supply-side, free-market, unregulated, trickle down, right-wing economics and dupe the rest of us into buying this lethal theory. Where there is a concentration of wealth, those with great wealth, wield great power in the market and therefore the market is not free, at all, but is controlled by those who have the most money.

What is the answer?

Is a controlled economy the answer?

It depends on what kind of control is imposed and at what levels.

In a totally controlled market economy, as in a Communistic

economy, a central authority determines what goods and service will be produced, and the central authority determines the price at which those goods and services will be sold on the market. But in order for this to work, there has to be enough purchasing power in the buying side of the market to afford the goods and services at the set price. This means that employment, wages and income also needs to be controlled to insure there is enough demand.

Generally it has been found that this type of controlled economy doesn't work well and that supply does not keep up with demand, so shortages occur. Part of the reason for this is that the decisions made by the central authority often do not reflect what the buyers want. Part of the problem there is no reward for those who organize and run the businesses, in other words there is no free enterprise so there is little incentive to work hard to make a success.

In a Communist economy there is yet another layer of control beyond the control of supply and demand. In a Communist economy all property and means of production are owned communally and there is no individual ownership of property or business. In practical terms, rather than communal ownership the ownership and control belong to the Communist Central Government and not to the people. This means that there is little incentive for people work or to innovate or to create. Moreover, freedom and self-determination are so fundamental to the human spirit that this type of authoritarianism is oppressive. Because power corrupts, Communism usually devolves into Totalitarianism. This system, then, is incompatible with democracy, which includes the freedom to start, to run one's own business.

But as we saw the completely unregulated free market doesn't work either.

Is Capitalism the answer?

What do we mean by Capitalism?

What is Capital?

Capital is simply stored value that can be used to produce goods and services in the economy. There are many forms of stored value. Capital can be stored as money in a bank account, as stocks and bonds, as land, as machinery, as raw natural resources, as a skilled labor force, as knowledge, research and development. Because the fundamental basis of an economy is the power of the human mind to create and the power of human energy to do, the fundamental Capital of any society is it people and their knowledge, abilities, energy and skills.

Every economy needs Capital. Even Communistic economies need Capital to invest in production. Usually the term Capitalism refers to an economy in which private individuals own and control stored-value. But again this is ambiguous because the nature of the economy depends very much on how that stored-value is distributed and how it is used or invested. The word Capitalist is used in a derogatory manner to mean someone who has a lot of money and exploits others, but this is a very narrow use of the word. We need to find new words to describe what we need to do to create workable, fair, flourishing economies.

The word Socialism has so many different, conflicting meanings that this just adds to the confusion. A Socialist Democracy is a completely different system from a Socialist Totalitarian system.

We need to keep in mind that the purpose of the economy is to produce healthy happy functioning creative human beings and to preserve and enhance the health of the natural environment on which every economy depends. To do this there must be broad distribution of purchasing power and an educated skilled, healthy population.

In the opinion of the author a healthy economy requires democratic governance, free enterprise, the right to own property, to start and to run one's own business as one sees fit within the law, fair judicial systems and non-corrupt legislative powers. Add to this the concept of the Commonwealth, that is, the ways in which we all pool our resources energy and money to provide for societal well-being. This is accomplished to a great extent by a tax system that provides for the general welfare and through which we invest wisely in projects and services that enhance societal and individual wellbeing.

The creation of a healthy economy also requires intelligent rules that regulate the manner in which financial and economic institutions operate. Laws that prevent great combines of wealth and power from accumulating huge amounts of political and economic power are necessary, because when wealth concentrates it begins to corrupts our democracy, our freedom and our economy.

Chapter Seventeen: Cosmology

Black Rock

Route 135, which we had been following, bears off to the right, and we veer onto Route 16. The sign says "ROUTE 16, 16 EAST"; and on the sign underneath, it says "BOSTON." I feel rising excitement, as we get closer to our goal.

We curve up a rise by a park with large hardwood trees and birches, and through another town center lined with cheering people, beautiful, sunny happy faces. We run on through the stoplights and by the Little League field, spacious lawns and large houses, with old mansard roofs.

There, behind the crowds, behind the stoplight, behind the railroad track, an immense rock wall rises to the left. An entire hill has been cut in half and hollowed out to make room for the railroad track and the road. The rock glistens purple and black, with flecks of quartz shimmering in the sun.

It's an astounding sight, this huge black, up-thrusting cooled and crystalized mantle of the earth standing here completely unnoticed, as if we choose to forget that the core of our earth is molten-hot. Grass and oak trees have grown back along the top, where the hill used to be.

Here for all to see are the bare bones of the earth exposed in dramatic testimony to our planetary essence. We often forget in the business of everyday life that we are denizens inhabiting a small planet, in a galaxy, in a universe, in a cosmos and that we have no idea why or how all this comes into existence.

I'd seen that All-That-Is has to be in the continuous act of creating

Itself into existence in this paradoxical, miraculous way. But what is the nature of this universe out of which we have evolved and within which we have our being? I had seen that it cannot be purely a material existence, because subjective experience could not arise within a purely material existence. Never the less it is instructive to look at how physicists explain the existence of the universe.

The "Big Bang Theory," so-called, has been widely endorsed for decades. This idea that the universe is expanding dates back to the 1920's to a man named Edwin Hubble. Astronomers noticed that the spectra of elements in distant stars and other galaxies appeared to be shifted towards the red end of the spectrum. That is, each element, when it's emitting electromagnetic radiation, does so in a characteristic pattern. Based on the spectra of the elements as we observe them on earth, as we look at the same elements in stars that are very far away from us, we note that in the distant stars the atomic spectra are shifted towards the red, that is, the wavelengths are longer than normal.

Scientist pondered what would cause the wavelengths of elements in distant stars to be longer than normal. They compared this effect of the lengthening of wavelengths of light from distant stars to what happens to the wavelengths of sound waves as for example when a train passes by.

When a train emits a whistle as it rushes by you, you hear the tone as higher as the train is coming toward you, and lower and lower as the train moves away from you. From the point of view of the observer on the train, the note is always the same; but *you* hear it first higher then lower because, as the train is coming toward you, the velocity of the train adds to the velocity of the sound wave, in effect pushing the wave along, causing the frequency to increase and the wavelength to shorten.

However, when the train is moving away from you, the velocity of the train in effect pulling the whistle along and stretching out the sound wave, making the wavelength longer and the frequency of vibration slower, which makes the whistle sound lower to our ear. Remember the frequency of the sound wave is the number of waves that pass a certain point in a given interval of time, and the wavelength is the length between adjacent peaks.

This stretching out of the sound waves is called the Doppler effect; and this same theory had been applied to distant stars. The shift in the spectra of the elements to the red has been interpreted as the lengthening of the wavelength of the light coming to us from distant objects that are moving away from us. The question then became what was causing the stars to race away from us.

It was then concluded that there must have been an explosion at some point in time and this caused all the stars to be racing away from some central point. Tracing it back in time physicists reasoned there must have been some time at which the entire universe was concentrated into a very tiny volume, which was called a singularity.

This tiny volume was unimaginably dense and when it exploded the force was so astronomically great that the universe sped away at great velocity. Some physicists suggested that the theory should be modified to include the possibility of expansion, not from a central point but from *all* points, like bread dough expanding. But it was noted that even when bread expands from every point, it also expands from the central point of the dough mass.

The Catholic Church endorses the Big Bang theory because it gives an external God one moment of creation; the Bang. Men like the Big Bang Theory because the Bang is the Male Orgasm, which ejaculates the entire universe into being with no need of the female, who originally had been the bringer of form. Materialists like the Big Bang theory because it is all in terms of matter, energy and forces. But, of course, there is no explanation of what created God or from where the singularity came.

From the time I first learned of the Big Bang theory in my physics class as a student at Tufts University in 1962, I felt that the Big Bang Theory was fundamentally wrong. I watched as over the intervening years the Big Bang Theory became more and more firmly imbedded in the lore of mainstream science and all who doubted were treated as heretical.

So as usual I found myself on the outside of the mainstream. Unable to find a place for myself in the existing structure, I was reduced to thinking my own independent thoughts as a solitary person, eking out an existence on the edges, trying to support myself doing other things, while feeling that my right work involved studying and thinking, and as always, questioning the prevailing mythologies and seeking to find new truths.

The Big Bang theory goes on to explain what happens each millisecond after the Bang. We find forces evolving and differentiating, and elements appearing. But there's nothing in the Bang to explain how forces appear and differentiate, or how the elements can come into existence, or how anything can have *form*, or how principles, or laws, or rules, and regularities of behavior that we call *Natural Laws*, come into existence.

Nor does the Bang explain how systems exist or become more complex, how atoms form out of subatomic particles, or how electromagnetic radiation is structured, or how all the energy in the entire universe was contained or existed before the Big Bang in this singularity, or how the energy and matter of the entire universe was compressed into such a small space, or what initiated the Bang.

To add to all the other unbelievable and incomplete assumptions made in the Big Bang theory, it was the discovered that, not only were the distant stars moving away from us, but that their speeds were continuously increasing.

I scarcely knew where to begin in challenging this huge tangled mess.

According to Relativity Theory, the moving away from us of a distant star is equivalent to our moving away from the distant star, that is, there is a relative motion between the star and us. In fact if the star is increasing its velocity away from us, then we are increasing our velocity away from the star, that is to say that there is a relative acceleration between us.

Since acceleration is proportional to the force acting between two bodies and inversely proportional to the masses of the two bodies, this means that if we believe the Big Bang Theory there must be an assumed force acting between the distant stars that is pushing us further and further apart at faster and faster speeds.

In other words, this acceleration of distant stars is inconsistent with the conventional Big Bang theory where the force of the original explosion occurred at a past time and the stars continue to move away from each other at the constant speed they acquired from the initial explosion. In the original explosion theory, the velocities of the stars would remain constant.

However, if the stars are moving away from one another with ever-increasing speed this would imply an assumed force that continues to act between the stars causing them to increase the speed with which they are moving apart. There is no explanation of what this continuing force might be or how it must act to push the stars apart at ever-increasing speeds.

Moreover if there is a continuing force acting to push the stars apart as required by the observation of the increasing velocities of distant stars, then there is no need of an initial big bang to explain why the stars are moving apart. The stars would be moving apart because of a continuing force acting between them to drive them apart, not because of any big bang.

So we have to move beyond the initial Big Bang explosion theory.

When we look at the alternative hypothesis of a force continuing to act to drive the stars apart, we are confronted with even deeper problems. We are now looking at a hypothetical universe that is continuously being driven apart by some force that is causing the distant stars to accelerate away from one another. We know that as material bodies increase in speed, their apparent masses increase and we know that the upper bound on the speed of a material object is the speed of light.

Therefore we are left with a hypothetical universe in which, as the stars are driven to higher and higher speeds by this mysterious force that is assumed to be acting to drive them apart, their masses are increasing, and since they can never travel faster than the speed of light they cannot accelerate indefinitely. As their speeds approach the speed of light their masses, as measured from a central point or from other slower moving stars, would appear to approach infinity.

This would mean that the masses of distant stars would act to retard any light emitted from those stars and thus produce a spectrum of light that was continuously exhibiting a longer and longer wavelength. This would indeed appear as a red shift and continue on into the infrared range from very distant stars.

In addition, it is well known that when there is a clock on a coordinate system that is moving relative to us, or in a gravitational field, the faster the relative motion, or stronger the field, the slower a clock appears to tick, to an outside observer. This would produce an apparent red shift, if we consider the emission of waves, from activated atoms, as a clock. So the observed red shift can be explained by saying either that the stars are moving away from us, or that the stars are getting heavier and heavier and thus they create an ever increasing gravitational field between themselves and the rest of the universe, the further away the stars is. But there would have to be an upper bound on this, or the mass and gravitational force would become infinite.

But this leaves unexplained the mysterious force that hypothetically acts to drive the stars apart, and fails to explain what happens as the masses of distant stars approach infinite mass, at which point they would weigh more than the entire universe. Nor does it explain what would happen as the speeds of these distant stars approach the speed of light.

Confronted with this ugly mess of unlikely hypotheses, I decided to go back to the original observation of the red shift and to question the assumptions that followed from that. What is observed is simply that the wavelengths of the emission spectra of the elements from distant stars appear to be longer than they should be based on the wavelengths of those same elements as measured on the earth, and that the further away the star is from us, the longer the wavelength appears to be shifted to the red.

Can there be any explanation for this observed shift in the spectral wavelengths of known elements other than the Big Bang theory?

I realized I had to go deeper, and that the real key to understanding the red shift lies in understanding the interaction of the observer with his or her gravitational horizon. I decided to look again at what acceleration actually is.

As we saw, one of the examples Einstein used in thinking about the General Theory of Relativity was the equivalence between these two situations: In one situation, there's a person in an elevator way out in space away from gravitational fields, and that elevator is being propelled at an ever-increasing velocity, faster and faster. From the inside of the elevator, the person thinks she's standing in a gravitational field that is pulling her to the floor of the elevator. She drops objects and finds that they always fall towards the floor with the same acceleration. And she concludes that she is in a gravitational field, and the mass she experiences is gravitational mass.

To the observer on the outside, seeing that the elevator is not in any gravitational field but is being pulled by a hypothetical rope affixed to the top of the elevator, faster and faster, she will reason that the object is falling to the floor, not because of any gravitational field, but simply because the floor of the elevator is moving at ever increasing speeds toward the object that has been released from the person's hand, and that what is being observed is the inertial mass of the body in space.

Clearly gravitational mass and inertial mass are always equal because they are simply different ways of measuring the same acceleration.

This sets up an equivalence between accelerating reference frames and gravitational reference frames.

This is relevant to understanding the red shift, because the phenomenon of rushing away at ever increasing velocities - that is, of accelerating away - is in fact equivalent to the presence of a gravitational field. And so we have an image of gravitation describing something as moving away at ever increasing velocities, while staying in the same place. Keep in mind that place is not an absolute position but is always relative to some designated reference frame.

The presence of a gravitational field distorts the way space and time, mass and energy, and hence frequency, are measured. Or to say it differently a gravitational field is a distortion in space and time. Or to say it still more differently, our measure of space and time defines the presence of a gravitational field. In Riemann physics, a gravitational field is a distortion of space-time. The gravitational field is described by a kind of geodesic warping of space-time.

Thus an observer who is operating within a gravitational field is making measurements relative to a system of reference in which the space and time coordinates, and thus the frequency, mass, and energy coordinates, are distorted. The extent of that distortion depends on the strength of the gravitational field in which the observer is immersed.

This is all very well known to relativistic theorists; but I think the relation of the observation and its intrinsic reference to the coordinate system of the observer is something that hasn't been fully appreciated with regards to horizons.

I decided to look at the big picture, that is, to look at the cosmos of All –That-Is. The All-that-Is has no outside edge, which means that there can be no central point, or to put it differently, every point in the universe is the central point.

Since every point is the central point there can be no absolute central point from which some hypothetical explosion occurred, which is further evidence against the Big Bang. But this brings up an interesting point. Suppose that no matter where you are standing in the cosmos it appears that the rest of the cosmos is arrayed around you, and that all the stars are moving away from you with ever-increasing speeds.

Is there another possible interpretation of this phenomena?

I think there is.

Suppose, by analogy, you are standing on the surface of the earth, which is a sphere. Now as you look out from your vantage point you will see your horizon arrayed around you in a large circle. Someone standing on your horizon will see his horizon arrayed around him and you on the furthest reaches of his horizon. So each observer has a horizon that is relative to that observer.

To each person standing at the center of her horizon, objects farther and farther away appear to be smaller and smaller. The farther away an object is the smaller it appears. Conversely, to a person who appears to be on her horizon, she appears to be a tiny dot. The sizes of objects don't really change, only the appearance of distant objects seems to change relative to the person in the center of his or her horizon.

By analogy we look out and see the universe, indeed the entire cosmos of universes arrayed around us with us at the center and our horizon on the periphery. To a person standing on the periphery of our universe, he or she thinks that they are at the center and we on the extreme edge. Thus, not only is every point in the universe the center of the universe, but every point in the universe is on a horizon as viewed by an observer on one of the infinite centers of the universe.

We see the spectra of elements on earth as being what we would call normal but we see elements on the periphery of our horizon arrayed around us as being shifted to the red. Likewise the person on our horizon would see the elements on their planet as emitting normal spectra but would see the spectra of elements on earth as being shifted to the red.

That is to say the observations are completely symmetric and relative to each observer. This is exactly the case we saw in Special Relativity where each observer on relatively uniformly moving coordinate systems looks over at the other and sees measured lengths shortened in the direction of the relative motion and each sees each other's clocks as ticking off slower times.

However, when you look out into the universe, you are making your observations not from a uniformly moving coordinate system, but from a coordinate system in a gravitational field. But a gravitational field is equivalent to an accelerating coordinate system. But this is just what we see on the periphery of our space-time horizon: We see the entire gravitational field of the universe arrayed as a horizon around the center of each point in the universe. But this is just what the redshift is. I believe the red shift is an artifact of the way in which we as observers are interacting with the totality of the mass of the cosmos arrayed around us, in a system where every point is the center of the cosmos and there is no outside boundary to All-That-Is.

Just as on our earthly horizon, distances and sizes appear to shrink the further away the objects are until they are beyond the horizon of our vision, so in the cosmos, objects on our horizon appear to be distorted in space-time in a manner that we can interpret as gravitation, or acceleration, of distant objects that would cause an apparent redshift without there being an actual expansion or racing away of the stars themselves.

What we are seeing is an artifact caused by our interaction with the distortion of space-time in a gravitational cosmos in which every point is the center and there is no outside boundary. Indeed in my hypothesis, space and time or space-time are not the fundamentals at all. Space and time and space-time are the ways in which we human measure what we perceive as our environment.

We project the neurological correlates that our brains use to help us navigate through the world of what we perceive as objects and distances onto a cosmos that is in my opinion based on a much more fundamental system in which I hypothesize action and interaction are the fundamentals, not space-time, force or mass.

In my system velocity is not created by composing distance traveled per unit of time. Rather it is the other way around: velocity is primary and fundamental and space and time and space-time are decomposed from the basic velocity parameters. Where there are no forces, the velocities remain unchanged. Only when interaction occurs do velocities change and these interactions are what we measure as accelerations and masses or forces.

Just as there can be no central point of the universe, there can be no center of mass of the universe because there is no outside boundary. This means that the center of mass of the universe is at every point in the universe, or to say it differently, every point in the universe is the center of mass of the universe.

This means that when we view our horizon we are viewing it from our relative center of mass for the entire universe. Thus the apparent gravitational field of the entire mass of the universe is arrayed around us at our horizon. This is true of every point in the universe.

It is well to remember, here, that the entire mass of the universe of all that is, is much greater than the sum of the masses of the stars. In fact the mass of the universe is immense and contains enormous amounts of what has been called dark matter, which has not been understood. It is very possible that as light passes through this dark matter, it loses energy and that this too may contribute to a shift towards the less energetic end of the spectrum, which is the longer wave-length red shift.

The further away the star is, the more gravitational "dark matter "it passes through to get to us, and so the more energy it may lose and the more shifted to the red its spectrum would be.

So to summarize, in my theory, the redshift is not caused by the actual racing away of distant stars or by a big bang. The redshift is an epiphenomenon of the way we interact with the totality of the gravitational cosmos arrayed around every point, in a cosmos that has no outer boundary and where every point is the center.

The mass of the cosmos appears to accumulate at each horizon. The gravitational field of the cosmos appears to compile at each horizon around each point in the cosmos. That is, the horizon is the curvature of space-time due to the presence of the gravitational field of the universe of All-That-Is. But, what is that curvature? It is not an absolute curvature of something physically real out there. It is a relative curvature a seen from each different point.

The further away from our relative center we probe, the stronger the gravitational field at our horizon *appears* to be. Therefore, the more distorted space-time seems and the more light coming from these regions appears to be shifted to the red. Hypothetically if we go far enough the apparent mass is so great that the light from these regions never reaches us.

But remember, all these appearances are relative to each observer who is from her own perspective at the center of mass of the totality of mass of the entire system, which has no outside and in which every point is the center. This concept of gravitational horizons and warped space-time is also relevant in understanding and explaining so called apparent black holes, which again are apparent regions of increasing gravitation and warping of spacetime over an event horizon that is relative to the various observers.

Since velocity is the ratio of the interval of the distance traveled to the interval of elapsed time, when the ratio of space to time is distorted, so is the apparent velocity. It is as if every point in what we have called "space" were instead a velocity vector, with the direction and length of that vector proportional to the observed gravitational field at that place, from the relative viewpoints of each observer.

In fact "space" does not really exist out there at all, any more than time does. Space is the way we interpret what we see. We cannot image an object with no outside. What is really there we can never know objectively, but in terms of the accuracy of our models, what is really there, in the opinion of the author, is more analogous to an array of velocity vectors, rather than "space."

Therefore, in the opinion of the author, the redshift, and the apparent expansion of the cosmos, is an epiphenomenon, an illusion, an interplay, of the observer with the observed. This racing away at ever-increasing velocities while staying in the same place, is the way we, as observers, interact with gravitational mass, that has been called the curvature of space-time. Remember that this so-called curvature is relative to each and every point in what I've called the velocity-vector array. It's not some explosion; this so-called "expansion" is an illusion. It's not expanding at all. It's all an appearance. We need to deepen, and to refine, our fundamental conceptions and models of what we have called space-time. Once we do this there is no need of a Bang to explain anything. There never was an explosion; there never was a Big Bang. There never will be.

CHAPTER EIGHTEEN: LANGUAGE

Route 9 Sign

Crowds pack the sidewalks all through Wellesley and Wellesley Hills. People cheer with unabated enthusiasm. I feel, around me, the pack of sweaty, lean bodies of the other runners. I'm running from the inside out, listening to every nuance of each cell of my body burning energy and oxygen, gauging my reserves. My legs and arms are moving around the central, still point of my body; I'm balancing always balancing.

"To route 9," the flat sign ahead states... "Newton Up Falls."

We follow the other sign to West Newton and Watertown along Route 16, passing right over Route 9. "Isn't it funny how a bunch of marks on a board can convey meaning." I marvel. What is language? I wonder. How is it that we humans can communicate with language? Amazingly, many animals have languages in the sense of a potpourri of sounds, intonations, and body movements through which they signal and communicate with one another, but the extent and development of humans to speak and write a complex systematic, grammatical language is unique. How remarkable when you think about it. Language is the way knowledge and the technologies of society are passed down from generation to generation. Although we have a number of ways of communicating, language is the most complex way we communicate our thoughts, ideas, feelings, plans, perceptions, wants, needs and knowledge to one another.

What is language? I wonder.

A language is a systematic way of representing thoughts by

symbols. But what are thoughts? A sentence represents a complete thought we were taught in grade-school. But what is a complete thought? A complete thought as expressed in a sentence has a subject, verb and usually, but not always, an object. Why? Because that is the way we think. But that isn't the only way we think. We can think verbally, but we can also think in visual images, felt senses, feelings, intuitions and abstract representations. We can store a memory and recall it at will. We can imagine. But clearly one way we think is expressed in language.

The structure of grammar and syntax reflects the structure of our mental processes, which correspond to the organized activity of our brains/ nervous systems. We talk about nouns, verbs, subjects, objects, adjectives, adverbs, predicates, conjunctions, clauses, phrases, relationals because that reflects how we perceive and think, which reflects the function and structure of our minds/brains.

What, then, can language tell us about the structure, organization and operation of the brain, or at least part of the brain? What is this thing we call a thought? And how is it related to the brain?

The shape of the human mouth, tongue, and larynx makes it possible to make a great number of different sounds. But sounds don't make a language. These sounds are merely symbols. The sounds we make represent, or stand for, something else. In the context of a structured syntax and grammar, these sounds serve to *represent* thoughts. The speaker associates his or her thoughts with the sounds, and then when the listener hears the sounds in the context of a given linguistic structure, she or he can associate it with his or her own thoughts and so thoughts can be communicated between minds. It is really very ingenious.

Later people invented a way to make marks that could signify ideas. The marks could be put together according to a system of grammar, which was implicit in the spoken language. So language, both spoken and written, symbolizes and represents a series of thoughts. On reading or hearing the symbols, which have been associated with certain thoughts, the reader or listener can reconstruct the thoughts of the speaker or writer in his or her own mind.

What, then, does the structure of language reveal about the structure of our brains? And again, of course, that all-present question which is never asked — What is thought, and how does your thought, which is an incorporeal, subjective experience relate with your brain, which is a mass of cells, composed of molecules and atoms? And how can the brain represent to itself, in its own language, it's perceptual and conceptual subjective experiences?

I had seen that you can never know directly what the "outside world" is. All you ever know is your subjective experience of your interaction with whatever is out there. Your subjective experience is created by, in and through your nervous system and brain and its interaction with whatever is out there.

We've seen that the blue sky is not really blue out there. The BLUENESS is created in your nervous system and presents itself miraculously to you as your subjective experience BLUE. So language isn't about an objective outside world. It is about your subjective experience, which is created in, by and through your mind/brain as you interact with whatever is out there. Later you can think or dream about it by re-visiting the subjective representations that your brain and nervous system have created and stored.

Basic to understanding language, then, is the understanding of subjective experience. How do subjective, mental experiences occur? How are they structured? What are they?

Take the simple idea of "dog". Already you have an idea of what I mean by "dog". How do you do this? Dog, you say is a noun, which refers to a specific physical object having reality in the outside world. But is it?

"DOG" is an abstract idea, a concept, with which you have associated a certain set of sounds, a fricative "d" sound with the tongue pressed against the back of the upper teeth while making a muted sound in the throat. A rounding of the lips and exhaling of soft air produces the "o" and the guttural "g" at the back of the throat ends the sequence of sound, which you associate with the abstract idea "DOG".

From now on I will designate with capitals DOG the internal subjective experience of dog. While dog will refer to whatever the external referent is. Quotation marks will designate the abstract mental concept "DOG"; while "dog" will designate the set of all dogs out there.

How dare I say that "DOG" is an abstract idea in the face of generations of philosophers who declare that, "There is no such thing as an abstract dog?" I answer that I am able to do this because it's not the dog that's abstract, it's the idea, the concept "DOG" that's abstract.

Einstein used an example to illustrate why he thought ideas are not abstractions, but are representations. He said that when you check your coat at a restaurant, the attendant gives you a check. This check represents your coat, he said. Whereas when you make soup from bones you boil them down into something else. This is an abstraction. You abstract the essence of the nutrition from the bones. So he said that thought or an idea was a representation, like a coat check, not an abstraction, like soup.

But this isn't really correct.

What is abstract? Abstract means "taken from" or drawn out of. An abstraction draws out the essence of something. What is an essence? An essence is a collection of characteristics that define the referent in question.

When a child learns a language, she learns categorical sets of ideas. She sees various examples of dogs—short, black ones, tall, shaggy ones, brown ones and spotted ones. Her mental apparatus is such that she has no difficulty in abstracting, that is, drawing out, the characteristics all that the dogs have in common and separating out the characteristics that differ from dog to dog. Thus, in my opinion, she does much more that simply associate a specific dog with a representation as in the coat check example. Her brain, effortlessly and naturally finds the qualities that all the objects called, dog, have in common. That is, she deduces or takes from the specific examples and makes a general category that represents all dogs, that is, all objects having these characteristics, but not other characteristics.

She sees examples of cats and she notices that, like dogs, cats have tails, ears, four legs and fur, but she doesn't confuse cats with dogs. She notices that cats have retractable claws and climb trees, and dogs wag their tails when pleased and so forth. Later she will learn that dogs and cats belong to a larger category of quadrupedal mammals.

So categories differentiate and overlap in layers of inclusion and exclusion. Later, as her ability to abstract becomes more finely tuned she will learn set theory about conjunctive and disjunctive sets.

Our language enables us to associate symbols with these abstract sets of things and events and to represent the objects of our thought and their relationships with language, syntax and grammar. So we both abstract and we represent those abstractions by symbols, words, sentences and discourses.

This ability to abstract categorical sets from the observation of relatively few individual examples is a mental capacity that arises from the very structure and function of our mind/brain. It is this ability that is the basis of our capacity for language. And indeed, it is basic to our capacity for recognition.

The nervous system is very good at finding similarities and differences at all levels.

The nervous system is especially organized to abstract and create certain qualities out of the blips of energy impinging on its receptors. Out of these blips the brain/mind constructs its subjective picture of the world. This is a remarkable feat. We have no idea how it does this and in particular how subjective experience results from the organized firings of neurons in these highly organized brain structures. And yet, I believe that it is through elaborations of this basic neuronal ability that the higher brain acquires the ability to think in abstract categorical sets that underlies the ability to express thoughts in language.

One of the methods the brain uses to achieve abstraction is the comparison of inputs. Neurons are constructed to be able to compare inputs, to respond to differences and to detect and enhance contrasts. To compare and to measure differences and similarities between inputs is a strategy even the most primitive nervous systems use.

The seeking and finding gradients of certain chemicals in its environment is essential to the survival of one-celled organisms. For example, some organisms seek sugar. How do they accomplish this?

They follow gradients by comparing the inputs and outputs of two or more receptors.

How does the organism compare inputs or outputs? If you have two receptors that are sensitive to sugar and are located some distance apart, and one of the two receptors feeds on to a third neuron in an excitatory fashion and the other one feeds on to the same third neuron in an inhibitory fashion, then that third neuron will be able to detect the exact ratio, or difference between the two input receptors. If the organism is wired so that the left receptor is inhibitory and the right receptor is excitatory the organism will "know" whether there is more sugar on the left or on the right and will adjust its course accordingly.

These comparator cells are ubiquitous in the nervous system at all levels of complexity and this enables the organism to find the ratios, or differences, between inputs at a multitude of levels of operation.

Similar comparator neurons in the higher brain centers can compare the inputs of complex functions that represent subjectively the different objects and events in the environment.

The young girl can compare images of dogs and cats, cows and horses, and her nervous system will detect the similarities and differences. From these myriad comparisons of similarities and differences the brain builds up abstract concepts that pertain to different classes of objects and events, like "DOG" and "CAT".

So, basic to language is the mental capacity to form concepts, to abstract categorical sets, to distinguish like features and unlike features in any collection of objects and based on similarities and differences to generate a category of sets based on defining characteristics.

What sort of thing are these abstract categories? The concept "DOG" is not a visual image. What is it then? As soon as you conjure up a visual image you are dealing with specifics. You can't think of a specific abstract dog.

Whenever you think of a specific dog it has specific characteristics. You can visualize a small, short-haired dog or a tall, black, shaggy dog, but you can't visualize the concept "DOG." When you think of dog in general, that is, when you think of the abstract category "DOG", what are you thinking of? It's not so clear.

You are holding the concept "DOG" in your mind, and it has a definite meaning. If I say "The dog jumped out of the pen." You know exactly what I mean. I can linguistically elaborate by adding concepts for example, "The red setter, leaped out of the chain-linked enclosure." Now you have a more specific visual image. But however detailed, the linguistic description is, it is still made up of concepts abstracted from your experience. I could say. "The cocker spaniel jumped out of the picket fence pen." Both of these more specific statements are included in, and represented by, the same abstract presentation embodied in the sentence: "The dog jumped out of the pen." So abstraction, contrary to what Einstein said, is fundamental to our ability to express ourselves in language. In fact our nervous system performs the operations of both representation and abstraction.

These conceptualized mental categories are the basis of linguistic sets, that is, they are the conceptual, abstract sets, which form the basis of linguistic representation.

The syntactical, semantic and grammatical systems, through which we structure our abstracted concepts, symbolize, and reflect, the structures of our subjective experiences, which, in turn reflect the structure of our brains. We think in terms of actor and acted upon. This is reflected in the syntax of subject and object. We see objects and perceive motions. This is reflected in the linguistic structure of nouns and verbs.

Although the entire brain is in some sense involved in the processes of perception and conceptualization that underlie the subjects of our discourse and the determinations of meaning, implicit in semantics, two areas are known to be specifically relevant in language. Wernicke's area, located in the temporal lobe of the cerebral cortex, between the visual and auditory areas, is necessary in the process of understanding both spoken and written language, that is, in semantics and syntax. Broca's area, located in the frontal lobe, with connections to the motor cortex, is involved in the ability to organize syntax and to speak language.

A mistake that philosophers have made since the time of Aristotle, with his Categories, and Plato, with his Shadowland of Forms or Templates, is to attribute the abstract categories of human thought and perception to the "outside" world.

In truth these categorical sets don't exist "out there" any more than do color or taste. *The categorical sets, with which we think, and which we symbolize by language, are the product of our mind/brain and its interaction with whatever is out there. These categorical sets exist solely in our subjective experience.*

Aristotle and many subsequent philosophers, except maybe Berkeley, thought of the essences of categorical sets as being substances in physical reality.

I had come to see that color, and all the sensory qualities, as well as the categorical sets themselves, exist only in our subjective experience, as a result of the way our brain structures its interaction with whatever is out there.

What language does is to symbolize these systematic subjective experiences not only with words, but more importantly, with a systematic syntax and grammar. Grammar and syntax are systems that reflect the way we think. Onto these syntactical and grammatical systems we map our subjective interactions with the world out there, as well as our internal thoughts and experiences. We then organize and express our thoughts in terms of these grammatical and syntactical systems, which we then represent by sounds and marks, which we understand through our ability to decipher the semantic meanings of the symbolic representations of a given language.

The manipulations that we perform on these syntactical, semantic and grammatical systems analogizes our systems of thought. This is not unlike a mathematical system, which we construct, and to which we then refer certain aspects of "the outside world." We represent one system with another. We construct a system and map another system on to it and in this way try to describe, or rather model, reality. These operations are similar to what the nervous system itself does, which makes sense because our thoughts and our languages reflect the structure and operation of our nervous systems.

The brain is a system that creates within itself a representation of another system, namely the "outside" world, not as a one-to-one mapping, but as an internally consistent system, which creates its own qualities and quantities to symbolize or represent another system.

Keep in mind that your subjective experience is exactly the firing of neurons in an organized manner in the organs of the brain, and yet this subjective experience is, as viewed subjectively from within, a totally different type of experience from our observations of the objective firing of neurons from the outside.

227

We have no idea how subjective experience or mind, arises from the activity of the brain. But we know that brain is all there is. There is no insubstantial stuff in the brain that has, or is, the subjective experience. There's no little man in there viewing the TV screen and pulling the levers that activate our muscles. The brain, itself, perceives, thinks, feels, decides, initiates and coordinates action. I talk about this elsewhere and follow this observation to conclusions about what the nature of all that exists must be.

Aristotle sought, and some philosophers, to this day, look for the essence of tableness out there in the world. Some thought that each specific table out there in the so-called real, physical world must contain some essence of tableness within it. Plato conceived of linguistic categories as being the ideas of God, which were the realities behind the shadow images, which we see.

Most people, including scientists and philosophers, still do not understand that subjective experience is created in our minds through the interaction of our nervous systems with whatever is out there, and that we then project this image back onto the world.

The sense of there being an objective physical reality out there, which is as we perceive it to be, is so compelling that our entire language reflects this misperception. We talk about sugar being sweet. Fire being hot; the sky being blue the grass being green and so forth, convinced beyond a shadow of a doubt that reality out there is as it appears to us, when in reality it is a construct of our own nervous systems representing itself to us subjectively.

This is not to say our nervous systems are making it all up in some solipsistic manner and nothing exists out there. This is not the case, except in cases of schizophrenic delusion, or psychotic episodes where people are hallucinating, seeing visions or hearing voices as though in a trance. Rather, our nervous systems are interacting in a regular, repeatable way with the environment, and from these interactions are constructing their subjective representations.

However, it is true that there is, in reality, no objective blueness in the sky. BLUE is a product of our minds/brains.

The same is true of chairness or tableness or treeness or dogness. These are conceptual categories that our minds/brains abstract from our interactions with whatever is out there and, in a similar way, create our subjective experiences of "COLOR".

Even when you look at a particular table you see your subjective experience of it. And when you think of a TABLE or speak of tables you are speaking of your conceptual categories. The "essence" of tables is simply the defining characteristics of the categorical set which you name "TABLE". The "essence" of tableness doesn't exist out there in the "real physical" world.

Think for a moment of the sentence: All the tables in this room have four legs. You know exactly what I mean. But how do you think of all the tables in this room? You have no idea whether they are wooden tables, iron tables, marble or glass tables, large tables, high tables or low tables. Yet you have no difficulty understanding what I mean. What is it you are thinking of when you think of table? Are you symbolizing that thought with a visual image of a particular table? Or are you thinking of all the tables in this room in a way that doesn't specify what they actually look like?

When I think of all the tables in this room I do not have a specific visual image, yet I am thinking of something very definite that has a well-defined meaning. I can imagine any type of table I please and visualize it. I can even look at it from any view I choose. I can imagine myself under a large wooden table or sitting at a small glass-topped table.

But there is another way I can think, which involves no visual images and yet which is quite exact. I can think of all the tables in the world in a way that has a well-defined meaning even though I don't visualize a single table. I can think the thought: the woman is writing at the table. This thought has a well-defined explicit meaning even though I don't visualize or even know what woman, what table or where the scene is.

What is it that I'm thinking when I think of these things? It is well-defined, it carries a definite meaning, but it's a non-visual, abstract thought, which is a very subtle thing and hard to describe exactly what it is that conveys the meaning.

The essence of tableness is in your conceptual, categorical mental thought, not in the table, not in some shadowy realm beyond tables. In order to be classified as a table, an object (as subjectively experienced by you) has to possess certain characteristics (as subjectively experienced by you). If it has these qualities, it qualifies as a member of the set of all tables.

The more we come to understand about the brain, the more we will understand how language reflects the operation of our brain. Indeed we can deduce probable operational modes of the brain by looking at the languages we have invented to represent our thoughts.

So language gives us a doorway through which we can look into the workings of our own brains and be amazed that the human brain has evolved over billions of years into something that can think abstractly and represent those abstractions with symbols, words, sentences, syntax and grammar.

CHAPTER NINETEEN: KNOWING

The Free Library

We are strung out in long lines and small groups now, running hard, focusing inwardly. We pass over Route 9, and here, just on the right, behind a line of spectators is a fieldstone building. I squint and read the sign: "The Wellesley Free Library."

Free Library, I think, what a beautiful concept. This idea that every town would have a library, open to the public for free is fundamental to democracy. Democracy depends on one thing above all others: the freedom of the human mind, a freedom hard won after centuries of religious intolerance and thought suppression.

What is this drive to know that characterizes Homo Sapiens? In myself, this drive to know had shaped my entire life. I have always been insatiably curious. I wanted to know the truth of things. I voraciously read as much as I could get my hands on. I wanted to experience all that I could. I wanted, not just know things, but to understand things.

During the years I studied at the Tufts University School of Special Studies from 1962 to 1965, I thought about the mind and the nature of the physical universe. On my trip West in 1964, and the years that followed, many insights came to me.

When, in 1972, I began to work with Jerry Lettvin, the famous neuroscientist, at Massachusetts Institute of Technology, I continued my quest.

"Jerry, what does it mean to know?" I had asked. His answer had surprised me.

"To know," he said, "It's necessary to have a system that's capable of existing in two states. When it changes state in response to an input, it knows something."

But, is it enough for a system to just change state in response to an impinging input of energy for it to be knowing? I mused.

How does the system *know* that it has changed?

A TV, for example, is made up of millions of component parts, which change state in response to external input. But the TV has no knowledge of its own change of state, as far as I knew.

How can a system know of its own change of state? I mused. What sort of system knows of its own change of state? Or rather, for what kind of system does an internal change of state become or comprise knowledge?

Is there something in the system that knows of the change of state?

Then how does *the-part-of-the-system-that-knows* know?

Whatever knows of the change of state of the system would have to change its own state in response to the change of state of the system.

But then in what sense does it know of its own change of state? There would have to be an inner knower that would change state in response to the change of state of the knower. This would lead to an infinite regress of knowing systems each changing state in response to the change of state of the system in which it is embedded.

I'd seen that all we know of the external world is our internal subjective experience of our interactions with it. I'd seen that there is no little man in our brain watching the TV screen of our changing neuronal states and converting those neuronal states to subjectively perceived thoughts, feelings and sensations. Rather the brain is perceiving its own activity from within, with what I called a self-reflexive inner view of its own activity. All we see, probing from the outside of the brain with voltage-sensitive probes, are blips of neuronal activity.

In the perceptual system, this regress of perceivers had led me to the astounding conclusion that there is not one perceiving entity at the top that is viewing the TV screen. Rather, the system *as a whole* perceives its own changes of state from *within*.

I had been led to the astounding conclusion that the brain is experiencing itself from the inside as subjective experience. The system as a whole perceives itself from within. The system is reflexive and self-viewing. The system is reflexively viewing itself as a whole and the ambiance of this self-viewing is not just little dots on a screen, but it the full flower of the wonderful, colorful subjectively represented world we see, hear, smell, touch, taste, feel, think and dream about. How can this be? How can a material object like the brain view itself subjectively?

In what way are knowing systems the same or different from perceiving systems. Perception, as the word is usually understood, entails a nervous system with sensory inputs from sensory receptors.

Jerry's answer indicated that he thought that any system that changes state is a knowing system. This is much broader and more inclusive than perceiving systems. Knowing systems, as Jerry was conceiving them, would include mechanical systems and systems that, as far as I could see, had no inner subjective experience of their own knowing. So he was using the word "knowing" in a more general sense than I would.

To Jerry a thermostat could be a knowing system. But to me it appeared that the system has to know of its own change of state from *within* itself, otherwise, it has no knowledge of its change of state. Or rather, that change of state *is* its knowledge, but in order for that change of state to be knowledge to the system itself, the system has to know its change from within itself. Otherwise the system would depend on an external viewer to know of its change of state.

The notion of an internal view is subtle. Even a viewer located inside the system looking at the system arrayed around him would be looking at the outside of the inside of the system and would thus be external to the system he is viewing. The only way a viewer can truly be inside the system is if she or he is the system, viewing itself in this curiously self-reflexive manner that is prior to the subject-object split.

This self-viewing partakes of the same self-reflexive quality as the self-creating matrice in that what is done is what is doing, what is creating is what is created, what is seen is what is doing the seeing and what is known is doing the knowing.

I was thinking outside of the perspective of modern science, but I realized it is absolutely fundamental to making a model of the universe that more accurately reflects reality.

The first problem was in the definition of knowing and in what comprises a knowing system.

It seemed to me that mechanical systems can never know their own changes of state subjectively from within. When we watch a heat-seeking, rocket it looks as if it knows what it is doing as it unerringly adjusts its course to follow the heat gradient. But does it have an inner subjective sense of knowing? I didn't think so.

In a television set, or a computer, there are myriad subsystems that change state. But I doubted if a TV set or a computer could know of its own changes in the sense of having a subjective view or experience of those changes. Only the human being who designs, builds, and looks at the TV, or the computer, and its parts, knows subjectively what the machine is doing.

The computer responds to the various inputs automatically and these inputs trigger multiple levels of changes of state in the subsystems. Jerry would say that the TV or the computer is a knowing machine because they are systems that are capable of at least two states, which change state on the occasion of appropriate input.

I could see that I was at odds with the conceptual foundation of physics and the artificial intelligence community in that they believe that a man-made, mechanical system of sufficient complexity, like a robotic computer would be able to have a inner subjective experience. I didn't agree, but I wasn't sure. It seemed to me that any in-silica replication of a knowing system would lack that essential innerness. But it crossed my mind that if systems were constructed of living parts, like cells, that they might be able to acquire some sort of subjective innerness.

I had seen that in nature there are systems that in some sense build or create themselves. That is, they put themselves together in a manner to achieve the end goal of functioning as complete, whole systems. They transform themselves through the continuing interactions of their parts into systems that function as integral wholes.

I had seen that these systems are in some sense teleological, that is, they function in the present in order to accomplish some future goal. In the embryo, the notochord forms in order to become the spinal cord of the adult animal. The reason for the development of the notochord is to become something else in the future.

I had used the Greek word, "Teleos" to designate these types of systems, and had conceived of them as formatively intelligent in the sense of being teleological or end-seeking. I called non-living systems that put themselves together, like molecules in a chemical reaction, "Teleostemic," and I called living systems, all of which build themselves, "Teleosystemic."

I thought about this end-seeking behavior in nature in which entities interact with one another. These interactions have traditionally been thought of as propelled by invisible forces, but I can also think of many these interactions as end-seeking, or gradient following behaviors that involve a succession of continually changing states. Such interpretations are Teleostemic.

When I watch a drop of water run down a windowpane, I see how it jiggles and weaves back and forth as it encounters obstacles in its way. It always moves in such a way to maximize its gradient of descent. That is, it choses its path of least resistance. In effect, it is continuously summing the net forces acting on it at each moment. A speck of dirt stuck to the window exerts a force on the descending droplet and bends its course. Or we could say the drop of water and the speck of dust interact in such a way that the sum of the product of their masses and changes of velocity remains constant. Since in this example we are assuming the dust is firmly affixed to the glass, we note that it is the water that we observe to change it motion.

The droplet interacts with its environment as it moves. The droplet and the earth exert a mutual force of attraction on one another. Since the mass of the droplet is less than the mass of the earth we observe the droplet to change its motion relative to us, who are affixed to the earth. That is to say there is a force of interaction between the earth and the droplet that creates a gradient and the droplet follows this gradient. When it encounters the force of interaction of another object, it changes its motion, still following its gradient.

In the general theory of relativity, instead of considering the gravitational force between the droplet and the earth to be acting at a distance on one another, we consider, following Riemann's theory of gravitation, that gravity is imbedded in the four-dimensional structure of space-time itself and that the water droplet and the earth are subject to the local four-dimensional tensor field. But the result is the same in terms of gradient-following behavior.

To a child, it appears as if the droplet is finding its way down the windowpane. It looks intelligent as it continuously seeks its gradient of least resistance. It appears to make decisions as to how to move. However, we say that it has no free will, that is, it cannot decide which way to move. It has no consciousness that we know of and no inner subjective sense of knowing as far as we can tell. Yet it behaves in this seemingly intelligent manner as it actively seeks out its gradient of least resistance.

So what do we mean by "knowing?"

Does the droplet know its gradient of maximum decent? Does the droplet have some sort of innerness of experience of its changes of motion in response to its interactions with its environment? We can ask the same question about a robot, or an automated machine. Do we mean by knowing, simply these changes of state that we observe, or do we mean by knowing some innerness of experience of those changes of state?

A computer holds in its memory billions of series of zeros and ones that represent other variables that stand for myriad quantities. Does it know this? It is a system that can exist in at least two states and it changes state when it receives appropriate input, so according to Jerry's definition it would be a knowing machine even though it is highly unlikely that it has any kind of subjective experience of its changes of state. It doesn't know subjectively that it knows, if it does.

Even though there may be other circuits in the computer that "know" whether some subset of elements contains certain sequences of zeros and ones, in the sense that this second-order knowing system changes its state in response to various configurations of the outputs of the first-order elements, can we say that these second-order circuits know the contents of some subset of elements subjectively? I doubted it.

Even in systems that have a subjective experience of knowing, there appear to be millions of automatic responses. Indeed, the one system that we know has a subjective experience is our own brain-mind and yet the majority of changes of state of our brain and the rest of our body seem to occur automatically, without our subjective awareness of these changes. So do we say the system of our brain and body knows much more than we do? And if so, does this knowing entail simply changes of state as in the case of the automatic dishwasher, which are entirely devoid of an internal subjectivity? Or, do all the components of my brain and body have an innerness of view accessible to themselves?

If we take the first alternative, that none of the components of the system of my brain-body have any innerness at all, and they are simply mechanistic elements that change state with no inner knowledge or experience of that change of state, then we are left with the question of how then does this inner subjective experience emerge from a juxtapositioning of subsystems that have no subjective innerness?

Elsewhere I have written that I believe that this subjectivity of experience cannot spring into existence from the juxtapositioning of mechanical, external parts that are devoid of any sort of innerness what so ever, no matter how complex.

Alternatively, we are left with the astounding conclusion that if the brain is capable of subjective innerness, so must be the parts that comprise it. This means that even a single neuron has the ability to experience its changes subjectively in its own way.

Carrying that logic one step further, if a single cell is capable of an innerness of experience, then the components that comprise the cell must also be capable of an innerness at their own level, since we are assuming that this innerness cannot spring into existence from the juxtapositioning of purely external, mechanical parts.

Of what is the cell comprised?

The cell is comprised of complex molecules and dynamic processes.

So do these then have a subjective innerness in their own way? To be consistent with this line of reasoning, we would have to say they do.

Applying similar logic to the next level smaller, we have to say that atoms, and subatomic entities too must have this innerness. This would mean that all the systems and subsystems of organisms that are capable of experiencing subjectively would also have to experience subjectively at the level and in the manner appropriate to them.

That is to say the atom experiences itself in a way that depends on its own dynamic structure and activity in interaction with its environment and that is a different level of subjectivity than the subjective experience of a complex molecule or a cell. And likewise subatomic particles and entities, that I have called "interactons," would also have some sort of innerness.

I posited that at each level of complexity, as the system gains external physical properties and abilities through the more organized and complex interaction of its parts, the system also gains more elaborate subjective innerness of experience from its own self reflexive subjective perspective.

So where does this leave us with a definition of knowing?

If we take Jerry's definition then any system that can exist in two states and changes state on the occasion of interaction, is a knowing system, without reference to whether it has an inner subjectiveness or not.

If we chose to limit the word "knowing," to designate only those systems that have a subjective innerness of perspective of some sort, however primitive, then a multitude of natural systems may have a subjective innerness. The problem is the only system we can definitively know has this subjective innerness of perspective is our brain, and this is a very high level of complexly arrayed subjective experience.

We can never know if any other system has a subjectivity of perspective, because the only way we could determine such a thing would be if we were, in fact, the system.

I had named systems that have this inner subjectiveness of perspective Noestemic. I had named living systems that have this inner subjectiveness Noesystemic. And, I had named living systems with nervous systems, Neuronoesystemic. Clearly all Neuronoesystemic systems are Noesystemic, but not all Noesystemic systems are Neuronoesystemic.

Now I was trying to formulate a relationship between systems that form themselves through their own interactions, which I called Teleostemic Systems when applied to non-living systems and Teleosystemic when applied to living systems, to Noestemic and Noesystemic systems.

My intuition was that only systems that can form themselves, that is, that are Teleostemic can have a subjective innerness. This would mean that systems assembled by some other agency, the primary agency being human beings, would never be Noestemic, that is would never have a subjectivity of perspective no matter how complex.

Further I posited that all systems that are Teleosystemic, that is, all living systems, all of which assemble themselves using the energy and materials of their environments, are Noesystemic, that is they have some sort of self-reflexive subjective innerness, however primitive.

Let us now look at the very smallest systems and see how they interact.

When photons of light are shone through a double slit and projected onto a screen, we see an interference pattern, as we would expect to see in the case of a wave. Waves are comprised of long chains of troughs and peaks that move, usually through a medium, but in the case of light, without a medium. When two wave patterns, one from each slit, combine, they create an interference pattern such that when troughs combine there is a dark band, when peaks combine there is light band, and when a trough and a peak combine they cancel one another out and there is a neutral band.

Amazingly if the photons are released one by one, over time, the pattern that emerges on the projection screen is still in the form of interfering bands of light, as if each photon takes its place on the screen as if it knows of the positioning of the photons that precede and that follow it.

240

If light is thought of as photon particles, then it should be possible to determine which slit any one given photon travels through, However, when one puts a measuring device at one of the slits, the wave pattern disappears altogether. This is to say that the observer, in making the observation, interacts with what is being observed and causes the observed and the observation to change.

Interestingly the same type of behavior is seen when electrons are shone through a double slit. This led physics to propose that these small entities have both wave and particle properties and led to the merging of quantum particle physics and wave mechanics. What was clear to me is that the interaction of the observer has to be factored back into the observation.

The Heisenburg uncertainity Principle says that when we observe a wave or a particle in motion, our observation changes the behavior of the particle or the wave so that the more accurately we know our measurements of its velocity. the less certain is our knowledge of its position. Conversely, the more certain we are of knowing the position of the particle or wave, the less certain we can be of its velocity.

In addition, the Uncertainty Principle says that in an interaction each interactant can know only one half of the parameters associated with that interaction. This means that when the physicist interacts with what she is observing, she knows one half of the parameters of that interaction from her point of view.

Astonishingly this must mean that that-with-which-she-is-interacting knows the other one half of the parameters of that interaction from its point of view. That is, each participant in the interaction, changes state on the occasion of the interaction, and so, using Jerry's definition, each knows half if the interaction from its point of view.

To know something it is necessary to change state, and to change state it is necessary to interact. This means that in any interaction each participant is the knower, or observer from its own point of view and each is the known, or observed, from the point of view of the other. This is not unlike the case in Relativity Theory where as observers on uniformly moving coordinate systems, like spaceships, pass one another at high speeds, each looks over at the other and observes the other's lengths to be shortened in the direction of motion, and observes each other's clocks to be running slower.

The observations are perfectly symmetric, in that each measures the other's lengths and time intervals to change, while thinking that her own lengths and time intervals remain unchanged. In reality, there is no objective change in lengths or in time intervals at all. The observations are relative to the moving observers. So in the most fundamental physical reality there is a built-in dependence on the interactions of the observers with the observed. This makes sense because both observers and observed are contained in the meta-universe of all that is and there is no objective place to stand and no way to observe without interacting and no interacting except an action-between two entities.

These photons in my theory represent the smallest self-creating systems, in which the collapsing magnetic fluxes create expanding electrical flux that collapse to form expanding magnetic fluxes in a mutually self-creating process that is the basic quanta of action or self-activity of what we call physical existence.

To be consistent, and to discover a monistic substance that bridges the mind/body gap, I would have to say that from the inside these quanta of action are, to themselves their own primitive subjective innernesses, and therefore are Noestemic and Teleostemic at the most fundamental level.

CHAPTER TWENTY: CONSCIOUSNESS

River and Bridge

A river stretches is long sensuous tentacles through the valley, reaching up under the road; deep, wet, murky river hiding the minds of a thousand snakes and amphibians, tiny insect larva, cool, smelly, dank, slow-moving, a thousand years of rotting leaves, dark, murky, slow, liquid, fluid, this deep dark river, sucking water out of all the hidden springs, the end result of all the seepage. The water droplets coalesce into one liquid mass, moving inexorably down towards the ocean, seeking their end, which is also their origin, the sea.

We run across the bridge at the bottom of the valley, the low point of the watershed.

Water is the symbol of the unconscious. Rivers, like the primitive minds that swim in them, reach back hundreds and thousands and millions of years, during which time the animal mind has enlarged and evolved, brain upon brain, pushing its convolutions outwards, folding. The cortex, the most recent brain, is folded over the mammalian brain, which itself contains the inner brain, the reptilian brain, and the brains before that. As the brain evolves, the ability to perceive, think and conceptualize evolves.

Crossing the river, we surge up the other side. Ahead I hear the screaming traffic on Route 128.

Up and up we push. Below us, the highway spreads out, reaching as far as I can see. A river of shiny metallic, automated machines, invented by this modern mind streams under the bridge..

And so we cross from the river to the bridge, from the most primitive consciousness to human consciousness.

What is this thing we call consciousness? Is consciousness the same as knowing?

I had explored the question of what is knowing using Jerry's definition of a knowing system as being any system that is capable of taking on two or more states. I'd seen that there are two aspects of knowing, one the external changes of state of the system and the other the capacity of the system to have some sort of self-reflexive subjective innerness.

When I asked Jerry about consciousness, he said that the brain is the machine and the mind is the processes of the machine. But I'd seen that the processes viewed from the outside are just processes. Process alone is unable to account for the subjective experience of the brain.

Much confusion swirls around the definition of consciousness, even before we get to question of what it is. What it is depends in part on how we define it.

To some, consciousness is an awake and sentient state. To be unconscious is to be unaware of one's surroundings and unable to mobilize a muscular response to one's environment. Sleep would be a form of unconsciousness in this view. But others point out that we are often conscious or aware of our dreams and can sometimes remember them, and this means that we are not unconscious in sleep, but simply in a different state of consciousness. Still others say that consciousness is attentiveness and that we can be sitting in a room concentrating on our computer and be unconscious of the conversations around us. Others would say we are in a conscious state but are unaware of the conversations even though we are conscious of the noise.

Some limit consciousness to human beings, while others say that even plants are conscious in some way. If we mean awake animals capable of making neuro-motor responses to the environment then clearly mammals, birds, reptiles, fish and insects can be in a state of conscious awareness. Although fly consciousness is different in modality from lizard consciousness, the fact of being perceiving animals with motor responses is the same.

Scientists have been searching for the seat of consciousness in the brain, as if consciousness resides in one particular organ or area. We know that most of the activity of our brain has to do with automatic functions like blood pressure, heart rate, hormone release, processing of sense information, processing of motor control and so forth.

We are not specifically aware of the activity of our cerebellum as such, but if our cerebellum is compromised, we are immediately aware that we cannot coordinate our motions. This same is true of the dopaminergic motor control areas like the substantia nigra. Ordinarily we are not specifically conscious of this area but when it fails to operate we cannot move coherently and we develop Parkinsonian symptoms.

Our visual cortex operates automatically. We take for granted the continuous theater of visual sensations that our visual processing system provides for us as we interact with our environments. We are aware of the subjective visual sensation but we are not conscious of the individual firings of neurons that make visual imagery possible. Even in our dream state we are presented with an inner movie of visual images. Our brain both creates the movie and views the movie. We think we are the viewer, but, in the case of dreaming, we are also the movie, the screen, the producer and the director of the movie.

This brings up the question of who or what is this "We" or "I" that I think I am who sees, feels, thinks, hears and decides to move my arms or legs? Who is this "I" to whom I'm referring when I say, "I feel cold," or "My leg hurts," or I'm going to run." Who is the "I" who says, "I had a dream last night?"

In our sleeping state the different parts of our brains communicate with one another in visual images. These visual images vary from organ to organ and from area to area in the brain. When sleeping, I can be aware of intricate abstract patterns of colored lights,

245

or of cartoon-like representations of geometric shapes, or of fully formed recognizable objects in motion that carry out bizarre combinations of activity and interaction, or at times there can be a very realistic presentation— so realistic that I think I am awake and participating in something that is really happening.

All these subjective experiences are created by and viewed by different parts of my brain, and they are types of conscious awareness that are different from states of wakeful awareness and voluntary movement. So we have to expand our definition of consciousness to include several types, or states, of consciousness.

And of course, we are confronted again, when asking what consciousness is, with the unexplained fact of subjective experience— this innerness that I have previously called in general "Noestemia," in living systems, "Noesystemia," and in animals with nervous systems, "Neuronoesystemia." How is it that a material object like the brain can have an inner view of the firing of its own neurons in the first place?

In order to be mind, these brain processes must view themselves from the inside in a self-reflexive manner that has been over looked by materialists. That is, the same patterns of neuronal activity that we measure from the outside as tiny voltage changes in neurons are, from the inside, subjective experiences. I had come to see that these voltage changes do not create some insubstantial thing called "subjective experience"; these voltage changes *are* subjective experience to the brain.

How can this be? As soon as we drop the idea of subjective experience being some supernatural, insubstantial, non-physical other substance, we are confronted with an even more fundamental problem: How can a material system have within it, a subjective experience?

Let's backtrack a moment and see why I discarded the idea that subjective experience is some independent, insubstantial, non-physical other substance, whether inhabiting the brain as an independent spirit, as spiritualists and animists thought, or whether created by the firing patterns of neurons, as present day neo-dualists think.

This is a proof by contradiction. Let's assume that subjective experience is a separate, independent, non-physical substance. Since neurons are physical objects, this hypothetical, independent, non-physical subjective substance would have to be capable of interacting with a physical object, namely the neuron. That is, changes in this hypothetical independent, non-physical, other substance would have to cause changes in the neuron that would lead to changes in neuronal firing patterns and, conversely, changes in the neuron and in the neuronal firing patterns would have to cause changes in this hypothetical independent, non-physical, other substance.

If this hypothetical independent, non-physical, subjective, other substance is capable of interacting with a physical object then this non-physical, subjective substance would have to be a physical entity or process, (in order for it to interact with a physical object and its processes, like a neuron) but this is a contradiction.

That is, we start with the premise that subjective experience is an independent, non-physical, other substance, and we have shown that it must be a physical entity, which is a contradiction. Therefore subjective experience cannot be an independent, non-physical other substance.

Notice, we assumed that non-physical entities cannot interact with physical entities. Is this true? Yes it is true that non-physical entities cannot interact with physical entities because the definition of a non-physical entity is that it cannot interact with physical entities and thus there is no way of detecting it by interacting with it with physical probes.

So in conclusion, there is no independent, non-physical other substance that comprises a subjective experience, which exists exogenously and inhabits the brain, or which exists endogenously and is caused by, or causes, the firing patterns of neurons.

That is to say the firing patterns of neurons is all there is and these firing patterns can be viewed from the outside with probes as patterns of voltage activity, or the very same firing patterns can experience themselves self-reflexively from the inside subjectively.

Not only are the dualist wrong, as we have just seen, but the materialists are also wrong as the following argument will show.

Materialists claim that the nervous system is made matter and there is nothing else. All there are neurons that are made of molecules that are made of atoms, and that therefore no inner view is possible, required or necessary. The idea of subjective experience and inner view, to materialists, is just a fairy tale.

Let's look closely at the materialist's contention. First of all, what is matter? We define matter to be that which is composed of atoms and molecules.

If we define matter as being made of atoms and molecules, then the actual processes and motions of molecules and atoms are not themselves made of atoms and molecules. And so, by definition, motions and processes, although predicated of material objects, which are made of atoms and molecules, are not themselves material, per se.

What are motions and processes then? Here we must distinguish between what is material in the sense of being composed of atoms and molecules and what is physical, in terms of being posited of the external world.

We can say that the physical world is comprised of atoms and molecules and their motions and processes. Thus we add an entire operational mode of existence to matter when we say matter *and its motions and processes*. Processes, while physical, are not material because processes are not composed of atoms and molecules. But note, physical processes while being non-material are not independent of the objects of which they are predicated.

Thus, all material objects are physical but not all physical phenomena are material. The set of all physical phenomena is a larger more inclusive category than the set of all material objects.

So we can say that the brain is comprised of atoms and molecules and their processes and activities, that is, the brain is a physical phenomena, made of material atoms and molecules and non-material, physical processes and activities. So if materialists are saying that all that exists are atoms and molecules they are wrong. If they say all that exists is atoms and molecules and their processes and activities then they've added an entire new dimension to matter.

If materialists are saying all that exists is matter and its processes and activities then they are not strictly materialists, but could be more accurately described as "physicalists." They would maintain that all that exists is the external physical world, comprised of atoms and molecules and their activities and processes, and that subjective experience does not really exist at all except as an illusion.

That matter and physical processes, as we have conceived them do not have, and are not capable of, a subjective innerness of view, is not a problem to the materialists or the physicalists. Why? Because for them subjective experience doesn't not exist.

But what does it mean, "to exist"? If all they admit is physical existence then subjective experience doesn't exist.

In what way can subjective experience exist if it is not a physically existant object or activity?

In my view all that exists is atoms and molecules and their motions and processes in vast arrays of living cells that comprise the brain. There is no other substance in the brain. However, I believe that there are two perspectives on the activities and processes of these cells.

There is the outside view and the inside view.

When we view the brain from the outside we see a mass of living cells made up of atoms and molecules and their processes and activities, which is the physical perspective. When we are experiencing those very same cellular activities and processes from the inside in this paradoxically self-reflexive way then those same activities and processes are mental, subjective, experiences.

These subjective experiences cannot be separated from the activities and processes of the neurons of the brain. They have no independent existence of their own. Subjective experiences are simply a different perspective on the same activities and processes that from the outside we take as physical. That is to say the activities and processes are all that exists, but these processes are, to themselves from the inside, subjective experience. Thus physicality refers to the external view and subjectivity refers to the internal view of the same activities and processes.

If we are going to use the word, "processes," to refer to the external view then we need a new word to refer to processes that are also subjective experiences to themselves. We can call activities and processes that can be viewed from the outside and also experience themselves subjectively from the inside, "noestemaprocesses." Alternatively we can keep the word processes and understand that some, but clearly not all, processes and activities can, and do, view themselves subjectively from the inside in this identity-self-reflexive manner.

The subjective experience does not cause the brain's activity. The subjective experience *is* the brain's activity viewing itself, subjectively from the inside. The brain's processes and activities do not cause subjective experience. The brain's processes and activities *are* subjective experiences self-reflexively viewing themselves from the inside.

So the materialists and physicalists are right in saying that there is nothing besides the brain and the brain's processes and activities. But they are wrong in saying that this subjective, self-reflexive, innerness of view does not exist. It exists, not as a physical object and not as a non-physical insubstantial stuff. It exists as a self-reflexive point of view of an activity on itself.

What do I mean by a self-reflexive, subjective innerness of view?

If we think of a brain, we see a pinkish mass of tissue. We explore it further and find it composed of neurons, which are cells that are specially evolved to develop and transmit voltage potentials along their membranes. These voltage potentials result from the flows of charged potassium and sodium ions across the cellular membranes.

Many neurons are capable of sending electric signals to other cells via a long axon that develops a series of firing patterns when sufficient voltages reach its axon hillock. The neuron also possesses a dendritic arbor, a tree-like formation that receives inputs from other cells.

We also find supporting cells, called astrocytes, that surround, nourish and protect the neurons, participating in the maintaining, sending and receiving of voltage potentials. This amazing organ from the outside looks like a physical object, some of whose processes and activities we can measure by means of magnetic resonance. We find that specific areas and modes of brain activity are associated with specific subjective experiences.

Now imagine we want to go inside the brain. We become very small and are able to enter into the brain and look around at its inner workings. Will we be able to experience what the brain is experiencing subjectively?

No.

Why not?

Because we are still not inside the system. We are still a separate entity viewing the inside of the brain from the outside. Being physically inside the major brain structure, we have a more detailed view of the outside of the complex system, but we are not inside.

How then can we view this brain from the inside in the sense that I mean?

There is no way that we, as a separate entity, can view the subjective experiences of this other brain, because the only way we can truly be inside, in the way that I mean, is to actually be the brain.

This is monumental. This means that the brain's self-viewing of itself from the inside is prior to the subject-object split. This is a self-reflexive, self-viewing that is completely outside the bounds of modern science and outside the purvey of most philosophical and psychological discussions.

This self-reflexive, self-viewing is the fundamental basis of consciousness. In this self-reflexive, self-viewing, that which sees is exactly what is seen, subjectively. The processes are, to themselves, subjective experience. There is no split.

Now that we have established what we mean by this subjective, identically-self-reflexive innerness, let us look at human consciousness for a moment. If, as I believe, all neurons have a subjective innerness unto themselves, that is to say they are noesystemic, this innerness falls very short of our complete human perception, conception and cognition. The innerness of a cell, in this case a neuron, is a primitive subjectivity.

However, I believe that just as cells can combine into multicellular organs of increased complexity, so these innernesses can combine into new dimensions of complex subjectivity.

In my view, consciousness is layered, in that at each level the dynamic processes of the components of a conscious system, are, to the components themselves, a type of innerness of experience or view, and as these systems compile and become more complex so do the innernesses of experience.

One of the classic textbook examples is of a Mr. X, an artist, who due to a head injury became unable to perceive color. Interestingly, all the information from his retina regarding the wavelengths of light was intact. He did not lose his ability to subjectively perceive. Rather his perception was of lurid compositions of brightnesses of gray.

This illustrates my point. The intact parts of the visual processing system have their own subjective experiences that compile as the system compiles. The part of his visual system that subjectively perceived color was missing, and so the rest of the visual processing and the layers of subjective experience that normally would underlie the color process became revealed.

Much has been written on the search for that part of the brain in which subjective consciousness resides. However, I think this pursuit is misguided. Subjective experience does not, in my opinion, reside only in one part of the brain, but is distributed throughout the brain in its various modes and dimensions. However, only certain of the brain's activities identify themselves as "us." We are who we think we are. And who we think we are is some subset of the brain's on-going activity and dynamic processing.

The remaining question is who is this "I" who has this final conscious awareness? This "I" is that part of our brain's activity and operation that identifies itself as us. Descartes said, "I think, therefore I am." I say, "In so far as I think, I am that which thinks I am." That is to say I am the configuration of dynamical activity of my brain that is conscious of being conscious. Or to say it differently: These dynamical, recursive circuits of self-generating activity identify themselves as who I am.

In the brain there are recursive circuits of activity along loops of projection neurons that feed from the cortex to the basal ganglia to the thalamus and back to the cortex. These loops maintain a topographical mapping, one on to the other, and are in a continued state of activity during waking consciousness. It is here that I believe lies our consciousness of being conscious. Of course input from every other part of the brain including the cerebellum, hippocampus and entorhinal cortex, as well as from the vast array of memory banks coded in the structures of clusters of pyramidal, cortical cells feed into these recursive circuits.

Most of us have had experiences where we've reacted quickly to something, only to recognize a few milliseconds later what it was. This is because we can react through neuronal circuits that go directly from sensory input through the lower brain areas and spinal cord to the motor reflex.

These lower areas per se do not identify themselves as "us," although these lower centers send and receive signals to and from the higher level cortical levels. That is to say that although these lower centers, in my view, have subjective experiences in their own manner, per se, these activities do not identify themselves as "us."

With the discovery that a compromised reticular formation, an organ at the base of the brain, results in unconsciousness, there was much talk of this organ as being the seat of consciousness. But I believe this is an error and that the reticular formation is just one of many switches that can interrupt the flow of information to and from the higher cortical levels in the recoursive loops of activity among the cortex, basal ganglia and thalamus.

So in summary, I think that consciousness is a layered function of compilations of the self-reflexive, subjective innerness that characterize all the cells and organs of the brain. Just as the physical brain as viewed from the outside has organized itself into orderly systems of nested systems, each systemic layer, and each organ develops its own characteristic self-reflexive, subjective innerness of view. These self-reflexive, subjective innerness of view comprise our perceiving, thinking, feeling and all the other aspects of consciousness.

Consciousness then derives from and is comprised of all the activities that we associate with mind, which are the subjective, inner self-viewings of the layered processes and activities of compilations of the dynamical, organized structures of the brain, in which the activities and processes are to themselves the subjective experiences that identify their own self-activity as us.

Chapter Twenty-One: Health

Newton Wellesley Hospital

Once we cross route 128 we are inside the circumferential highway, part of the close knit suburbs that surround Boston and are known collectively as "Greater Boston." Boston is ahead, now, not as far away as it was. We are getting closer and closer. Each time the clock ticks off a little less than seven minutes, I'm a mile closer to the finish. I feel good; I feel as if I can run on like this forever. The temptation is to speed up, to cavort, to celebrate, but I reign myself in.

The suburbs share in the propriety of Boston proper, unruffled, methodical quintessentially civilized, self-controlled and above all reserved. And here we are a band of wild half-naked runners in white underwear careening through this unflappable propriety, arms and legs thrashing, nostrils flared, eyes focused within. We are a wild band. Staid and proper Bostonians have left their comfortable homes and are standing on their front walks screaming, cheering, clapping, roaring as if somehow this spring marathon ritual releases some ancient wildness too long repressed.

On the right a brick building appears — the Newton Wellesley Hospital.

We all know what it means to be sick.

But what is health? We can tell when a plant, for example looks healthy. It leaves are full and vibrant; it seems to have a vigor about it. A healthy animal has clear eyes, lustrous skin and hair, energy and a general sense of balance and well-being.

A healthy organism is one in which all the coordinated processes, parts and functions are working in cooperation to maximize the well-being of the

organism. Again we see a circularity in which the well-being and proper
functioning of each part contributes to the well-being and proper functioning
of the whole and the well-being and proper functioning of the whole
contributes to the well-being and proper functioning of each part. Moreover,
each part in the whole functions not only to maximize its own well-being,
but also to maximize the well-being of every other part.

For example the healthy heart functions in such a way as to maximize its own performance in pumping blood, but if the heart were to try to maximize its own good at the expense of other organs, the lungs, for example, or the liver, then the organism would become unbalanced and sick and this would adversely affect the heart. So it is in the heart's own best interest to maximize its own functioning not only to benefit itself, but also to benefit every other organ and to benefit the whole. This is the classic win-win situation that we see in virtually all whole systems. A win-lose, zero sum situation does not work in the context of whole systems.

We can apply the concept of health in many other spheres than hospitals and human health. We can define what a healthy ecosystem is and we can distinguish the healthy ecosystem from the sick ecosystem. We can see the difference between a healthy society and a sick society. We know what a healthy economy looks like and what a sick economy looks like. We know when our political system is healthy and when it is corrupt and unhealthy.

Being able to analyze situations and systems in terms of health can be productive in terms of problem solving. Thinking in terms of health and sickness can clarify our goals. If our goal is to create healthy human beings, we need to know how to do this. We need to look at physical health, mental health, emotional health, social health, environmental health and spiritual health and to discover what conditions conduce to total health and what conditions make us sick.

As we come to understand how our individual mental, spiritual, emotional and physical health interfaces with the social, economic, political, environmental and spiritual health of the family and society in which we live, and how our total health depends on the ecosystem in which we as human exist, we see how such vital issues such as clean air, clean water, non-polluted food, oxygen-producing and carbon-absorbing plants, oceans, rivers, mountains, forests and continents are all part of the wonder and beauty of being alive here on planet earth. We see how the inter-related systems in which we live affect and determine our own personal health.

Let us now look at health in these inter-related systems.

What is a healthy person like?

Individual health, as we saw, is comprised of mental, emotional and spiritual health as well as physical health.

We all know what physical health is. We see a robustness and vigor, a positive attitude towards life, the skin, bones, organs and muscles are all functionally optimally and in synchrony with one another. The physiological functions, including heart rate, blood pressure, glucose levels, cholesterol, and all the functions that are measured in the annual physical exam are normal. In additions there are no diseased conditions present, like cancer, diabetes, Alzheimer's Disease, parasites, the flu, AIDS, or the thousand other functional and pathogen carried diseases that flesh is heir to.

What is mental health?

The more we learn about the brain the more we understand that physical, mental, emotional and spiritual health are connected with brain health. A healthy, well-functioning brain leads to mental, emotional, physical and spiritual health and good mental, emotional, physical, and spiritual health enhances the health of the brain.

The brain is made up of billions of living cells, neurons that conduct electrical signals along their membranes, and supporting cells, like microglia, astroglia and schwann cells. That such a thing as the human brain has evolved and functions at all is nothing short of miraculous. When a few molecules go wrong, or a few connections fail in the brain, major diseases like alzheimers, parkinsons, obsessive compulsive disorders, addictions, schizophrenia, and bipolar disorder can result. Behavioral abnormalities and criminal behaviors can result from brain abnormalities.

Conversely, stress, abuse, drugs, toxic and addictive substances, as well as brainwashing or cultism can produce negative physical changes in the brain. On the positive side, meditation, exercise, safe, loving human environments and cognitive therapies can result in positive physical changes in the brain. Brain health then is crucial to emotional, mental and spiritual health.

The brain is the physical manifestation of the mind and so our thoughts both result from and cause changes in our brains.

When we learn something, new connections form among the neurons in our brains. These are real physical changes in our brain cells that represent and remember what we have learned.

Brain health and its relationship with behavior is something that is only beginning to be understood.

What do we mean by emotional health?

Our emotions are directly controlled by our brains and hormonal systems, which in turn are affected by our emotions. The emotion of fear, for example, releases corticosteroids, like epinephrine or adrenalin, into the blood that affects the parts of our brain that control blood pressure, heart rate, arteriole diameter and myriad other functions. It is almost impossible to separate our emotional health from the physical and mental health of the body and brain.

Continued emotional stress causes changes to the physical structure of our bodies and brains. Cultism and the practice of certain beliefs, as well as substance addictions cause changes in our physiology that take many months of therapy to repair.

Creating environments that support emotional health is a major challenge in family therapies, and is an important often neglected aspect of school and work.

What then is spiritual health?

Spirit refers to the invisible causes that people have long thought are behind the visible events that we see manifest in what we call the physical world. Ultimately our spiritual sense has to do with the mystery of our existence and the sense of awe we have when contemplating the beauty and majesty of the cosmos. We find ourselves here in our bodies on the earth. We come into this world and we pass out of this world. The fact that we and everything else exists is a miracle that surpasses our understanding and our ability to explain.

Our sense of the infinite wonder of existence is what we call our spiritual sense. When our spiritual sense is awakened we see the beauty, mystery and wonder in ourselves, in each other and in all of existence. This is a state of spiritual enlightenment, which is also a state of mind that is connected to our brain processes and our fundamental ability to perceive.

A healthy person has a sense of spiritual awareness, that is a sense of the larger picture, the wholeness of the cosmic miracle in which we have our individual existences. This sense of awe and spiritual awareness fills us with love and a feeling of connection to everyone and everything. This feeling of love and connection helps us to heal and to stay healthy. The brain processes that are connected with this spiritual awareness heals our brains and therefore conduces to our emotional, mental and physical wholeness and health.

When we speak of health then we are speaking of wholeness and the functional processes that are necessary for the optimal continuance of the entire system.

Let us now look at what we mean be health in other contexts in which the word is not usually applied. The concept of health and sickness can be instructive when analyzing a multitude of systems including political systems, social systems, economic systems and ecological systems.

What does a healthy political system look like?

Politics is about how power is partitioned and distributed in a society. Politics, therefore, is about the structures through which we are governed, or, in the case of democracies, govern ourselves. To govern means to regulate.

A healthy government governs for the benefit of the governed; that is, a healthy government governs for the good of the whole of society and for the good of each and every individual.

The good of the whole of society and the good of each and every individual are two sides of the same coin. When a government governs for the perceived good of a small elite at the expense of the whole, it is corrupt. Or when a government governs for the perceived benefit of one faction or one group to the detriment of other groups or factions then it is dysfunctional in terms of its ability to produce the greatest good for all.

To be healthy, a government must govern for the benefit of all, in an inclusive manner in which the same laws are applied to everyone, the laws are fair and for the benefit of everyone and in the interests of the common good, the enforcement is equitable, the judiciary is even-handed. In terms of structure: there is adequate housing, food, clean water, clothing, waste disposal, police protection and health-care for everyone.

The infrastructures necessary for the proper functioning of commerce, transportation, information systems, education, protected property ownership, and so forth are intact. These functions and services of government are paid for by everyone contributing according to their abilities to pay, in the form of taxes. In a healthy political system, taxation is the means though which people cooperate to provide themselves with the services they need to maintain a healthy society.

We know what unhealthy governmental and political systems look like: The government is ruthless. People have no freedom of speech or of the press or in theocracies, no freedom of religion. The state rules for the benefit and power of those who rule at the terrible expense of those who are ruled. Taxes no longer function for the benefit of all, but are the means of the rulers for robbing the ruled. There is no justice, no fairness or equitability. The individual is a captive of the corrupt governing authorities.

In an unhealthy political system, the government, for example, in a fascistic state is controlled by corporations and in some cases religious hierarchies. In state communism the state controls all aspects of society and owns all the property. Both of these systems are the antithesis of democracy and comprise totalitarian dictatorships. In both cases human and civil rights are non-existent and there is no individual freedom of action or thought. These forms of oppressive political systems are devastating to societies and to the human spirit and therefore not healthy.

Often these corrupt governments are a result of national or revolutionary wars in which the conquerors impose an absolute, oppressive, punishing regime on the conquered. The corruption can also occur from within as special interest groups or gangs of criminals and thugs obtain control of the governing mechanisms. The citizenry becomes captive to the corrupt gang of rulers.

In some cases one group, sect or religion seizes control of the government and kills or disempowers the members of every other group. This is not an inclusive government and results in deep divisions in society that create fundamental instabilities. This is a sick political system that results in a sick society that in turn continues to manufacture a sick political system.

There are a number of distributions and structures of regulatory governing authority that can produce healthy societies.

When a monarch labors incessantly for the well-being of her or his people, this can lead to a healthy society in which the monarch is beloved by her or his people, there are fair and just laws, individual freedoms and a high level of individual and social well-being.

More often than not, however, monarchies and aristocracies corrupt societies and rule for their own power and wealth at the expense of the rest of the population. This produces an unhealthy imbalance in society.

Plato believed that the government most able to provide the maximum well-being for a society was rule by a class of elite, philosopher-kings, who have the intelligence and character to rule for the benefit of the whole of society. He mistrusted democracy because he thought ordinary men lacked the insight and knowledge to be able to determine the best course of action to create the healthiest society. This was the natural aristocracy that Thomas Jefferson believed would arise in a meritocracy where everyone had the opportunity to rise to his best potential. Of course neither Plato nor Jefferson included slaves, women or property-less men in their definition of citizen.

Dictatorships and totalitarian regimes impose the will of one leader and his military enforcers on a citizenry that has absolutely no individual rights or freedom. This oppression of the human spirit can provide stability in the sense that the warring factions of the state are held in check by the ruthless, military power of the dictator. It looks like peace because the physical violence is suppressed, but in fact it is a state of frozen warfare.

In cases where people are unwilling to overcome their sectarian or ethnic conflicts and work together to create an inclusive democracy, a dictator can provide a stable society. If the dictator rules for the benefit of society, as was the original intent in the theory of communistic governance, then a dictator may actually benefit a society, for a time. An enlightened dictator, or military government can make a gradual change to a more democratic system with individual rights and freedoms. But, unfortunately, in most cases, the dictator eventually becomes corrupt, or paranoid and increasingly ruthless, and the society disintegrates into poverty and oppression.

Religious theocracies are totalitarian governments and are neither healthy nor free because a small elite holds absolute power over virtually every aspect of individual life—a power that is ruthlessly enforced. In religious theocracies oppression, coercion of thought and action destroys the human spirit and leads to a deep pervading sickness in the captive society. Ultimately the theocracies become so corrupt and ruthless, that the society disintegrates and is torn apart by sectarian violence, revolution and war. As we saw in the essay on war, the author believes that war is the final stage of societal corruption.

Anarchy is the absence of governance and it results in a state of violent chaos where there are no laws, no police protection, no organized way for citizens to provide the structures and functions that underlie a society's ability to function, like roads, schools, sanitation systems, health care, property rights, conflict resolution methods and all the systems that we provide through our government. In anarchy, the most violent ruthless elements of society run rampant, often in gangs, terrorizing the populations, murdering, robbing, raping, and plundering the citizens who no longer have a way of protecting themselves.

Constitutional Democracy, though not perfect, is the best way yet invented of creating an inclusive governing authority that guarantees the rights and freedoms of each and every individual, no matter to what group he or she belongs. This idea of individual liberties in which an individual is free to do what he or she wants provided he or she does not break the law or cause harm to another, is a new evolution in political thought that underlies the creation of truly inclusive, healthy, just, balanced, functional political systems and societies.

We have seen what a healthy political system looks like. What does a healthy economy look like?

A healthy economic system has to include everyone. An economy, as we saw, is the inter-related ways in which everyone makes a living. Without a livelihood a person cannot obtain the rudiments of life, food, water, clothing and shelter. Those who are completely abandoned by the economy, for whatever reason, end up destitute and eventually dead. This is true in all economies, from the most primitive, basic, survival level economies to the most complex, technologically advanced economies.

This is why in most societies there are provisions for including those who cannot provide for themselves in the economy through family support, or government intervention, or some other means of insuring that basic food clothing and shelter are available to everyone. When that fails to occur we see people dying of starvation and/or exposure.

A healthy economy is therefore inclusive and everyone has some means of sustenance, even if it is charitable or provided by the state.

Since livelihood involves work and knowledge, whether it is knowledge of how to trap a wild boar to eat, or whether it is knowledge of advanced computer design, or knowledge of agriculture and animal husbandry, we see that individual livelihood is fundamental to a healthy economy.

Because education is the way we learn the skills necessary to survive, education is fundamental to livelihood, whether it is how to make a spear, or whether it is biochemical research. It is through education, that is, teaching and learning, that the techniques inherent in the technologies we use to provide what we need and want are passed down from generation to generation. To the extent that an individual acquires and applies his or her education and skills he or she becomes a working member of an economic system.

Besides learning the techniques and technologies of the past, it is also necessary to continue to invent new technologies that then form the foundation for an expanded resource base and the cores for new business organizations.

We saw that businesses are organized activities in pursuit of livelihood and are the basic units of every economy, whether it is a one-person business, like Granny knitting sweaters that she sells, or a multinational corporation with thousands of employees. So the invention of new technologies and the creation of businesses are fundamental to healthy economies.

When an economy is flourishing and healthy we see broadly distributed purchasing power, broadly distributed property ownership, individual initiative, private enterprise, an infrastructure that supports commerce, laws that regulate and enforce fair business relations contracts. Government, bank and private investments are regulated in such a way that funds are invested in enterprises that create real value in terms of human and environmental well-being, and not in money-making schemes that accumulate wealth with no underlying value created.

We might call this condition of health, well-being and sufficient economic success as, "whealth." Whealth is wholeness, health, well-being, which includes adequate material well-being as well as a sense of wholeness, and physical, mental, emotional and spiritual balance and well-being.

What is environmental health?

When we look at a polluted lake we see dying fish, sediments, slime, oily residues, toxic chemicals and a dead ecosystem. This is environmental sickness. When we breathe air that is sharp, irritating, full of toxic chemicals we know that the ecosystem is sick and that we who are immersed in the sick ecosystem become sick. If we drink polluted water we become sick. If the soil is contaminated with plutonium residues we see a dying wasteland and we know if we come in contact with this soil we will become sick.

We know that the air, water and soil that our earth provides for us are the givens of nature on which we depend for our lives and that when these ecosystems are sick we become sick.

We also know that the major sources of air, soil and water pollution are caused by human beings, whether it is a primitive village that uses the same lake for its waste as it uses for its drinking water, or burns off rain forest to plant its crops, or whether it is an industrial chemical plant or oil refinery or plastics manufacturer that pumps its waste into a stream, or a coal-burning or nuclear generating plant that releases its waste gas into the atmosphere or ocean.

In the USA, as in Europe and in many other nations of the world, we have passed legislation to prevent and to clean up environmental pollution and we see that when toxins are removed, that nature heals itself, and indeed aids in the purification of water and air by its own regrowth. We as human beings, who have evolved here on earth and depend on nature for every breath of air we breathe, every drop of water we breath and ultimately for every bite of food we eat, need to reconnect our conscious awareness with our deep dependence on nature.

Our own personal health directly depends on the health of our ecosystems. This does not mean to return the earth to pre-human conditions. We can transform desolate dessert into bountiful gardens, we can plant and replant great forests, we can protect areas for wildlife and still have room for billions of human beings. We can invent technologies that preserve, protect and even enhance natural habitats and provide us resources for the future.

There is no reason why human beings cannot build beautiful civilizations that function in perfect harmony with nature. Indeed, living in harmony with healthy ecosystems is the only way that we will create healthy lasting societies and civilizations.

Chapter Twenty-Two: Causality

Junction of Routes 16 and 30

Our conversations are brief now. We are turned inward, balancing our bodies. The cells of our body tingle, as they deliver us the smooth, steady energy we need to run mile after mile after mile—muscles working in harmony, billions of tiny nerve messages coordinating every muscle perfectly for maximum efficiency.

The bottoms of my feet are feeling hot.

Out of the corner of my eye, I notice the Woodlands rapid transit station. Here we are at the junction of Route 16 and Route 30, otherwise known as Commonwealth Ave. A policeman motions all the runners to the right. "Atta go, girl! They'll never catch you now!" he booms. I smile thinking of how I'd been afraid the police would arrest me.

The runners get smaller in the distance, and then vanish completely as they turn the corner.

To me, a junction like this is a choice point. I think of all the times in my life I have made choices. What would it have been like if I had taken the other path? What causes us to choose one thing over another thing? This idea of alternatives and choices runs right through human life and into the natural world. These are questions of causality: What causes things to happen the way they do? Why does something happen one way and not another?

We search for explanations as we ask; Why?

What is cause? In what consists an explanation? When you look around the room you see tables, chairs, a rug and windows, but nowhere do you see a cause.

What sort of thing is a cause? What sort of existence does it have?

When I was a child I used to wonder whether the fire caused the log to burn or whether the log burning caused the fire.

Then I learned that the explanation is that the heat generated by the joining of oxygen gas in the air with the hydrocarbon molecules in the wood releases energy in the form of light and heat. The heat then triggers the continuing reaction of oxygen with the hydrocarbon molecules.

The molecules re-form themselves into a lower energy configuration in which two oxygen atoms join with one carbon atom to form carbon dioxide and two hydrogen atoms (from the hydrocarbon molecule) join with one oxygen atom to form water. Thus the log burning *is* the fire. What we see as flame is the electromagnetic radiation being released in the visible spectrum from the breaking of the hydrocarbon bonds.

You say the heat causes my hand to feel warm. But unless my nervous system is so constituted that I can have the subject experience of warmth, the heat cannot, in and of itself, cause my hand to feel warm.

Causality, then is contextual, it is the confluence of events which come together in such a way that this event occurs.

Cause is fundamental to our reasoning ability. To reason is to find the causes of things and then to explain happening through reasons.

You reason from the observed phenomenon back to the assumed invisible causes behind the physical, observed phenomena. It is so natural that you do it without realizing it. You see the observed phenomena and you deduce the cause. You know the cause and you predict the result.

Through the scientific method we discover which events are causally connected and which are not by doing experiments in which we vary one parameter while holding others constant and note carefully the results. Thus we learn which phenomena are connected in such a way that observation B occurs if and only if observation A occurs, but not if C occurs, for example.

Whenever you ask for a reason, you are referred to a cause that explains the phenomena. Why is the sky blue? Because the particles of dust scatter the light rays. You are referred to a context of explanatory theory that explains the precedent context, which in turn causes the event in question.

Aristotle, the ancient Athenian philosopher, set out four criterion that any explanation must fulfill. To explain something you must specify the following four causes:

1. The material out of which it is made, for example, the statue is made of marble.

2. You must name its formative principle, that which defines, its form, that is, the shape of the statue— what I would call the intrinsic structure or activity through which the identity of the object or process is achieved and maintained.

In the case of the statue the form is imposed from the outside by an agent other than the statue. In the essay on form we saw that in nature we find systems that form themselves through the interactions of their parts.

3. You must detail the efficient cause, that is, the forces outside itself that bring it into being, for example the sculptor and her chisel.

4. Lastly you must define the teleological cause, that is, the end to which the entity functions, that is, its purpose or reason for being, for example in the case of the statue, to decorate the town square, or to commemorate a famous person.

When we analyze the function of a machine we search for the causal relationships among its parts. Let's look at a hydroturbine, for example. We see the falling water hits the blades and causes the turbine to rotate. The action of the rotating turbine then causes a coil of wire to rotate inside a magnetic field. The magnetic field acting on the electrons in the wire causes the electrons to move, thus generating electricity. In this description the forces that act are delineated as the causal explanation for how the machine works.

We see that there is a series of causal links in which energy is transformed through the interactions of the parts of the turbine. These causal links form the efficient causes that can be traced from past to future, from the originating force through the subsidiary forces.

However when we ask the question why is there a hydroturbine? Our answer is not, "...because the action of the falling water causes the rotation of the axle that causes the wire to rotate in a magnetic field." When we ask: Why is there a hydroturbine our answer takes an entirely different form. The answer is: "The hydroturbine exists *in order to* generate electricity. The hydroturbine exists *for the purpose* of generating electricity." In this case we are invoking a teleological cause, that is, we answer in terms of the end to which or the purpose for the hydroturbine functions. This is not to imply that the hydroturbine itself has a purposeful intent; rather it is to point to the purpose of the designers in creating the hydroturbine.

There has been much controversy over teleological causes because of the confusion between the different meanings of the word, "purpose."

The purely functional teleological explanation in no way implies that the machine or any of its parts has a conscious intention or sense of purpose. This end-to-which explanation is simply a functional explanation in which it is understood that, in the context of the machine, each part functions to some end that is part of the general operation of the machine.

This function involves a process. A process is a sequence of activities in time. Thus the functioning of each part of the present machine operates to bring about some future result. The future is anticipated in the present design and operation of the machine.

To summarize, we see that the action of the machine can be

described in terms of the forces, that is, the efficient causes, that act in a sequential manner to make the machine work. In addition, the function of the machine can be described in terms of the functional purpose of each part in bringing about the purpose to which the machine functions, that is to generate electricity.

In addition to this functional teleological description, the second meaning of the word, "purpose," is as a conscious intent or intentionally purposeful activity. We might say that the engineers' purpose in designing and building the hydroturbine is to generate electricity to power cities. In this case we are referring to the subjective, mental intention of a person. We don't say that the generator caused the man to build a hydroturbine. We don't consider this use of the word, "purpose," a functional explanation, but rather as a statement as to the mental state of the people who decide to design and to build a hydroturbine. They hold a conscious purpose in their minds that informs their actions.

Because the machine has no conscious purpose, in science, the explanations are always in terms of efficient and material causes, because when we use teleological explanations there is an ambivalence as to whether we are speaking purely functionally or whether we are invoking some conscious purposeful intent either on the part of the natural system itself, as in animistic lore, or on the part of a Great Supernatural Designer and Creator, as in religious lore.

However when we speak of self-forming biological systems it is not so easy to avoid resorting to functional teleological explanations. When we ask, why does the heart beat? The answer is in order to pump blood to all the cells of the body, which is a functional teleological explanation. We can say, the heart beats because a nervous impulse has been transmitted from the brain to the node of Ranvier and this causes the heart muscles to contract and relax. This is a explanation in terms of efficient causes or forces, but it is less than satisfactory as an answer to the question.

271

We see that teleological explanations describe the given phenomenon by referring to a future result that is accomplished by the present action, whereas the invocation of efficient causes explains the present event by reference to past events that have led up to the present phenomenon.

The fact is that all we know that exists is the present moment, which is poised between the past and the future. Thus a full explanation must include both the past and the future in its causal reach.

Exactly where the present moment is in time is a matter of great confusion since the past seems to flow seamlessly into the future in such a way that no matter how small a segment of time we take, we never seem to catch the exact point of that change that comprises the present.

Let us examine this idea of force, for a moment. Force is the generalized efficient cause. We speak of the force of gravity causing the ball to drop. We speak of the force of the collision causing the ball to move. We speak of electrical and magnetic forces. We can make shorthand notations of all the forces acting in a certain region of space and time by conceiving of a field. A field is a calculation of what the force on a unit object would be if that object were there. In a gravitational field that unit object is a unit mass. In an electric field, that object is a unit electric charge.

In my essay on interaction I pointed out that the invocation of invisible forces to explain why things change is in some sense metaphysical in that all we know is that an interaction has occurred. An interaction is an action between in which the interacting participants change their motions, or states or configurations. When there is no interaction the participants continue on indefinitely in whatever their present state is.

We assume that there is an invisible force acting because we see a change in motion, state or configuration, but this assumption is unwarranted. We have no way of detecting or measuring a force except through detecting and measuring the change that it is thought to cause. It is handy to think in terms of force. It helps us to analyze the observed changes, but we could as well speak of units of interaction.

Following the flow of energy also helps us to analyze changes. We can see and measure energy as the various transformations occurs in complex interrelated phenomena, as we did with the hydroturbine.

What is energy? Energy is defined as the capacity to do work. In physics Work is defined as the exertion of a Force over the Distance moved. So that if you push against an stationary wall although you are expending energy you are doing no work. The energy you are expending can be calculated in terms of the capacity to move the wall if the wall were moveable.

Energy is conceived of in two main forms: 1. Potential energy that exists within a field, or within a system of potentially moving parts and 2. Kinetic energy that is a function of the object's motion with respect to its environment. For example a rock poised at the top of a hill has a certain amount of potential energy because it has the potential to fall, that is, to move within the gravitational field of interaction. When it actually is in the act of falling it has kinetic energy. The amount of kinetic energy it exhibits as it falls is exactly the same amount of potential energy it had stored in the rock-earth system.

The amount of kinetic and potential energy the rock has depends on its mass and on the strength of the field or interaction. The distance the object falls in a given time depends on its velocity, but in the case of a freely falling object the velocity is constantly increasing. A constantly changing velocity is called acceleration. We know that Force equals the Acceleration times the Mass of the body that is accelerating, or more accurately, Force is equal to the change in the Momentum of the falling object relative to the earth in time, where

Momentum is the product of the Mass times the Velocity.

Since Energy is defined as the capacity to do work and Work is defined as the exertion of a Force over the Distance moved, and since Force is measured as the Mass of an object times the Acceleration that the force causes, or more exactly, Force is measured as the change in Momentum that that applied force causes over time, this means that Energy is measured as the change in Momentum that the force applied causes multiplied times the Distance the object moves. So the amount of energy stored or released in the system both defines and depends on the interactions of the masses that comprise the system.

In an electric or magnetic field, the interactants include the electric, magnetic and electromagnetic interactions among the components of the system.

This brings us to a fascinating aspect of physics. Despite the long resistance to describing phenomena in teleological terms, there is a quantity that is called, "Action." Action is defined as Energy acting over a Time interval, such that the product of the amount of Energy multiplied times the length of the Time interval is called the Action. Because, as we saw, Energy can be described in terms of Mass and Velocity, we can also describe Action as the product of the Momentum, which is the mass multiplied times the Velocity, multiplied times the Distance over which the momentum continues.

More exactly, Action is defined as Energy acting over a Time interval. But Energy is defined as Force applied multiplied times the Distance through which object moves as a result of the applied force. Since Force applied is equal to the Change in Momentum per unit Time Interval, we see that Action is equal to the Change in Momentum divided by the Time Interval all multiplied times the quantity: the Distance moved multiplied times the Time Interval. But the Time Interval in the numerator and the Time Interval in the denominator cancel. Therefore, Action can also be described as the Momentum multiplied times the Distance over which the Momentum continues.

In systems dynamics, remarkably, the system in question tends to evolve in a way that minimizes the Action, that is the system changes in a way to reduce its Momentum times the Distance it moves, which is to say, the system changes in such a way as to minimize its Energy times the Time over which the energy acts.

If we conceive of configuration space as being a sequential description of the configuration of the system at each moment in time, we can see that the system follows its gradient, that is it's path of least resistance along its Action parameter.

This is a teleological explanation because it is describing the present in terms of the future. The system re-configures itself *in order* to minimize the function of its Momentum multiplied times Distance, or Energy multiplied times Time. This in no way implies that the system has a conscious purpose or that any supernatural being or creator has a conscious purpose, or that human beings have anything to do with this at all. Never-the-less, it is a teleological explanation in which a present phenomenon is described in terms of its tendency to become something in the future.

It is also interesting to note that at the very smallest level of physical interaction, the indivisible quanta are not quanta of energy but are quanta of Action. This observation is further support for my idea of using the fundamental concepts of Action and Interaction from which to build up our models of the physical world, and not space, time, velocity or mass, all of which I believe can be better described in terms of, the more fundamental, Action and Interaction.

In physics, causality takes on another dimension.

In physics, event A has to precede event B in order to be its efficient cause. Or to say it differently, event B has to follow event A in order to have been caused by it. In terms of efficient causation, the past precedes the present. Even in teleological causation the present precedes the future.

Since the discovery that electromagnetic radiation travels at a constant speed as measured by all uniformly moving observers, and that the speed of light defines the top speed at which a material object can travel, the causal connections among events has taken on a new dimension.

The discovery that no massive object can travel faster than the speed of light, is expressed in the Lorentz equations. The Lorentz equations show that as a massive object travels faster and faster it becomes, or appears to become, heavier and heavier, that is its mass appears to increase.

We need to remember that speed is always relative to the observer who is measuring the speed. So when we say the massive object is traveling faster and faster, we mean that the relative speed between the observer and the object being measure is greater and greater.

For an observer co-moving with the massive object the relative speed between this co-moving observer and the massive object is zero, and hence, to this co-moving observer, the mass of the object remains the same. We examine this in more detail in the essay on matter.

Here the point we want to understand is that because the speed of light forms the upper bound of all possible measured speeds for massive objects, this means that the measures of time and the measures of distance are always conjoined and constrained by the fact that the maximum ratio of the distance traveled to the time elapsed is "c," the speed of light. That is to say that a material object, starting from point A, cannot get to any place B, that is outside the region of space that can be reached by a beam of light that starts from A and reaches B.

This division of spacetime in to regions that can or cannot be joined by a beam of light is called the "Light Cone."

This has profound implications for the causal connections of events in spacetime.

Why? Because an event at A at time a cannot cause any event B at time b that is outside the region of spacetime that can be reached by a beam of light starting at A at time a, if that causal connection requires the traveling of a material or energetic object like a wave.

Yet, more recently, it has been discovered that apparently some types of information are transmitted instantaneously as if there were no space or time separating events that appear to be widely separated in space and time.

For example, when a laser is directed at a certain type of crystal a pair of photons can be simultaneously released such that one photon has an angular momentum, or spin directed in one direction and the other has a spin directed in the opposite direction. When these mated photons are separated even by thousands of miles, and you changed the spin on one of them, the other one instantaneously changes it's measured spin. That is, the two photons behave as if they were still conjoined and not separated by space or time.

According to physical theories, if distant events are independent, then for one event to cause another, there would have to be some transmission of energy or force between them. According to relativity theory, no transmission of energy or force can be accomplished instantaneously, but rather has to travel at the speed of light or at a lesser speed.

If distance events are not independent, then we have the question of what conjoins them?

In our example of the mated photons there is no detectible delay in time between the reversals of polarity of the two electrons even though they are widely separated from one another. How can this be? It changes our intuitions of space, time and causal connection.

In the case of the conjoined photon pairs, they continue to act as a whole system even when separated by thousands of miles and theoretically by millions of miles. Their entwined angular momentums are conserved no matter where they are located in space and time or in spacetime. This is apparently action at a distance although nothing is transmitted between the twin photons.

The unity of the conjoined photons precedes and is more fundamental than our measures of space, time and spacetime. In my theory of interaction preceding space, time and spacetime this is no problem.

In the case of the conjoined photons, in order to measure the spin on one photon we have to interact with it. That interaction then defines either the position or the velocity, as well as the spin, of that photon or some combination of these factors. Before that interaction we have no way of knowing where the photon is or how it is behaving or indeed, even if it exists.

We assume it exists in some way. Physicists describe that existence as the probability of finding that photon somewhere in space and time or spacetime. Some even go so far as to say the photon doesn't exist until we interact with it, and our interactions with it bring it into existence in some absolute way.

Clearly this depends in part on what we mean by existence. Its existence before, during and after interaction is different, that is, its existence takes on different forms. We cannot know of its existence in some absolute manner. We only know our perspective on our interaction with it. We assume that it exists in some way independent of us, and independent of our interaction with it. We assume that its form, or mode, of existence changes on interaction with us, or with anything else. But to say that we in some way bring it into existence out of nothing or in some absolute manner is to credit ourselves with an anthropomorphic power that far exceeds reality, and confounds ontology with epistemology, that is, confuses what we posit to exist with what we presume to know.

But the fact remains the instant we interact with one of the paired photons in such a way as to change its spin, for example with a magnetic field, the other photon, thousands of miles away flips it's spin as measured by an experimentalist at the distant site. Rather, when the experimentalist measures the distant photon, she finds that its spin has already flipped. The change is so fast that it cannot be observed in process.

If, as I say, interaction is prior to time, space and spacetime, where does that leave time, space and spacetime? Where does it leave causality?

We have seen that time and space do not exist out there as some extended physically real entities. Time is just the number of ticks on a clock and space is just how many unit measuring rods we can lay out between events. We have seen that our measures of the number of ticks and the number of measuring rods between events varies depending on our reference frame. This is Relativity Theory.

We also have quantum theory that sets out the parameters of interaction for very small entities. These theories are the frameworks in which we have understood the causal relationships among events and by means of which we measure and interact with these events in predictable ways.

So we see how our assessment of causality and causal relationships depends not only on context but also on our theories and models of explanation. We explain events and phenomena by invoking causes. But causes are not things, and they have no existence out there in the physical world. Causes are relationships among events that are interpreted in the context of our explanatory models and theories.

However our discussion would be incomplete without a brief discussion of the concepts of the uncaused cause and the self-causing cause. Aristotle wrote about the uncaused cause. He reasoned that in a sequence of causal events that stretched back into the past, each succeeding event would be caused by some preceding event. For example if a rock is moved by a lever, the lever contacts the rock and the movement of the lever is transmitted to the rock and causes the rock to move. But what causes the lever to move? The lever is attached to a wheel that turns. The turning of the wheel causes the lever to move. But what causes the wheel to turn? The wheel is attached to an axle, but what causes the axle to move? The axle is attached a horizontal pole. But what cause the pole to move? The pole is attached to a donkey by a harness, so the movement of the donkey causes the pole to move. What causes the donkey to move? A boy leads the donkey around in a circle, so the boy causes the donkey to move. And what causes the boy to move? His father has promised him three gold coins if he leads the donkey around. So we see a chain of causality.

For Aristotle in analyzing the motions of the natural world, he observed that one motion caused another motion, but what was the final cause? What was causing the entire chain of motion? For Aristotle is was the uncaused cause that moved the natural world. This final cause was not caused by anything else. It was the originator of motion without itself being moved. For this cause there was no explanation.

Part of the problem was that Aristotle and the ancient philosophers erroneously believed that a massive object would stay in a state of rest unless something acted on it to cause it to move. We now know that this is an error. Newton's brilliance saw that a massive object remains in a state of constant uniform motion unless acted on by something that *changes* its motion, that is, either its speed or direction of motion.

In contrast, I've talked about the concept of self-causation, specifically with respect to a natural existence that creates, the therefore causes itself in a paradoxically reflexive manner. This idea of self-causation is different from the ancient concept of the un-caused cause, because the uncaused cause is without motion or activity. It, itself, is unmoving.

In contrast, my concept of self-causation is perpetual activity and motion. Self-causation is not only in the past but is presently and immediately active. Self-causation is an activity not caused by anything other than itself. It is identically self-reflexive, meaning that its causality is paradoxical in that what is caused is also what is causing. The acted upon is also the actor. And it is reciprocal and reflexive in that this self-causality is ultimately prior to time and space in the sense that its past is also its future and its present.

This brings us to the fundamental point about causality. Our understanding of the causal relationships among events is expressed in the theories that we create to explain phenomena. And conversely the theories we invent depend on our discovering the causal relationships among events.

Homo Sapiens is a theorizing animal species. Our theories can be right or wrong. Our survival and advancement as a human species depends on the accuracy of our theories, with which we connect the interrelationships among events in the correct causal context and allows us to control outcomes.

Vital to our survival and progress as a human race is our ability to discover the causal relationships between events and among contexts and conditions. This is true not only in the physical and biological sciences and medicine, but also in the human sciences of sociology, politics, economic, anthropology and psychology, where finding the conditions and causes of the various political, economic, social and psychological events and outcomes is crucial.

For example, in economics, our ability to find the causal relationships between monetary policy and economic outcomes determines our ability to create economic systems that work for everyone and produce healthy societies. Our ability to determine the consequences of various political decisions is based on our appreciation of the causal relationships among causes and results.

To discover the causal relationships in sickness and health is vital to our individual well being and is the subject of on going medical research. Our models of the interlocking causal relationships among events is absolutely vital to our happiness and success as individuals and as societies not only in science but in all areas of our lives. Improving the accuracy of our causal models on all levels is therefore a matter of which we are all vitally concerned.

So causality is conditional, contextual, multidimensional, relative, relational and interactive and depends our ability to find the consistent conjunctions of multiple events and contexts that produce the same results in a repeatable fashion. The scientific method of experimentation, observation, consistency and the ability to manipulate the variables in predictable ways is used to ferret out the mysteries of causal relationships that are not always obvious. These causal relationships then serve as the handles through which we control events and implement technologies.

CHAPTER TWENTY-THREE: MATTER, MASS AND ENERGY

Heartbreak Hill

For some time I have been hearing the other runners talking about Heartbreak Hill. I'm not sure what Heartbreak Hill is or where it is; I just keep on running, following the other runners. "Heartbreak Hill. That's a killer," I hear one guy say. His friend answers, "Yeah," I seek relief for my burning feet by on the a pleasant grassy strip that follows along Route 30, otherwise known as Commonwealth Avenue, a broad, open road.

I'm surprised to see so many spectators. The road starts up here; I guess we've run somewhere around eighteen miles, give or take a mile or two. It feels good to be running up after all that downhill work. I wonder if this is Heartbreak Hill.

I've been reigning myself in, keeping my speed in check, feeling the weight of responsibility on my shoulders. Here I am making a bold public statement to change the way people think about women. If I collapse or fail to finish, I'll set women back another fifty years.

Now, heading up hill, I'm pushing myself, rather than holding myself in. I feel the weight of the earth pulling me back and down. The road flattens out. If this is Heartbreak Hill, it's nothing compared ot the mountains I've run over. But in the next moment, the road begins to rise again. I push hard against the pull of gravity and after some time the road flattens out again. "Whew, glad that's over," I think. It's not a particularly steep hill, but coming as it does, so late in the race, it feels harder than it is. A few moments later, the road begins to rise again; and again I feel the fierce tug of gravity pulling me back and down. Again I push, and again reach what I think is the top, only to find a few moments later that another rise confronts me.

Finally we crest the top and the road starts down. Now I have to resist the force of gravity pulling me forward. My quadriceps, strained from miles of downhill, now complain at the renewed strain. It's harder coming down Heartbreak than it was going up! Often, I'd marveled at the force of gravity and the massiveness of the earth that tugs so persistently at us.

What is gravity? I'd studied physics at the Tufts School of Special Studies and had wondered at what actually causes the massiveness of material objects. I'd spent hours throwing rocks up into air the watching the perfect parabola that unfolds as the rock arced up, reaches the top of its trajectory and then arcs down again. I'd wondered what mass really is. How is it that material objects have mass?

After much thinking, I'd gone to my physics professor and had asked him why, if gravity is the only force acting on a mass, doesn't it just fall straight down, very suddenly from the top of the trajectory. Instead, it gains speed, only gradually, as it falls, as if there is a force acting to keep it from speeding up. He said that in his twenty-five years of teaching I was only the second student who had seen that. He said that if I were a man, he'd suggest I go into physics. Then he told me that there are two types of mass— gravitational mass that pulls between two massive bodies and inertial mass that keeps massive objects from changing motion. These two masses are always equal, he said.

I had puzzled over this for hours. It occurred to me that inertial mass and gravitational mass were just two different ways of measuring the same thing, namely the connection of the massive object with the rest of the mass in the universe.

"What is it about a material object that gives it is mass? What does it mean to say that an object is material? Is matter the same as mass?" I wondered.

Historically matter has been considered as the material or stuff out of which something is made. The statue is made out of marble. The house is made out of bricks. The boat is made out of wood. In the same way, matter is taken to be the stuff of which the universe is made.

Material objects are considered to be made of atoms and molecules, to have mass and to exist out there in the physical world.

Is matter the ultimate substance out of which the universe is made?

Matter is not the fundamental, ultimate substance out of which everything is made if we define matter to be that which is made of atoms and molecules, because molecules and atoms are made of something smaller and more fundamental.

There is some confusion around this point because materialists define "matter" as that ultimate substance out of which the universe is made. But this is a tautology because whatever it turns out the universe is made of the materialists have already named it "matter." This is why we specifically define matter as that which is made of atoms and molecules, so we can avoid this trap.

When we say material objects have mass, what do we mean? Are all material objects massive? Are there entities that have mass but are not material in the sense that they are not made of atoms and molecules? How does a material object "have" mass. Is mass the same as energy?

To answer these questions, I asked: Are there entities that have mass but are not made of atoms and molecules? And I answered: Yes, a moving wave-particle of light has mass but is not made of atoms and molecules. Therefore mass is not the same as matter and not all entities that have mass are made of atoms and molecules. Therefore there are non-material entities that have mass, for example, as we saw, electromagnetic radiation. Interestingly this reveals that electromagnetic fluxes, which are much smaller than atoms and molecules have what we call a physical existence but are not material entities.

Are there any objects made of atoms and molecules that do not have mass? No there are no material objects made of atoms and molecules that do not have mass. Why not? Because atoms and molecules have mass, and therefore objects made of atoms and molecules have mass.

So in conclusion we see that mass is a property of material objects, but not all entities that have mass are material.

What then is mass and how do objects and entities have it? As we saw there are two kinds of mass, inertial and gravitational. So mass is both the resistance to changes in the motions of entities, and is also the attraction between entities that have mass.

But what about the entity gives it its mass?

The famous equation from Relativity Theory shows us that Mass is equal to the Energy contained in an object divided by the square of the speed of light, that is, the speed of light multiplied times itself. This is more commonly written as, the Energy of an object is equal to the Mass of that object times the speed of light squared.

Is mass then the same as energy?

What is energy? Energy, we saw, is defined as the capacity to do work and work is defined as the exertion of a force on an object times the distance that that force moves the object. So a donkey pulling a cart is doing work, but a donkey pulling a boulder that doesn't move, although he is exerting energy is doing no work. This seems strange. In the first case the energy of the moving donkey and cart is kinetic energy and in the second case the energy of the stationary donkey is potential energy, that is energy that could do work if it were actually moving something. We saw previously in the example of the system of the rock and the earth that the potential energy that the rock has at the top of the hill can be converted to kinetic energy when it falls.

So energy is a property of systems of interacting parts. There is no such thing as disembodied energy floating around. Energy results from, and is a measure of, the interactions of the parts of a system. Systems are comprised of collections of interacting parts. So therefore it must be that mass, too, results from the interactions among the parts of systems of interacting parts. *So both Mass and Energy are not things, but are properties of systems.*

To be more specific, the external or kinetic energy that a massive object has in a gravitational field derives from its gravitational interaction, as a whole system, with the system of masses in which it is imbedded. And, the internal energy of a massive object derives from the internal interactions of the parts of which that system is composed. Both inertial mass and gravitational mass, then are systems quantities. The inertial mass and gravitational mass of an object are always equal because both the inertial mass and the gravitational mass are the result of different ways in which we measure the interaction of the massive object with the gravitational mass of the entire universe in which it is imbedded.

When we speak of the rest mass of an object, we mean the internal energy that that object has when we measure it from a coordinate system that is co-moving with that object. When the object is at rest relative to the coordinate system from which we are measuring it, we say it has no kinetic mass or energy relative to us. Therefore its entire mass/energy is a measure of its rest mass and rest energy. This rest mass derives from the internal interactions that are inside the object whose mass and energy we are measuring.

When we measure the mass/energy of an object from a coordinate system that is moving relative to the object, we note that to us, it appears that the object has gained mass and energy. We are now measuring the sum of its rest mass and its kinetic mass/energy, as its total mass energy.

How is it that merely by moving relative to a massive object, we can increase its apparent mass? ... The answer is that all these qualities and quantities are systems properties and when we interact with something we are part of the system of interacting parts that defines and create the measurement that we are making and the qualities we are measuring... That is to say that mass and energy are not properties of objects, but are properties, both of the internal interactions of the parts of these systems, and of the interactions of these objects with everything else including us the observers.

There is nowhere outside of what we are measuring to measure from, just as there is nowhere outside the perceiver from which to perceive. This means that the there is no way to get an objective view of what we are perceiving or measuring. Every measurement we make requires an interaction with what we are measuring and that interaction changes the state of what we are measuring.

This becomes most clear at the smallest levels of interaction in quantum physics as we saw with Heisenberg's Uncertainty Principle that says that the more accurate is our measurement of the velocity of very small entities the less accurate is our measurement of position, and the more we hone in on position the less definite becomes our measure of velocity. Each interactant can "know" only one half the parameters of that interaction from its own point of view in its own way. The same is true when we measure mass and energy, we are part of the system that we are measuring and our act of measuring requires an interaction that changes the state of what we are measuring.

When we split an atom, we breach the threshold energy that is holding it together and it releases a plethora of subatomic particles and radiation that was its internal mass and energy. Its internal energy and mass has become external. Its rest mass has become converted to the masses and kinetic mass/energy of all the resultant particles and radiation that is released. No mass/energy is lost; it is simply converted from one form to another, from the internal mass/energy of a system of interacting parts to the external mass/energy of the independent parts interacting with the rest of the universe.

We note that when parts begin to interact to form a system, they begin to pool their potential energies. This smaller system of interacting parts, with its pooled potential energy, then interacts, as a whole—the individual parts being constrained by their interactions within the system—with the entire universe in which it is imbedded. When the smaller system disintegrates, what was the *internal* mass/energy of the smaller system of interacting parts becomes *external* mass/energy as the parts, now separately interacting with larger system in which it is imbedded, as each component of what was the smaller system begins to interact independently with the entire universe into which it is released. However we must also include the energy that escapes as light and heat in our measurements of the total mass and energy of the systems involved.

Thus, although mass and energy measure different characteristics of systems, they derive from the same underlying fact: namely the strengths of the interactions among the internal parts of the smaller system, plus the strengths of the interactions between the smaller system, as it interacts as a whole, with the system that imbed it. This is why I say we need to take interaction as more fundamental than energy and mass.

Interestingly and importantly, we note that for light, and all electromagnetic radiation, the rest mass is zero. The light wave particle, also called the photon, acquires mass/energy only through its motion. When a photon is released it goes from zero velocity to the fastest speed possible for a massive object in no time. It is in effect born, already traveling at the maximum speed possible. This is remarkable. What can it possibly mean?

In some sense the photon does not exist until it moves because its existence is in fact as a mutually self-creating interaction of expanding and contracting electric and magnetic fluxes neither of which exist before created by the action of the other. So then, how to these photons exist within atoms before they are released? The answer must be that they don't exist as photons, at least, not as traveling photons.

Can there be any other type of photons beside traveling photons, that is, what would a stationary photon look like if it were possible? To get at the answer to this question I asked: What has the speed of light to do with mass and energy?

The discovery of the speed of light squared as the conversion factor between the measure of Energy and the measure of Mass is a direct result of the Lorentz Equations as applied to the Newtonian expressions for the relationships between momentum and kinetic energy. Even in classical physics it was known that there is a relationship between the energy and the mass of systems. To be specific in classical physics the Kinetic Energy of an object is equal to one half its Mass times the square of its Velocity.

Remember that the Dutch Scientist Lorentz created his equations based on the observation that the speed of light is the same for all observers on uniformly moving coordinate systems no matter what their velocities. This stunning fact remains an enigma. Why should this be?

However, by plugging the Lorentz equations, which contain the constant the speed of light squared, into the classical equations we find the speed of light squared appearing in the equations that relate relativistic Mass and Energy, namely, in this case, the Energy equals Mass times the velocity of light, "C", squared. That the velocity of light turns up in these basic equations that relate the energy and mass of a system indicates some deep property of mass, energy, space and time that in the opinion of the author has not been properly appreciated.

What happens if we view light, not from a uniformly moving reference frame, but from an accelerating frame, or equivalently, from a reference frame that has a gravitational field associated with it, like the earth? We looked at this in the Essay on Cosmology, but here we see that although the forward speed of light appears constant, the beam of light is observed to curve, relative to the observer in an accelerating or gravitational frame.

Here we see that light, which is an electromagnetic radiation has wave properties when it is traveling but "condenses" to a particle-like entity when interacted with. This type of "condensation" on interaction does not appear in the fundamental descriptions of spacetime and gravitation, which describes spacetime and gravitation as continuous fields or manifolds.

Quantum physics, however, conceives of a spacetime or manifold of discrete probabilities of finding a quantum of action at a particular place when it is observed, that is, when we interact with it.

What then is the relationship between electromagnetism and quantum physics and gravity? Both electromagnetism and gravity are explicable in terms of interactions, but the interactions seem to be somewhat distinct, that is, there seems to be two different types of interaction involved, gravitation and electromagnetism. And yet, here is light, an electromagnetic phenomenon that links the gravitation of material objects to spacetime, mass, energy and velocity.

Indeed, as we saw, Riemann geometry accounts gravitation as geodesics of spacetime, that is, in General Relativity Theory, it is the curvature of space and time or spacetime itself, that creates what we measure as gravitational force.

No massive object can travel faster than the speed of light. Some say that no information can be transmitted or transferred or communicated faster than the speed of light. The author doesn't agree with this last statement and we looked at this in the Essay on Causality, where we saw that in the case of photons with paired opposed spins, the flipping of one spin is mirrored immediately in the flipping of the other, no matter if they are separated by great distances.

This is reminiscent of the fact that a photon is born already traveling at the fastest possible speed. This says something fundamental about our measures of space and time, and is why I feel that space, time, mass and energy are not fundamental, but can be explained more fully by my theory that takes Action and Interaction as fundamental.

But how do we do this?

How do we create a physics in which dimensionality is not fundamental, but in which Self-Creating-Self–Activity, that is, Action, and Action-Between are fundamental? First we need to realize that dimensionality is simply our way of ordering the events according to how our own nervous systems interpret the data we encounter. We are wired, so to speak, to navigate the external world by means of place cells in our hippocampus that keep track of where we are in any given perceived environment. So naturally we apply this methodology to our attempts to navigate the conceptual world of cosmological and subatomic physics.

Events are happenings, in which there is a change, but every change requires some sort of interaction. So in effect events are the signposts of interactions. And interactions are actions-between two or more entities, in which each causes a change in some state, or motion, of the other.

However, there is an alternative in which space and time and spacetime do not exist, and are not taken as the fundamental explicands, and in which electromagnetism and gravitation can be explained in terms that do not involve geodesics, and events can be described not using the multidimensional spaces of string theory or other theories that are based on dimension.

In my theory, light is fundamental. Light, that is, electromagnetic radiation, I take as the fundamental self-creating, self-activity of what we call the physical universe, remembering that physical refers to an outside perspective on our interaction with what is there. I believe that the motion of electromagnetic radiation, is not "through" space and time or spacetime, but that the motions of traveling photons actually create what we measure as spacetime.

Moreover, in terms of mass and energy, light is an entity that has no parts, or rather, it is purely the interaction of its two fluxes neither of which exist before they are created by that other. If you could take apart the two fluxes they would cease to exist. The photon at rest is indivisible and has no rest mass, therefore it is comprised of no interacting parts. Where does it come from then?

What would a photon at rest actually be?

In my theory, the only way a photon could be "at rest," is if it is confined through interaction with another entity. I conceive of s-photons as being stationary in the sense that two, or more, photons interact with one another in such a way that their motions are confined to close orbits in which they are traveling at the speed of light around one another. I conceive this as multi-dimensional figure eight patterns or sinusoidal orbits of pulsing expanding and collapsing magnetic and electric fluxes. These s-photons, in my theory, are the fundamental, indivisible quanta of action, which then interact to build up other subatomic entities including all the so called subatomic particles, and finally the electrons, positrons, neutrons and protons that interact to form atoms, and thus serve as the basis of both matter and antimatter, depending on their spins and on the directions of their orbits.

This explains why and how when an electron and a positron, which is an antimatter electron, collide, two photons appear. Conversely, when two photons interact they can form an electron and a positron. In my theory, electrons and positrons are composed of interacting s-photons with opposing spins. The huge force that these subatomic particles display results from the extremely strong interactions that an interacting pair of s-photons have with one another by confining each other.

These s-photons are not really stationary, but rather are confining one another through their extremely powerful interactions into fast moving orbits. They might better be called c-photons, for confined photons but this is too confusing because "c" is used to denote the speed of light. Therefore we name them s-photons.

So these self-creating-self-activities in my theory manifest as fluxes of interacting, electromagnetic mutually self-creating, self-inducing fluxes, which are not the activity of some "thing", but rather are the self-activity of activity itself. The activity exists prior to the subject-object split, prior to the split between what we name with nouns and what we name as verbs. Here the subject and the object, the actor and the action and the acted and the acted upon are one and it is out of this fundamental unity that I believe all matter is formed through compiling in ever more complex systems of systems of systems of nested systems of these interacting s-photons. This is what I call my photon theory.

Chapter Twenty-Four: Religion

Boston College

The Boston skyline shows through the trees as we curve around Boston College. A lovely church spire rises towards the sky. Historically, churches, temples, mosques, and other places of worship have formed an integral part of the social landscape of virtually every society.

What exactly is religion and why has it been so important to the human psyche?

Religions seek to explain the world of events in terms of unseen supernatural powers. Religions bind people together in a common framework of beliefs. Religions usually involve a set of customs and practices. The ultimate event that religions seek to explain is existence itself. We seek reasons for events. We seek reasons for existence. We seek reasons for our own birth, life and death. More than reason, we seek comfort and aid through the events of life and death.

Fundamentally all religions are speaking of the same thing — the miracle, mystery and wonder of creation. Contemplation of this mystery brings us spiritual enlightenment and a sense of awe at the Divine source of our being and of all being. Each religion has as its core a spiritual path, which helps people to access this sense of the incomprehensible love out of which all existence is continuously being born — this is the mountain. Different religions are different paths up the same mountain. The problems arise when people forget the mountain and become immersed in the paths.

Historically religions have served both to join people together and to split people apart. For those sharing the same religious beliefs, the religion binds them together. For those who believe differently, the story is quite different. For millennia, wars have divided along the fracture lines between religions, and religious leaders have sought and obtained immense political power.

Theocracies have functioned throughout history as political institutions and often oppress entire populations and engage in murderous assault on those who refuse to convert. This has been true of the Christian Church in Medieval Europe, where the Inquisition and religious wars resulted in forced conversions and the murder of millions of innocent people in the name of God and the Church.

In modern secular constitutional democracies, freedom of religion and separation of the church and state are fundamental constitutional provisions. But in religious theocracies the situation is reversed: The church is the state and the state is the church. So when we study the history of religions we are often also studying the history of political empires as well.

The distribution of power between the Church and the State can vary. In tbe case of State Religions, we find parallel power structures in which a religious hierarchy and a political, secular, civil hierarchy exist side by side in the same state, as was the case in European monarchies. In these cases the relationships between State and Church vary from an uneasy truce, to a cooperative effort, to outright warfare, to the domination of the state by the Church or the domination of the Church by the State. Again, it is important to distinguish between the political power of the religious hierarchy and the religious beliefs and customs inherent in that religion.

When we think about religions, we can divide religion into five aspects that blend together in various proportions to define that particular religion: 1. The Doctrines, Beliefs and Myths that become reality for the true believers; 2. The Customs and Mores followed by the adherents of that religion; 3. The Rules of Behavior that are implicit in that religion; 4. The Politics, power structure and organization of the religion, which can be divided into: a. the internal political structures and, b. the external power that the particular religious group wields in society and 5. The Spiritual Path revealed in the context of the religion.

These categories overlap as they pertain and are used to analyze a particular religious organization. The most important is the fifth and last category, the Spiritual Path, but it is also the most decimated when political motives, ambition, greed and corruption disrupt the spiritual aspects of the religion.

One of the oldest world religions is the Hindu Religion based on the sacred texts that includes the Vedic Scriptures, the Upanishads and the Bhagavad Gita. While this religion defines a culture of music, verse, mythology, and worship of the Brahma and subsidiary forms of the Divine, it has existed through the centuries in the contexts of multiple forms of civil governance that include monarchy, colonization by the British Empire and modern constitutional democracy, it has generally not engaged in conquest or violent overthrow or forced conversions.

Buddhism, an outgrowth of the Hindu Religion, generally preaches tolerance and peace. Its sacred texts are the writings and teachings of the Buddha, who lived in the fifth century B.C. Generally Buddhism does not attempt to create a Theocracy, but exists within the contexts of whatever civil governance is prevalent in the nations in which it is practiced. In terms of the organizational structure of the religion, the Dalai Lama is chosen by the priests and is not democratically elected.

The Hebrew or Jewish Religion embodies not only spiritual practices but customs and practices that are carried on to this day around the world and has functioned as a theocracy during parts of its existence. Parts of this religion were incorporated into the Christian religion, and of course the Old Testament is taken directly from the Hebrew Bible. The Jews however do not recognize Jesus as the Messiah for which they are waiting.

One of the largest and oldest of the Christian Churches is the Catholic Church, which is structured as a top down hierarchy in which the lay person has little power. In the Catholic Church, priests and other high officers of the church are required to take an oath of celibacy. The dogmas, doctrines and services are structured by the hierarchy, as they have been centuries. The liturgy is based on the life and death of Christ as interpreted and represented by the Church based on the Gospels. Mary, the Mother of Christ, plays an important role. The Pope is taken to be God's representative on Earth and is chosen by the College of Cardinals, in an internal process in which the laity has no power. Historically the Catholic Church has wielded immense political power in the nations in which it operates and has as its final goal the conversion of the world's population to Catholicism and the unity of the world as God's Kingdom on Earth, ruled by the Catholic Hierachy, which is currently split into the Eastern Orthodox and Roman branches.

During the 1600's after Luther's revolt from the Catholic power structure a panoply of Protestant Churches began to spring up, the first being the Lutheran Church in Germany.

The Anglican Church or Episcopal Church, is a protestant Church, which broke off from the Catholic Church during the reign of King Henry VIII of England, but which still follows much of the Catholic Doctrine. The Anglican Church is not only the Church of England but includes membership throughout the world. Priests are not required to practice celibacy. The service is similar to Catholicism, but this church does not recognize the Pope as its head, nor is it part of the Catholic Power structure.

In most Protestant Churches the minister is chosen through a majority vote of the congregation, and the services are centered on the teachings of the Bible. The minister preaches to the congregation during services that include prayer and singing.

The Society of Friends is structured as a consensual democracy in which decisions are made by the entire congregation, which discusses matters and comes to a consensus. Their beliefs center around the idea of a Living Presence that is accessed through silence. In their meetings, which are characterized by long periods of silence, anyone can speak.

In Christian Science, the meeting includes readings from the Bible and readings from the works of Mary Baker Eddy. The major teaching is that God is a divine being, who is directly accessible through prayer and is capable of healing. This healing power is based on the ability of Jesus to heal as delineated in the New Testament.

The Mormon Church, although Protestant in nature, is a highly structured top-down hierarchy, in which the members have little power to affect policy decisions. Beliefs and behaviors, rules and the mythologies of the Church are provided by the texts written by Joseph Smith in the 1800's and interpreted and presented by the hierarchy of elders. There is little room for individual beliefs.

Various Evangelical Fundamentalist Christian Religions focus on literal interpretations of the Bible and on the belief in the imminent Second Coming of Christ accompanied by the destruction of the world and the Rapture in which true believers will be taken up to meet God.

The Islamic religion is based on the Quran, which contains revelations to the Prophet Muhammad by what he regarded as the Archangel Gabriel, during the early part of the 6th century AD (CE). The Quran sets out the doctrinal principles of Islam and has been the subject of much subsequent interpretation, diversity of opinion and conflict of internal sects. For over a thousand years, from the late 700's CE to around 1,200 CE, during what was known in Europe the Dark Ages, the Islamic Empire flourished across Northern Africa and the Middle East as a center of culture, science and religion. The Islamic world then fell into decline, while the West emerged from the Middle

Ages into the modern era. As one of the world's largest religions, Islam, in the 21st century, has become the focus of attention as civil wars and terrorism tear apart Islamic Theocracies in transition to modern, democratic secular states.

A plethora of religions, religious practices and cults exist throughout the world now and from time immemorial. Egyptians worshiped Ra the sun god creator 2,500 years BC. The Persian Religion of Zoroasterism in 1,500 BC, predated Judaism, Islam and Christianity. Zoroaster conceived of Ahura Mazda as the supreme benevolent creator, whose opposite was Ahriman the destroyer and bringer of chaos and evil.

Before all these religions, there was the ancient Mother Goddess who ruled the heavens and earth for thousands of years.

Interestingly Germany and Italy, the protagonists in WWII, comprised the remnants of the Holy Roman Empire, and the dictators of these two nations, though opposed by the laity, were funded and supported by the Church Hierarchy. In some sense then WWII can be seen as the last final gasp of the old Catholic Hierarchies and the governments they supported, in their fight against the rise of modern democracy.

The situation with the Islamic Religion in the 20th and 21st centuries has some resemblance to the fall of these preceding theocracies. We can understand the Arab Spring as the first blow in a revolution of people who want to live in modern democratic states as they struggle against the traditional theocratic rule of the Muslim Hierarchies.

As in all Revolutions, we see an angered citizenry rising up against the abuses of an oppressive government. The uprising then becomes violent with the use of force of arms against which the ruling powers fight. Into the chaos of the revolutionary war, steps the most violent ruthless elements of society, no longer kept in check by the oppressive government.

Since generally rebel forces do not have a governing structure, authority and power, they are defeated by the more ruthless factions in what miscarries into civil wars, as society fractures along ethnic, religious and group lines that had been repressed by the autocratic government. Into this government-less vacuum, gangs of thugs and opportunists pour, as chaos prevails. Out of this chaos, more likely than not emerges a dictator, who may be a benevolent transition to democracy or conversely, may impose a ruthless rule on the populace.

We saw this in the French Revolution of 1798, from which emerged Napoleon, who then, with the support of the Catholic Church, marched his armies across Europe. We saw this in the Russian Revolution of 1917 out of which Stalin eventually emerged. Stalin imposed a totalitarian regime, murdered millions of the most creative people in that society and opposed the Catholic Church. We saw this again in the Chinese Communist Revolution out of which Mao Tse Tung emerged. Mao killed millions of the entrepreneurial class in China. These were not religious revolutionary wars per se, but the pattern is all too familiar.

In United States the situation was different, because the colonies had centuries of semi-autonomous democracy prior to the Revolution. Most importantly, the Founding Fathers had the foresight to provide a Constitution and a functioning system of civil government, in which freedom of religion was a fundamental tenet. Because of this no Theocracy was able to emerge.

So we see that freedom of religion can only exist within the context of a strong secular, civil, democratic governance that guarantees the freedom of religion, that is, the freedom of every individual to worship, or not, in a manner of their own choosing.

Where does this leave us with Religion? We have discussed the power structures implicit in religious organizations and we see that such power structures are not dissimilar to the power structures that we have seen in civil societies, whether dictatorships or democracies.

The questions then become:

1. Can religious organizations, in terms of beliefs, ethical prescripts, habits, politics, rules of behavior, customs, mythologies and spiritual life, be separated from the governmental power structures, politics and organizational frameworks of the societies in which they are imbedded?

2. Can the religious organizations adapt and reform themselves to bring their beliefs and practices into line with modern constitutional democracy, the social and legal norms of modern civilized, egalitarian societies and the United Nations declaration of human rights that insure freedom of religion as one of the basic human and civil rights?

History has shown us that the embedded power structures of the various religious organizations react violently to prevent such a shift to democracy and secularism. What has always been essential is the need for an enlightened populace, to lead the way in demonstrating that the beauty and spirituality of a religion can flourish without the oppression and governmental structures of a Theocracy. Rather, each religion can function as one of many religions, in a secular democracy committed to individual freedom and human rights.

We have discussed the political power of organized religion. Now let's look at the laws dictated by a particular religion. Laws are prescriptions for human behavior. To be effective, the laws must be understood, accepted or acquiesced to (willingly or unwillingly) and obeyed by the people that the laws regulate.

In the Talmud, which comprises one of the sacred books of the Hebrews, a multitude of prescriptions for diet, dress, marriage, punishments for transgression, and even a rudimentary criminal code are set out.

The Ten Commandments comprise one of the best known ethical, moral and legal code in the Jewish and Christian world, including such prescriptions as "Thou shall have no other gods before me; Thou shall not make idols; The shall not take the name of thy lord in vain; shall not kill; Thou shall not commit adultery; Thou shall not steal; Thou shall not covet; Thou shall not bear false witness against your neighbor...."

In the New Testament, in addition to the Ten Commandments, Christ sets out a moral and ethical code for all time and all people in saying: "Thou shall love thy neighbor as thyself and Thou shall do unto others as you would have them do unto you." This is not a legal code, but is a moral prescription for attitude and behavior that is based on empathy and love and when followed includes the most important aspects of the fundamental laws of human behavior.

The Quoran sets out Sharia Law as the fundamental legal, ethical and moral code for Muslims. In the 21st century a worldwide debate around the Islamic Religion focuses on the fact that many prescriptions thought to be interpreted from Sharia Law are forbidden by criminal and civil law in modern constitutional democracies. Since the huge majority of Muslim people are peaceful and law abiding, there needs to be some clarification and adjustment in the interpretations of these writings and rules.

The doctrines, customs and beliefs inherent in a religion, serve as justification for the laws and ethical prescriptions. For example, in the Catholic religion it is believed that in order to avoid going to hell, a soul must be blessed by the Church. Coupled to this, the Church teaches that human life begins at conception and that, therefore, if there is a miscarriage of an embryo, it must be blessed by a priest or it will go to hell. In this case the belief informs the behavior of the believer, of Catholics and of Evangelicals in opposing abortion.

For non-Catholics, and non-Evangelicals, an embryo, although living, is not yet human; it is merely a collection of dividing cells that has the potential to become human only if it is carried to term. So we see how different beliefs, color our interpretations of reality as well as inform our behaviours and our laws.

Religious proscriptions against the use of contraception has resulted in massive overpopulation in some of the poorest areas of the world, and has exacerbated poverty, illiteracy, despair, disease, hunger and warfare. Nature's solution when a region has over-populates its resource base, is war, famine and disease. This is not a pretty way to achieve the balance that nature demands.

When people produce myriad children that they cannot afford to feed, cloth, shelter or educate, the result is human tragedy. A farm that can produce enough for five people, when populated by twenty people is unsustainable. With the advent of the AIDS epidemic, condoms offer a protective barrier that can help to prevent the spread of the disease. The proscription against condoms condemns millions to unnecessary disease and death.

In the 5th century AD there was a doctrinal split in the Christian Church over whether Christ was wholly divine or whether Christ was part human and part divine. This split was the subject of a war in which millions of people perished. We see the power of doctrine and belief.

We have discussed the fourth, third, and second categories listed above. Now we will address the first item listed: 1. the Doctrines, Myths and Beliefs of Religions. These doctrines, myths and believes in some cases, as we have seen, result in behavioral prescription and in interpretations of reality. In addition, each religion has its stories, myths and beliefs that purport to explain and describe historic events.

In the Old Testament we find stories about talking snakes, Noah's Ark, a burning bush, a Whale's belly inhabited by two men, and the like, which are stories that symbolize and represent certain aspects of human existence. We have a beautiful passage in Genesis in which a supernatural God creates the world in six days and rests on the seventh day. Taken as an allegory it is a moving description that gives an a feeling of inspiration and appreciation of the immensity of the

Creation.

For true believers every word of the Bible is taken to be the word of God and therefore literally true. This persistent belief in a holy text is seen in the Muslim religion as well.

For Muslims, the Great Prophet Muhammad is the only true Prophet of Allah. Allah is believed to be the supreme, supernatural being who created the world and who oversees the private lives of all good Muslims.

In the New Testament of the Bible, we have the stories of Jesus.

In many cases these stories and myths are orally transmitted from generation to generation and form a common bond and history of a people. In some cases these stories and myths are included in the sacred texts of a religion that not only set out the laws and practices of the religion, but also embody the stories that are learned by generations of those who practice the religion and serve to form a common belief system that is shared by the in-group and serves to bind the group together.

The Mormon religion, for example, provides a strong sense of community and a code of morality and health that forbids alcohol and mind-altering drugs. In addition to these healthy proscriptions, however, in terms of beliefs and mythology, the Church has an entire doctrine of faith that includes a concept of reincarnation of human beings as gods, and of God as pre-existing on another planet to name a few. These beliefs and myths become reality for the true believers and serve to bind the faithful together and to separate the group from those who do not believe these doctrines.

Therefore, as we have seen religious beliefs join the in-group together and exclude the out-group. The trouble occurs when each religion, sect and subgroup maintains that it alone has the true and right way and that other groups, and beliefs are not to be tolerated. In these cases each group, claiming to be the one truth belief, sees every other belief and every other group holding different beliefs, as a threat. Worst of all is the case where a group seeks to enforce its beliefs, mores, customs and laws on every other group. We can see the chaos this causes when numerous opposing groups engage in this behavior.

Unless there is a strong, civil government that imposes tolerance and forbids the harming of one group by another, these groups devolve into warring tribes. This is the brilliance of democratic self-governance that allows diversity, forbids discrimination and enforces equal rights and uniform laws on all persons and groups within the society.

Having now examined the political, doctrinal, mythological, and social aspects of religion, let us now look at the most important aspect of religion, the spiritual dimension.

The most important aspect of religion is the spiritual path that leads the believer to a feeling of connection with the mysteries of existence, life, death and love. The foundation and core importance of religion is not the political power, the mythologies, the customs, mores, beliefs, doctrines, sacred texts or laws, but is the connection with the mystery and wonder of the miracle of our existence and the ultimate cause of creation and the awe that such a comprehension invokes.

We all naturally have a sense of wonder in the fact of our own existence and of the existence of the world we see around us. It is this feeling of connection with the Divine that the human soul craves. This is what draws us to religion. There are many paths to this feeling of awe and love that connects us with the Divine.

For the devout Catholic, meditating on the Virgin Mary brings a sense of love, safety, and gratitude. For the Christian conceiving of the infinite, unconditional love of Jesus gives comfort and assurance in a tumultuous world. For the devout Muslim the call to prayer and the reading of the Quran creates an immediate sense of the presence of Allah. For the Hindu, participation in tantric yoga and religious ceremony brings an immediate sense of peace and connection with the Divine Spirit. For the Buddhist, meditation produces a sense of calming presence and connection with the divine processes of life that transcends death. For the pagan, viewing the rising and setting of the sun can produce a sense of universality and of a divine existence expressed in nature. The agnostic and the atheist may not believe in a deity, but may feel a spiritual connection with existence. A pantheist sees God in everything, everywhere. No doubt primitive human beings wondered at the mysteries of birth, life, death and nature and felt the presence of the Great Spirit. For centuries, the Mother Goddess filled the spiritual hunger of the human spirit.

Beyond the explanations, beliefs, and mythologies that people invent and, the power structures, laws, and the sociology of organized religions, is the human hunger to be connected to the mystery and miracle of existence. The fundamental core of every religion is the experience of wonder at the miracle of existence. To experience this wonder and sense of awe directly fills us with the sense of the incomprehensible love out of which all existence is continuously being born.

This sense of awe and wonder we feel in contemplating the miracle of existence is the mountain, up which the multiple paths of religious practice lead. It is crucial that the world return to this universal sense of divine wonder and awe, that we realize that we are all talking about the same sense of the divine mystery and love, and that we stop fighting about the paths up the mountain.

Chapter Twenty-Five:
Information and Meaning

Coolidge Corner

We are now in the outskirts of Boston. I can sense the end up ahead. My pace slows down. I feel a painful jolt each time my foot hits the ground as my bleeding blisters scream out for me to stop. But I won't stop. If I stop now I'll set women and women's running back fifty years. I feel the weight of responsibility heavy on my shoulders. I have boldly set out to demonstrate what women can do. I'm challenging the prevalent beliefs about women in the face of cultural opposition. If I fail now I fail more than myself.

Since I am outside the world of sports and have no coach, I have never worn a pair of running shoes before—I'd always run in my sturdy leather nurse's shoes— so I don't know you are supposed to break shoes in. And worse, I'd been told in high school that if you drink water while exercising it will give you cramps. So on this hot sunny day, I've drunk no water for the entire race and am now severely dehydrated.

I have little idea of where I am. I'm just following the course. As I feel my pace drop off, I see that my three-hour marathon is lost and all hopes of winning the race have vanished long ago. Suddenly it seems we are in a tangle of overhead trolley wires in a very urban setting.

We run on and I notice that more houses are appearing along the sides of the road. We are approaching a town. Telephone wires signal the approach of civilization. "Talking wires," as Native Americans called them.

What a brilliant idea to convert sound waves in the air into electrical signals that can be transmitted over great distances. It wasn't until the 1800's that this technology began to be developed. The principle is simple. Vibrations in the air caused by the voice cause some medium — either liquid, metal, or transistor — to vibrate. These vibrations then cause variations in an electrical current, which are transmitted by wire to a receiving device. The receiver then translates the electric impulses back into airwaves by producing vibrations in a membrane. These air-compression waves then cause the tympanic membrane of the ear to vibrate. The vibrations of the tympanic membrane cause tiny motions in the organs of the inner ear, which motions are translated into voltage potentials in the auditory nerves. These voltage potentials are relayed to the auditory centers in the brain where they are subjectively experienced as sound.

The telephone carries information from one place to another and from the sender or transmitter to the receiver.

What do we mean by information? We go the information booth to learn where a certain doctor's office is, or in what room a given patient is. That is, we learn something we didn't know before. When I say that an article in the newspaper contains some valuable information, I mean that I learned something from reading the article. When I dial 411 for information, I want to learn what someone's phone number is. When the witness says that he was not informed of the leak until 7:00 AM on July 27th he means he did not learn that there was a leak until that time.

In all these examples we are talking about human beings learning something they did not know before. If Jane reads a book and she knows everything contained in it, she says that she did not acquire any information from reading the book, although she concedes that many people would find the book full of information.

We assume that we are talking about human communication when we talk about information. However, in fact many biological systems can be said to acquire and act on information. We know that when a dog is tracking a scent she is acquiring information and acting on it. When a male butterfly finds a female by following the gradient of pheromones that she releases, he is acquiring information and acting on it. When a bacterium follows the gradient of sucrose in its environment it is acquiring information and acting on it. Whether these organisms have a subjective experience of that information is another question that we discuss in other chapters. Let us assume for the present that, at least, that animals with nervous systems, in which changes occur in the sense organs and neurological processing apparati, some sort of subjectiveness of experience occurs. I have previously named these systems "neuronoesystemic systems."

In a living cell the chromosomes contain, in their DNA, the information that codes for the structure of proteins and non-coding RNA. That is to say the genes are units of chromosome that are structured in a double helix composed of the sugar, deoxyribose, like a spiral staircase. The steps of this staircase are comprised of four base molecules that join, two at a time, adenine with thiamine, cytosine with guanine. The arrangement, of these base molecules, codes the information that the cell utilizes for creating the various amino acids that will eventually form the proteins that are the building blocks of the cell itself.

Now let us consider the concept of information at an even more fundamental level. Suppose we have an electron traveling along in space and it encounters a magnetic field. Immediately, our electron changes direction. Because it changes direction, we can say that it has interacted with the field. But can we say that it has received information? Can we say that the field contains in its dynamic structure coded information that the electron can read? Clearly the electron has acted on receiving the information contained in the magnetic field. That is to say the interaction between the fields of the electron and the magnetic source contain information that changes the behavior of the electron.

The word "in-formation" is the noun, or subjective, form of the verb "to inform." To inform connotes an action taken. What does in mean to inform? Literally the word, "to inform," means to bring or give form to something. Can we say that the potter informs the clay when she makes a pot?

I have taken form to mean the dynamical structure of something through which it acquires and maintains the characteristics that define it as itself. In the case of mechanical systems, that form is imposed from the outside by an agent other than itself. In natural systems the form arises from the interactions of parts. When these interactions continue in a way that allows the system to act as one, then I call these whole systems or unitary systems. When the interactions are sporadic and temporary then the systems formed are naturally occurring but do not persist as whole systems. Whole systems gain characteristics and abilities that emerge from the continuing juxtapositioning and interacting of their component parts as a whole.

In the context of nervous systems, to be informed implies that there has been some neuronal activity that has formed a trace in the brain where neurons have changed in structure to form neural configurations comprised of synaptically plastic modifications. Synaptic strengths may be strengthened or weakened. Existing neurons can add synapses or retract synapses. Entire neurons can be added to, or pruned from, the various neural networks.

When we consider the information contained in spoken language we see that the information-containing message from the speaker is translated into air borne compression waves by means of the tongue and vocal cords that reflect a series of sounds that represent letters that are used to make up words that are strung together to represent the thoughts of the sender.

These fluctuating compression air waves then impinge on the ear of the listener, whose tympanic membrane vibrates in such a way to cause tiny voltage changes in the auditory neurons that are relayed to the auditory centers of the brain where they are subjectively experienced as sound.

The auditory centers relay the neuronal impulses to the higher brain centers, including the region known as Broca's Area, where the linguistic code for producing speech is located and Wernicke's Area, which is involved in understanding language. The person then understands the meaning of the sounds that embody the message and she can then be said to have received the information conveyed by the sender.

We see that in this process the information is translated and transmitted multiple times in multiple forms.

But what do we mean by "information?"

In the context of human communications, the word "information," historically has connoted the idea of idea. That is, to be informed is to conceive of an idea or image of something. But an idea is a subjective experience. So does information require a conscious being and an ability to subjectively know?

Claude Shannon, sometimes considered the father of information theory defines information in the following excerpt:

"The fundamental problem of communication is that of reproducing at one point either exactly or approximately a message selected at another point. Frequently the messages have meaning; that is, they refer to or are correlated according to some system with certain physical or conceptual entities. These sematic aspects of communication are irrelevant to the engineering problem."

So the formal definition of information does not require subjective experience or even conscious awareness, nor need the message have any meaning what so ever. In information theory, meaning is something a message may or may not have. A message then is simply a pattern that is conveyed from one place at one time to another place at another time. We might call information theory the theory of pattern conveyance.

We then look at the number of possible patterns that can be

conveyed in any given system and determine the likelihood that any one pattern will be, or is actually, conveyed. This is relevant to coding and decoding. Symbols are used to represent letters that are contained in the coded message and the task consists of finding the correspondence between the coded symbols and the language symbols so that the meaning of the message, if there is one, can be detected.

The hidden assumption in information theory is that there is an objective outside observer who can determine whether the pattern received by the receiving device is the same as the pattern sent by the sending device and who can measure the degree to which the pattern received differs from the pattern sent.

In information theory then the message is simply a pattern that is conveyed and information is just another word for the pattern. Meaning is something in addition to the pattern. (And interpretation is something in addition to meaning.) A unit of information, in information theory, is simply a collection of symbols that make up the pattern that is conveyed, it has nothing to do with conveying meaning. For example if you have a toggle switch that can be up or down, this system stores one bit of information, that is, the system can be in one of two states. To say it differently there are two possible patterns that the system can exhibit: switch up or switch down and therefore at any discrete moment the system exhibits one of the two possible patterns and this is called one bit; or you could say one pattern unit. To call this bit "information," does not at all coincide with our usual understanding of information.

In our usual understanding of information, we would say that the pattern may or may not convey information depending on the capacity of the receiver to interpret and to understand the information conveyed. In this more general view of information the word means, not just a pattern, but connotes the interpretation and understanding — what we would call the meaning of that pattern.

But the pattern means different things to different receivers, and the pattern sent by the sender may not involve any subjective awareness on the part of the sender. For example an ocean storm may create ocean waves that are transmitted in all directions. The storm is not aware that it is sending a message in the patterns of energy that it is creating. The waves are patterns of matter and energy that when received by various receivers can have different meanings depending on the ability of the receiver to interpret the patterns.

An experienced mariner will know from the shape and size of the wave-forms that there is a storm two-hundred miles to the south and that the fish will be driven towards the shore where the fishing will be good for about eight hours, giving the fishermen two hours to head home before the storm hits.

A landlubber will look at the waves and know only that he is terribly seasick. So are there different amounts of information in the waveforms depending on the capacity of the receiver to understand and interpret the patterns? As we commonly call information something that conveys meaning, we would say that the information contained in the waveforms varies according to the ability of the receiver to assign meaning to the patterns.

But in information theory, information means simply a pattern. The information theorist would say that what varies is not the information, or the amount of information, but is rather the meaning of that information. If we replace the word "information" with the word "message" and the word "message" with the word "pattern," we will see that information theory is not about what we commonly call information, at all.

The theory of meaning is an entirely different topic. Meaning is relative to the sender and relative to the receiver.

How then do we measure meaning?

Historically philosophical inquiry into the theory of meaning devolves into arguments about how we determine the truth or falsity of a proposition. In many of these philosophical arguments, the philosophers assume that there is an objective reality that can be objectively determined and that the particular proposition is compared with the objective truth, or objective reality, to determine its truth value.

The author has pointed out multiple times that although there may be, and probably is, an objective reality all we can know is our subjective experiences of our interactions with whatever is out there. So it is impossible to know what that objective reality is objectively, and therefore, it is impossible to correlate a given proposition with what is there objectively.

What we, as perceiving animals, do is to create subjective models of an external reality through repeated interactions with the external world, which we call the objective, physically real world, although these too are concepts. This is not to say that we live in a solipsistic world in which there is no external reality, or that it is impossible to create a workable perceptual and conceptual model of the external world. It is only to say that we need to keep in mind that we are creating models and not experiencing an external objective reality objectively. We only know our subjective perceptions and conceptions of our interactions with what is there.

Inside our brains and nervous systems our neurons and supporting cells form networks of interaction that act to model the inputs of our sensory organs and to create systems of living cells that represent to themselves their models of perceptions and conceptions that make up our understanding of the world of physical objects and motions, and our world of conceptual thought.

We have previously examined how it is that, amazingly, the activities in networks of living neurons, and supporting cells, are experienced from the inside as subjective experiences.

RED as we experience it is a subjective experience associated with the activities of certain brain regions under certain conditions of stimulation. Even when there is no input from the retina from impinging photons we have no problem imagining red, or actually having the subjective experience of RED, in our dreams, for example. And yet when we look at the brain from the outside all we see is the activities of networks of neurons. I have said that the subjective experience and the observed neuronal activities are exactly the same thing. What is different is only the perspective of the viewer.

The external viewer sees the outside, or what we would call the physical, material perspective. The internal viewer, not only views from within, but views self-reflexively, that is to say that the very activity of the neurons *is* subjective experience to the neurons and collections of neurons that identify themselves as us. This is difficult to understand, but it is this identity-self-reflexive nature of subjective experience that no one seems to see. This is why I say that we need to understand the bigger picture, in which the nature of the entire cosmos contains within it this identity self-reflexion in which what is viewed is also what is viewing and what is created is also what is creating.

So with this review, let us ask again what we mean by meaning.

Some philosophers say that something untrue has no meaning. But this isn't true. We know exactly what Goldilocks and the Three Bears means even though it isn't true. How do we know what it means? We know what it means because we refer the story to some context and to some system for translating the data that impinges on our nervous system into a system of coherent symbology. It is through these coherent systems of symbology that we represent the systems of meaning that we have learned, or experienced.

These systems of meaning represent some things or ideas by other things or ideas in structured ways that are approximately self-consistent. Whether these constructed systems have any relationship to some outside objective reality does not impinge on the fact of whether certain events, objects, ideas or experiences can be referenced to these coherent systems and contexts in which the represented items have meaning.

Many functions and mal-functions of the human psyche can be understood, once we see that coherent theories of meaning depend only on the context of the systems of interpretation through which we understand our experiences and not on some objective realization of external objective reality. A paranoid schizophrenic for example constructs an entire imaginary structure for understanding his experiences that to him is a self-consistent context in which his bizarre experiences have meaning to him. Many religious beliefs come into the same category in which a manufactured context is taken to be reality and through which referred experiences have meaning.

The belief that evil spirits cause disease and that by burning offering to invisible, supernatural gods, one can ameliorate sickness is an example of a context and system of beliefs to which, and in which, experiences have meaning and through which actions are taken based on this false system of beliefs. To the true believer, slaughtering a lamb and incinerating it is a meaningful act, intended to bring about healing. To the modern onlooker, slaughtering a helpless, terrified animal and burning it half alive is an act of sadistic cruelty.

So meaning has nothing to do with external reality and everything to do with reference to a context and a system of representations. The decimal number system, for example, is a context within which the symbols 2+3=5 has meaning. I could write *"#@ /. These are symbols that comprise a message, that is, a pattern that can be conveyed and so, in the context of information theory, is information. But this information is in the anomalous position of having no meaning.

The message can be perfectly transmitted from Sender A to Receiver B and the parameters of distortion, bandwidth and noise analyzed numerically. The number of bits of information can be counted, remembering that for a system that has two states, like a toggle switch that can be up or down, we consider that each state is one bit of information. If we have two toggle switches there are four possible patterns of up switch or down switch. If we have three toggle switches there are eight possible patterns of up switch or down switch. If there are four toggle switches there are sixteen possible patterns of up switch or down switch. In binary code the up and down switch can be represented by zeros and ones. So depending on the number of switches that can be up or down, the number of patterns that are possible can be expressed as powers of two.

These patterns are considered to be the possible messages that can be sent within this system. But nowhere is there any requirement that any of these messages have any meaning what so ever. How, then, do we assign meaning to a message?

We assign meaning to a message by making the symbols refer to some coherent context, which we already know or understand. We do this by representing one thing or symbol by another. If we say * is 2; " is +; # is 3; @ is =; and / is 5, then the symbols *"#@/ have meaning in the context of the decimal system of numbers and the processes of addition and equality. We now know that the message means 2+3=5.

Alternatively *"#@/ can have an entirely different meaning if we refer * to the word I; " to the word see; # to the word a; @to the word red; and / to the word house. Now we understand that "I see a red house" has a completely different meaning, even though the message, that is, the information, that is, the pattern of marks on the page is exactly the same, namely *"#@/.

This process of making series of one's and zero's represent other things in nested systems of reference is, of course, the foundation of computer technology. Thus a series of ones and zeros in binary code can represent a number in decimal code or a letter in the alphabet, or a mark of punctuation or a mathematical operation, or a line or a color. These numbers, letters, operations, lines and colors can themselves become units in a larger system in which these elements are further composed to represent shapes, words, motions and equations.

This compiling of systems of systems of systems in which the outputs of the more primary systems become units in the more complex systems, so that, as the complexity emerges, more and more properties emerge, is not unlike the processing in our own nervous systems. Indeed, we see a similar compiling of systems, in which less complex systems are further juxtaposed as the units of more complex systems, which possess properties and abilities not possessed by the simpler systems, in the process of evolution of living systems.

Indeed our nervous systems create themselves on the same principle in which sub-systems form the units in more complex systems. We have seen how, in the visual system, at the level of the photoreceptors in the retina, the each receptor, in any given unit of time, either receives or does not receive a photon. At higher levels in the ganglia cells, which lead up to the lateral geniculate in the thalamus of the brain, there are highly complex responses that involve compositions of multiple receptor-cell inputs onto neurons. Each ganglion cell has a concentric field, in which the cell fires when there is light hits the center of and inhibits when there is light in the periphery of the field, or vice versa.

In the primary visual cortex we have compositions from the inputs of these lateral geniculate cells, which fire when lines of various orientations enter their visual fields. Other visual channels carry color-coded impulses, and in higher levels of visual cortex these lines, which are juxtaposed to represent boundaries are composed, with the signals that represent colors, into what we experience as the colorful, moving, panoply of images that continuously parades through our conscious senses as we look around the scene.

Each of these neuronal compositions has meaning within the context of the system that is generating the compositions. As children we learn to understand our visual input in terms of objects, colors and motions. As we learn language we develop a further context of meaning through which we associate an image, relationship or motion with certain sounds made by the vocal cords. When we learn to read we further associate the verbal words with the written symbols that represent these objects, concepts, percepts and thoughts in a coherent systems.

The associative areas of our brains accomplish all this and stores these codes in our memory banks in various areas in our brains. As we live and experience events, our nervous systems then represent these events in multiple ways, abstracting similarities and differences and making files in our brains where these memories are stored and can then be recalled through re-activating the neural networks in which the memory traces were laid down when the events were experienced. So we have levels of nested contexts of meanings even within our own nervous systems.

Through the dynamic structure, organization and operation of our brains, we pattern and re-pattern the initial patterns that we receive through our sense organ receptors. Do these patterns and re-patterns comprise new information?

Clearly the cells in the higher levels of the brain's visual system "know" more than an individual photoreceptor, and indeed, know more even than the sum total of the states of all the photoreceptors at any given moment of time. According to information theory, no new information can be created in the system. That is, since information is a message and a message is a pattern, this would mean no new patterns can be created in a system. But this is not true, obviously, the system is constructed to create new patterns by juxtaposing the impinging patterns with one another and with previously stored patterns.

We need to understand that in the case of the nervous system, the dynamic structure and activity of the system itself, imposes form on the input. That is to say, information, or pattern, is not just in the impinging input, but more importantly is implicit in the operation of the system. This is not analogous to the simple transmission of a message through a medium from sender to receiver.

There are multiple levels of patterning that occur within the nervous system and brain as a result of the fundamental structure and activity of the system. This can be considered to be a form of information in that there are dynamical patterned structures and activities that are built into the system.

The impinging input of sensory patterns interacts with the patterns of inherent dynamic structure and activity of the nervous system and the brain. Thus the system contains within itself, as a result of its dynamic structure and activities, orders of magnitude more information than is received by the sense organs.

In addition, the operation of the system, over time, creates changes in some of its patterns, and it then stores these changes. These stored patterns interact with the incoming patterns to create new patterns in the associative regions of the brain where they are subsequently stored. This explains why higher-level cells are responsive to and can elicit much more complex patterns than the sense receptors themselves taken independently.

In terms of meaning, we see that at each level of processing in the nervous system the messages sent by the lower level cells impinge in patterned ways that are built into the dynamic, operational structure of the system in such a way that new capabilities emerge at the higher levels. We can say that at each level of processing new interpretations emerge in which the higher level cell codes new dimensions that have meaning at that level of processing, to the part of the brain that is doing the processing.

Within the nervous system then messages, that is, patterns of activity, have meaning and in fact acquire meaning as the coded messages are received through the structured channels in such a way that the receiving cells, which gather input from many transmitting cells, can compare and contrast the inputs in ways that generate levels upon levels of qualities that combine in ways that at each level transcends the patterns of input of the levels below, and translates the new patterns that are generated into neuronal states that acquire new meanings within the system. That is, the inputs are referred to new neuronal contexts that represent qualities that the nervous system itself is generating through its pre-established dynamic organizational structure and operation.

That nervous systems have evolved in the contexts of living organisms is a testament to the innate intelligence of nature.

What do I mean by intelligence?

Intelligence has two different but related aspects:

First is the self-formative intelligence of nature, which may or may not have associated with it any subjective innerness, or subjective experience. I call this Tellios or Intellios, because this type of intelligence is self-formative. Self-formative natural systems I call intellic, inteleological, or teleosystemic from the teleological, or end-seeking nature of such self-formation. This is, at its most fundamental level, a gradient-following activity through which the system creates itself as a whole through the interaction of its parts that only come to exist within the system that is self-creating itself. This is the paradoxical and self-reflexive nature of self-formation and self-creation.

The second meaning of intelligence, is subjectively, self-experiencing intelligence, which is this self-reflexive subjective innerness, this inner perspective of the activity of itself. I have called this noestemic or noesystemic and in the case of organisms with nervous systems, neuronoesystemic. I happen to think that this noestemic, noesystemic and neurosystemic aspect or viewpoint is something fundamental to the cosmos and not something that is or can be acquired by compiling systems that don't have this fundamental noestemic nature.

So we see how the definitions of information, meaning and

interpretation differ in the various contexts in which they appear and this gives us a better understanding of what we mean by information and meaning. Much confusion revolves around these differing concepts of intelligence. Clearly natural systems included both self-structuring, self-formative systems and self-perceiving systems. In nature all self-perceiving systems are self-forming, but not all self-forming systems are self-perceiving. But in all cases nature generates the self-forming and the self-perceiving systems without recourse to the supernatural.

CHAPTER TWENTY-SIX: SUBSTANCE

Citgo Sign

Feet searing with pain, I tiptoe through Brookline, to the sound of people clapping and calling words of encouragement, "At a girl! Keep it up. You're almost there." I am used to running barefoot on the beaches or in my well-worn leather nurses shoes on dirt and grass. The pavement is too hard. You wouldn't run horses on pavement. There's a feel to a crowd, like a huge living thing that breathes, moves, makes sound, feels and thinks. You can feel its body and the density of its thoughts.

Stucco buildings and a clock tower pass on the left. My attention is completely turned inward now to that quiet place to which we return to find peace, to the place of unending calm out of which all action arises. I am tired. My feet hurt. Last night's roast beef feels like a fist twisting my stomach. I want to stop. But I must finish. It was a promise I made to myself and if I can't keep my promises to myself, then who can I keep my promises to? And I promised all women that I would finish. If I fail now I will end up proving exactly the opposite of what I have set out to prove.

This is not one of my better runs. I wonder if anyone will be at the finish when I get there.

Each step is an act of will.

We are now approaching Kenmore Square. High above looms a huge sign that proclaims "Citgo". This is the clarion cry of the oil industry that has provided the energy for the world since the conversion from horse and wagon to combustible hydrocarbon power. Hydrocarbons have supplied the energy that has been the substrate of twentieth century civilization. Yet we know we must make a transition from coal and oil to renewable, non-polluting energy.

It is often thought that energy is the fundamental substance of the universe. However, I'd seen that energy, like mass, is a property of systems and therefore is not the most fundamental substance.

Is there a fundamental substance out of which everything else is made? If so what could this fundamental substance be like?

Substance means that which stands under. So our question is: What stands under existence? We have seen that this fundamental substance is not matter, that is, the smallest, most fundamental parts are not atoms and molecules, because they are made of something more fundamental and smaller.

For a moment let's see what happens when we ask: What would the smallest system or particle have to be like?

The first thing we notice is there is a logical non sequitur here. A system is an interaction of parts. But the parts are already smaller than the system that they comprise, therefore the system cannot be the smallest entity.

So we are led to the conclusion that the smallest entity cannot be a system made up of parts.

What could an entity compose of no parts be like? What sorts of entity is not composed of parts? What would the inside of such an entity be like? Would such an entity have an inside? If it has no inside what would it be like? Would such an entity have a form or shape? If so what would give it its shape or form?

Could the primal entity be like a bubble with a surface but nothing inside it? If it were a bubble, there would still be an inside, because the surface would divide the world into two parts, inside and outside. There would be an inside and outside surface of the film that defines the bubble. There would be a volume enclosed.

Could the smallest entity have a volume? Could it have

mass/energy? No it could not have mass or energy because mass and energy are systems properties, and we have just seen that no system could be the smallest entity. So the smallest entity could not in and of itself have mass or energy as such. The mass and energy would arise only if the smallest entity interacts with something else, perhaps another smallest entity to form a system. The system would then have mass and energy as properties.

Would the smallest entity have form? Form is a shape or configuration, to have a shape or configuration, means that it would have a boundary to define the shape or form. What would form a boundary? If there were only one smallest entity in existence, it would have no size and no boundary. There would be no inside and no outside, there would be no boundary with anything else because there would be nothing else, not even nothing.

We saw that the cosmos of All-that-Exists has an inside, but has no outside boundary because there is nothing besides All-that-Exists for it to form a boundary with. To form a boundary requires that there be an interaction, which defines a boundary between the entity that exists and something else, even if that something else is nothing.

So to have form or shape would require that the primal entity interact with something. This would form a boundary of interaction that would give the entity, and that with which it interacts, form. This boundary of interaction would define the shape and position and motion of both interactants. This is reminiscent of the quantum phenomena, in which, until something interacts with a quantum of action, it has no position or velocity. We can only predict the probability that a certain interaction will occur, and where and when we think it might manifest.

So the smallest entity cannot, itself, have any size or shape or position or boundary until, or unless, it interacts with another smallest entity or with something else besides itself. But, as we saw, if there is only one primal entity it can have no size and no outside and no boundary or shape or form. Form arises through interaction. So as soon as we have two primal entities they can interact to form a boundary of interaction that gives them both form.

Since All-that-Is has nothing else besides itself with which to interact, it, as a whole, can have no size or shape or form or location from outside itself. Only within it are form, shape, size and location ascertainable in the interactions of what is contained within All-that-Is. Therefore the All-that-Is is the original unity. It is One, because there is nothing else besides itself. In contrast, the smallest entity has nothing inside itself besides itself. Therefore it too is a unity for a different reason. The smallest entity is a unity because it is comprised of no parts.

What does this mean? How did there get to be so many parts to all that is? How are these internal boundaries of interaction formed? How did the primal smallest entities arise? And why and how are there so many of these smallest entities? How do they divide themselves out of the primal All-that-Is?

Did the All-that-Is start off as the smallest most primal entity with no inside and no outside? If it did it would have had to divide itself into two interacting parts in order to create itself into interacting parts that could then form boundaries. Would there then have followed multiplication through division as in biological systems? In the fertilized egg, for example, cells multiply by dividing themselves into two parts, which then interact to form more complex systems. Could it be that biology is actually more fundamental than physics?

When we think of the smallest entity, we are thinking of objects. But what if the smallest entity is not an object, but is a motion or activity? Are activities and motions comprised of parts? A dance, you might say is composed of a sequence of events, but these are not parts in the same sense that a house is built of bricks or a molecule is composed of atoms. The parts of a dance are not divisible entities in the same sense as the parts of a house.

We saw that while processes can be physical they are not material. So when we inquire into the smallest part, do we mean the smallest non-material, physical process that cannot be divided into any smaller processes?

In physics we saw that the quantum of action, for example the photon of light, is not divisible. It always occurs as an indivisible whole. We saw that light, in fact all electromagnetic radiation, is comprised of mutually self-inducing, self-creating collapsing and expanding electric and magnetic fluxes.

In my essay on matter, I proposed that these quanta of action are the smallest and most primal entities of what we take to be the physical world, remembering that physical refers to an outside perspective on our interactions with whatever is there.

Are the quanta made up of parts? Yes, in the sense that a quantum of action is comprised of an electric flux and a magnetic flux but no, in the sense that both of these fluxes are not things, but are activities, and neither of these activities exists until created by the other in the context of the whole electromagnetic activity.

Is there some more primal substance than these quanta? From where do these interacting magnetic and electric fluxes derive? Are the magnetic activities and the electric activities more fundamental than the quanta and if so, do they exist prior to their self-creating interactions?

We have seen many examples of systems in which the parts do not exist as such until they create themselves in the context of the system of which they are parts. We saw this in the case of the frog, and in fact all living creatures, in which the organs and organelles that make up the organism do not exist, as such, until they are created and create themselves as parts of the whole organism of which they are parts.

This type of relationship between whole systems and their component parts can be seen throughout nature and here we see it again at the smallest most basic level in which neither flux exists until created within the context of the system in which the fluxes are creating themselves as they create each other in this mutually self-creating manner that we see characterizes the entire Cosmos of All that Exists.

We saw in the essay on matter that there is a zoo of so-called elementary particles including electrons, positrons, quarks, bosons and so forth. As I studied physics I had wondered if there were some unifying concept. I thought of the "Interacton", which I defined as a dynamic pattern characterized by a certain organizational structures and activities that have the properties not only of mass-energy, but also of a self-generating, self-maintaining forms, which result when atoms are shattered into parts.

Of what are these Interactons comprised? As we saw, light, that is, the photon, or quantum of action, has so far proved to be indivisible. Moreover, the speed of light has the unique property of always appearing to travel at the same constant speed to all observers on uniformly moving coordinate systems. The speed of light in a vacuum also defines the fastest speed possible for a material object. Moreover, light has no rest mass. It acquires the property of mass, only when traveling. When a photon is released, it goes from zero velocity to the fastest speed possible in no time.

In addition, as we saw, a photon, or unit of electromagnetic radiation is comprised of mutually inducing, fluctuating magnetic and electric activities, neither of which exist until brought into existence by the other. Given all these unique and special qualities of light, I was led to hypothesize my "photon theory."

My photon theory holds that the so-called elementary particles are actually comprised of photons. In this regard, I hypothesized that there were at least two kinds of photons: 1. Traveling photons that I called T-photons and 2. Stationary photons that I called S-photons. The S-photons are not motionless, but rather are comprised of at least two photons in interaction with each other in such a way that the interaction generates enough force for the quanta of activity to confine one another and to prevent each other from traveling. When released, these photons escape at their characteristic speed.

These S-photon orbitals I hypothesized are like multidimensional figure eights in which the photons, or quanta of activity, are spread out in orbitals that in turn can join with other S-photons to build up into the various elementary particles or interactons, as I called them. Again, I conceived of interactons not as particles but a dynamic patterns of interaction.

I hypothesized that these quanta of action, which are the unitary photon, are the fundamental particles, or interactons, that join together to form the nested systems of subatomic entities, which combine to form atoms, which combine to form molecules, which combine to form living systems and all the elements and objects of what we call the physical world. This physical world is characterized not only by its material objects but also by its motions and processes.

I also observed that the fundamental entities must exist in a way that is prior to volume and dimension. I hypothesized that the fundamental entities that make up physical existence are action and interaction, and are not material objects at all.

I hypothesized that the fundamental physical substance is not a "thing," but is an activity.

An activity of what?

Certainly in the physical world when we speak of activity we have to designate a thing that is active. Our brains think in terms of objects and activities and our language represents these basic concepts as nouns and verbs.

But the type of activity that I'm thinking of must not be an activity of something other than itself, because then it would not be fundamental.

So I was led to the startling conclusion that the fundamental activity must be an activity of activity. The activity itself is the substance, that is, that which stands under. Therefore the fundamental substance of the physical would I concluded must be this paradoxical, self-caused, self-activity.

But there has to be more.

There must be, fundamental to physical existence, not only activity, but also there must be interaction between and among these primal self-activities.

Moreover, there must be the possibility of action and interaction such that action and interaction, that is self-activity and mutual interaction becomes actual.

But there has to be even more.

These primal self-activities must be able to interact to form systems that have properties over and above the interacting parts separately. That is, there must be in physical existence, the capacity for interacting parts to join together to form new systems that take on a unity of action as a whole.

Let's look again at this concept of oneness or wholeness and the processes through which systems in nature form themselves.

We have seen that the character of the most basic whole system, that is, a system that is not comprised of any smaller or more fundamental sub-systems, is paradoxical. It is paradoxical because a system is defined as an interaction of parts in such a way that the system as a whole takes on properties that the parts do not have. How then can we have a system compose of no parts?

In my Photon Theory I posited systems comprised of self-inducing interactions of magnetic and electric fluxes that don't exist until created by one another.

Now let's go one step further and ask: What does an entity not comprised of any interactions of any kind look like?

An entity not comprised of any interacting sub-systems what-so-ever would be a fundamental unity. Inside this unity there would be no time, no space, no volume, no mass, no energy, and none of the properties that emerge later through the interactions and compiling of systems. The only way of detecting such an entity would be to interact with it from the outside. As soon as there is an interaction, a boundary of interaction would form between the unity and something else. This boundary of interaction would then define space, time, energy, mass and all the properties we associate with systems of interacting parts.

Prior to such an interaction, however, the unity would have no location, and no boundary of interaction. Indeed it could have no boundary what-so-ever, because a boundary would contain and define its existence through interaction. Thus a perfect unity would be the smallest most fundamental entity, and, it would also be unbounded, and therefore the largest most fundamental entity. That is, such a primal unity would be prior to dimensionality. It would be simultaneously the smallest and the largest and dimensionless.

It is through interaction that form exists. The unity, therefore, has no form. We can therefore say: 1. The absolutely fundamental substance is absolute unity and is prior to form; and 2. The entire physical world is founded on interaction, which creates and defines form.

One thing alone defines no event, no time, no distance and hence no space. Thus we see that the fundamental unitary substance has no physical existence.

In addition we see that in the physical world there is no such thing as an unformed substrate. The substrate, of the physical world of matter and process, is the plethora of interactions that define and create form. These interactions presuppose actions, and so once again, we take action and interaction as the fundamentals of the physical world. *In addition we see that, prior to the actions and interactions that form the basis of the physical would, is the absolute unity, which is the largest and the smallest. Thus as we have seen, this unity is both the smallest constituent and the enormous whole of existence at once and is prior to the what we call the physical world of mass, energy, time, space, and matter.*

We talked about self-forming systems and living systems in another chapter. I called systems that organize themselves into existence, Teleostemic, from the Greek word, "Teleos," which means end seeking, or acting towards some end goal. Why? Because these self-building systems, as they build themselves, take actions that are towards the end goal of self-creating, or self-building an organization that at each moment in time transcends what it was before.

There is a circularity in which the activity and existence of each part is necessary to the activity and existence of every other part, which is necessary for the existence and activity of each individual part. *I called it a mutually integrated, reciprocity of cause and effect.*

We think in terms of the potter making the pot, having an idea, which she implements with her hands and tools as she acts to form the substance into the object.

We are at a loss to explain, or even to conceptualize, a system that arises from within, like a natural system, and forms itself. So we anthropomorphize systems, putting the purposefulness and the plan in a supernatural agent, or many supernatural agents, and positing a passive or inert material out of which the system is made. We reduce causality to the material cause, or clay, and systems to mechanical systems. But this is an error.

When we're talking about natural systems we're talking about systems where the potter is the clay. This doesn't mean the potter is some unformed material or inert substance. It means that whatever this substance is contains also whatever the potter is. This changes forever our idea of what substance is.

That which is being organized is also that which is organizing. That which is created is also doing the creating. That which creates is also that which is created. We have in nature, at the most fundamental level this kind of paradoxical self-action.

Just as there is no little green man inside a perceiving system looking at the TV screen, there is no little director inside any natural system organizing it. Just as the perceiving system perceives itself, natural systems are creating themselves through the interactions of the fundamental paradoxical self-activities that are not comprised of any parts.

These fundamental, unitary self-activities that are not comprised of any parts are prior, even to the self-inducing, fluctuating electric and magnetic fluxes that I hypothesize form the fundamental substance of the physical world. The fundamental substance that underlies existence is prior to the physical world. Remember that the physical requires an outside viewpoint, and therefore, an interaction.

At this level of being, the subject object/split doesn't exist. Instead there is a curious, paradoxical, unitary self-reflexion in which what is doing is what is done and in which self-activity is the activity only of its own activity. At this level of substance, the fundamental unity is absolutely primal.

This unity with no parts has no form, but as soon as it interacts with another unity, it has form on account of that interrelation. Therefore as soon as these entities without parts (these unitary, self-generating activities) interrelate so as to form a system they themselves have form, that is, they take on the aspect of form.

But the question then becomes: If we start with a fundamental unity that has no parts, no form, and in which there is no space, no time, no mass, no energy, how can it interact with another unity, since the unity is all there is at that level?

If there are two unities, how did the primal unity become split into two unities that form a boundary of interaction with one another that gives birth to form, to relationship, to space, time, energy, mass and ultimately to the entire physical world of matter and motion, of action and interaction?

Of course no one knows the answer. No one knows the answer to the question of why or how all this wonder and glory of existence comes into being. Anyone who says they have the answer is not telling the truth. The truth is it is the ultimate mystery of existence and it is this mystery that gives us a feeling of awe and wonder when we contemplate it. This fundamental mystery is the foundation of all spiritual practice, all valid religions and all science.

The more we discover and make our models of how this miraculous existence works the more amazed we are and the more love and admiration we feel for this primal self-creating existence that embodies our fundamental spiritual being in perfect unity with our fundamental physical being.

What we are discovering here is that this primal unity precedes the diversity of parts. It is not that we start with a diversity of atoms and that then combine to form molecules. It is that the atoms themselves are systems that arise from the interactions of subatomic entities that arise from systems of interactions of still more primal entities that I have called the fundamental self-activities of the physical world, that arise from a yet more fundamental unity that is not made up of parts and is not what we call a physical existence. What we call physical existence arises when these fundamental unities interact and form boundaries of interaction through which form is born.

But there is more as we see in the next essay.

Chapter Twenty-Six and Two Tenths: Dima

Finish

My feet are burning with pain and a cannon ball of last night's roast beef sits in my stomach. These last two miles have turned my sense of elation into a sense of failure. Sometimes it takes more courage to go on in life not having met your expectations and yet not giving up, going on anyway. My pace has dropped off drastically. I am running on will power, severely dehydrated. This is not one of my better runs.

As I turn into the brick canyon of Hereford Street, cheering spectators press into the street so there is only a narrow passages for us to squeeze through. The music of victory and celebration blasts out. People are hanging out of windows, cheering and drinking beer. Hundreds and thousands of laughing faces turn towards us. I'm passing through a birth channel into a new life and everyone is shouting, "It's a girl!"

Colors and sounds, voices, faces, warm bodies, coats, hats, the rectangular strip of blue sky, the smell of city, exhaust, the cool wetness of spring breathing up from the earth in alleyways overwhelm my senses.

Finally I turn the corner onto Boylston Street. The roar of the crowd, like a living being with thousands of arms and legs, fills the space between the glass and steel buildings. Human faces and eyes meet mine. The power of uprising emotions of joy, triumph and love washes through me erasing the pain, fatigue and thirst.

A press truck rolls with cameramen hanging off them move slowly along the side of the road filling the street with acrid exhaust. Rows of cheering people fill the bleachers. Rope barricades keep the crowds back. Colorful flags and banners ripple in the afternoon wind. Far above, the sun peers down with its brilliant, blind, all-seeing eye through the blue sky.

After thousands of miles, and two years of training, I'm coming home. I look into the faces of all these people and I feel the poignancy of human existence—an existence that is so enduring and yet so fragile. We are born at the start of every marathon, we run, we pass through and we die. At the end, we've run our race, we've done what we came to do and we blow away as dust in the wind.

I run across the finish line. The crowds are screaming. My heart is full. Two years ago I set out on this odyssey, faithfully following my heart for no reason that made sense to anyone. Then my solitary journey turned into a social transformation as I saw a way to help to overcome the false believes that divide us and imprison us, and to set people's minds and hearts free.

And here they are—these people.

A kind man throws a blanket around my shoulders. I feel the rough itchy wool next to my hot skin. A fellow runner puts his warm hairy arm around me and beams at me. The governor of Massachusetts, Governor Volpe, is here on the platform with his broad face smiling and hand warmly outstretched. I extend my hand and feel his firm grip as he congratulates me. Members of the press crowd around me.

I feel supremely happy. I've done what I set out to do and I can now hope that others will follow.

The end is a new beginning; just as death is birth into something new. I'm overcome with the immediate sense of being alive here on this planet at this moment, the wonder, mystery and miracle of existence filling me to the brim with joy.

And what is this mystery and miracle of existence? I have been thinking about this for years, feeling the awe and wonder of existence itself. I have been searching for the fundamental nature of all that exists which to me is not only physical and mental but is also divine.

I'd come to see that the creative power of existence is fully present, and divinely self-creating.

This insight that the Divine Self-Creating Miracle, is both entirely natural, in that it is self-occurring through no other power than itself, and is wholly Divine in the sense that we use the word "Divine" to indicate that which creates and sustains all existence, conveys a sense of sacred awe, holiness, wonder and deep appreciation. This was, to me, a revelation that healed the splits in our culture between man, nature and the divine.

The reason that we invoke supernatural powers and explanations is that we have not understood the true nature of Nature. All that Exists includes both what we have called nature, and what we have invoked as the supernatural to explain what we do not understand. However — and this is a vitally important point — unlike pantheism, which proposes that God is Nature, this philosophy, holds that a deity, which is supernatural being or cause cannot be Nature, because nature is not supernatural. Nor can Nature be a supernatural God, because a supernatural God is not natural.

Most importantly, our idea of Nature is incomplete and incorrect and therefore we cannot say that nature-as-we-currently-understand-it, can be the Divine Self-Creating Nature of which we are speaking. This is to say that when we think of nature as what we see out there in the natural world, our vision is so limited that we are not comprehending at all the true nature of what is comprised in All that Exists.

All we can know is our interaction with whatever is out there and so our idea of Nature is not what nature really is, but is only our interaction with, and our interpretation of, what is there. All that Exists, then, is beyond our current conceptions of nature, and so to say that God is Nature is not a correct description of reality, not only because a god is a deity or supernatural entity, but also because our idea of Nature is incomplete and limited.

What exists is beyond our ideas of Nature and of God. This primal self-creating-self-activity transcends our ability to know it, and yet in some sense is all we know, since we are It becoming Itself as us. It is neither what we have designated as nature or as God, but rather transcends and includes both what we have called nature, as what exists on its own, and God, as the ultimate cause. Yet this ultimate cause is not supernatural, but rather is totally natural in the sense that it exists by its own efforts and does not rely on some supernatural power that is beyond or outside of Nature in its largest sense.

This discovery of an entirely natural Self-Creating Power also changes all of science, which had previously been premised on the existence of an external, physical world that is as we conceive it, which is made by something other than itself, and is external, in its fundamental character. Here, we are constructing a science in which this transcendent Self-Creating Power of Nature is paramount and fundamental and is what stands under the workings of all nature from the smallest to the largest.

This insight of a transcendent, Self-Active-Self-Creating, and therefore Divine, perfectly natural existence is revolutionary and fundamental to the way we human understand the cosmos from the point of view of religion, science and nature.

Here we will review our explorations into what the fundamental substance of existence is. We have seen that in looking for an ultimate substance, scientists have looked for the smallest and most basic building block of matter. We discussed the drawbacks of this approach and saw that any system of parts would have to be comprised of smaller parts and therefore could not be the smallest.

We then looked at what a system not made up of parts would have to be like. We looked at electromagnetic radiation in which expanding magnetic fluxes create collapsing electric fluxes, which in turn create expanding magnetic fluxes, and where expanding electric fluxes create collapsing magnetic fluxes which in turn create expanding electric fluxes in a process of mutual self-creation in which neither flux exists until created by the action of the other.

We've focused on what the fundamental unit of physical existence would have to be like and showed that it is the manifestation of the intrinsic, self-formative ability of the Matrice.

We further saw the paradox in which the self-creating system acts as a whole to reflexively create itself and yet, in order to act to create itself, it would already have to exist. The Matrice self-forms itself, and yet it cannot do so until it has already done so, which is the paradox that transcends time and space.

This self-formative ability of the smallest systems reflects the paradoxical self-creativity of the whole of existence, which creates itself in this perfectly natural, divine act of Self-Creation in which what is created is what is doing the creating.

In this way we can explain the emergence of matter and its processes that are part of the so-called physical world. But this leaves out a fundamental aspect of reality, namely the fact that a material object, namely our brain, can have a subjective experience. How is this possible in a material world, or even in the physical world that contains not only matter, but also contains processes and activities that are not composed of atoms and molecules?

How do we explain the emergence of subjective experience in higher animals?

We have seen that in these higher animals there is no insubstantial other substance in addition to the processes of the brain. We have seen that simply to point to the processes of the brain is not sufficient to explain or describe this inner subjectiveness of experience. We've also shown that going inside the brain is not sufficient to explain subjective experience, because when you go inside, you see the outside of what is inside the brain but you still do not see or experience subjectively what the brain is experiencing subjectively.

We've seen that this innerness of experience is peculiar in that it is identically-self-aware. It is not that the firing of neurons causes something else called subjective experience. It is not that some invisible subjective experience enters into the brain on the occasion of brain activity. It is not that some other substance causes brain activity. The firing of patterns of neurons in the brain *is*, to the brain, subjective experience. This is astounding and it is inexplicable in a world comprised only of matter and its processes.

We saw that this is a type of circular causality in which the activity, not just causes subjective experience, but actually *is* subjective experience, from the point of view of the system whose activity it is. *From the outside, we see the firing of neurons, from the inside, the ensemble of neurons experiences a red sunset over a blue sea, with the scent of roses on a clear evening.* The very same activity can view itself in two ways: the inside, inner, subjective, self-reflexive-self-viewing; and the outside where one part of existence views something other than itself in the process of interacting with it from its own point of view. *This is not possible in a purely material world, as we have understood matter to be in an externally existing world.*

But where does all this lead?

It is this innerness of view that is the mystery of subjective experience. The material view is the external view. The so-called physical world is our view of the outside of the activities and interactions of the universe. So the question becomes: Can this innerness of view emerge in higher systems of living animals from the juxtapositioning of purely external views of matter and its motions?

The answer is that this innerness of view cannot emerge at higher levels of organizational complexity unless this capacity for innerness is fundamental to existence.

The key is the subjective, identically-reflexive-inside perspective, which

341

is characteristic of natural, whole, systems that create themselves, that is, in what we've call teleosystemic natural systems, in which the parts exist in the context of the whole and cohere into systems of continuing interactions.

We've called non-living systems that have a subjective innerness, "Noestemic," and living systems that have this innerness of experience, "Noesystemic.," and added to this a category of noesystemic animals that have neurons and nervous systems, which we called "Neuronoesystemic." All of these terms imply an innerness, but not necessarily consciousness.

All these explorations were necessary to lead us to the point of finding a truly unitary fundamental substance that is both physical and divine and has this subjective innerness of perspective.

With this review we can now construct a truly unitary worldview.

Clearly to be conscious, a system would have to be noesystemic, that is, capable of an innerness of experience or at least some sort of innerness. If we say that this innerness is a fundamental aspect of existence then we can construct a worldview in which we can conceive of a truly unitary fundamental substance. In this view the physical world is the external perspective; the subjective experience is the inner view; and the two are simply different perspectives on the same activities: the one being an interaction from the point of view of something other than the thing itself, and the other being the inner-self-experiencing of the system of its own interactions, activities and processes, within itself and with itself in interaction with whatever is outside it.

In this innerness there is a self-reflexivity in which the system-activity that is viewed is also what is doing the viewing, in the sense that the subjective experience is in fact the system-activity itself, reflexively-self-viewed by the system whose activity it is. Note that is not the activity independent from the system, but it is rather the system-activity, which is the subjective experience of that system; this is the innerness of perspective that forms the basis of subjectivity.

Since our goal is to find a unity that explains and stands under, not only material, physical existence, but also that includes this subjective innerness of perspective, we have to find a unitary existence, which is prior to the subject–object split, and prior to the verb-noun split. Such a unity heals the mind-body split and solves the mind-body problem.

The primal substance has to be unitary, not comprised of parts; it has to be a self-activity and this self-activity has to be, to itself, its own subjective innerness. Until it interacts with some other self-activity, it has no dimension, thus, it is prior to space and time. Only through interaction does the boundary of interaction form, defining the form of the interaction, and localizing each participant in the interaction and thus creating what we would measure as a space and time metric. We saw that this unity is prior to mass and energy, since mass and energy are properties of systems of interacting parts and this unity or monity has no parts.

And now we see that the innerness of perspectives of these monistic self-activities continues through the interaction, each participant having a subjectively inner perspective on the interaction, each being on the other side of the boundary of interaction that forms when they interact.

Could it be that the electric self-activities and the magnetic self-activities are in fact the different symmetries implicit in the interaction of the Unity with itself? Through these symmetries of the Unity in its interaction with itself, all of what we call existence is born. Thus the magnetic and electric would be different symmetries or viewpoints of the unity on itself. Out of this primal interaction of these two symmetries, one of which we conceive as matter and the other antimatter spring the mutually self-creating electric and magnetic fluxes of the fundamental unit of action, the photon.

The interactions, as we saw, define space, time and volume. By symmetry I mean that the right and left-handedness of the view depends on the observer, just as when we view a windmill from one side it appears to be rotating in a clockwise direction and when we view the same windmill from the other side it appears to be rotating in a counterclockwise direction. These different symmetries seem opposite, but in both cases, the windmill is moving in exactly the same manner. The difference is only a difference in viewpoint of the observer.

As the interactions compile, the original self-active unity continues to divide itself into sub-unities that are interacting with one another. *The fundamental nature of the entire self-active matrice is its divine, paradoxical self-creativity and so the fundamental nature of the self-active monity is that it is continuously creating itself into existence at all places at all times, prior to time and space.* Indeed the self-creating matrice creates what we measure as time and space within itself from the interactions of the unities into which it continuously divides itself. All the unities that result from the self-division of the primal monity are also characterized by the self-creating nature of the matrice.

This then is our answer the solution to our search for a fundamental, unitary substance or monity:

The fundamental substance is as a self-creating, self-existing, self-activity, which interacts with itself to create itself into interacting self-activities each of which is characterized by a subjective, self-reflexive innerness comprised of its own subjective perspective of its own activities as it interacts with other activities to form boundaries of interaction.

In addition to these symmetries of perspective that define and result in the division of the Unity into to two self-interactive aspects of electric and magnetic on the physical level, there is the innerness of perspective and the outer perspective that define the difference between what we call the physical or outer perspective and the subjective, which is what we call this subjective innerness of perspective, which in the view of the author is fundamental to existence.

This is the monistic substance for which we have been looking, which is fundamental to the emergence both of what we call the material, physical perspective and the inner noestemic perspectivea. This monity, when there is only one monity, comprises all of existence, and is completely inner, with no outside boundary, and nothing outside of it, not even nothing. Indeed there is no such thing as outside. The universal unitary monity is entirely inner, unto itself and has no form and no dimension, no mass and occupies no space nor time outside of itself. Since it is self-creating, it is in fact the Divine-Self-Creating-Matrice.

We must note that to interact, a monity must have a boundary of interaction that defines it, and both separates and joins it, as a whole, to everything outside of it. As it divides itself into sub-monities, it retains its self-creating activities, but now, form emerges as the boundaries of interaction of the sub-monities, each of which is a unit of self-activity, comprised of no parts, unto itself.

In our photon theory, the mutually self-creating, interacting electric and magnetic self-activities form themselves into the basis of what we call the physical world as we see it from the outside. But it must be that from the inside these self-activities are to themselves subjective innernesses and therefore what we have called noestemic. That is to say, the photons, or quanta of self-activity, which we detect by interaction with them, from the outside, as the smallest physical entity, are to themselves, from the inside, noestemic, characterized by this subjective innerness, which in more complex system, can, as we see, compile into subjective experience.

These inwardly, self-reflexive, self-activities are the fundamental unity interacting with itself in such a way to create itself. It is natural, since the fundamental nature of all-that-exists is its self-creating, that the fundamental unit of existence is in fact this same self-creating. And it is natural that, since in the cosmic totality of All-that-Exists there is no outside, only inside, that this same insideness should be fundamental to the basic unit of existence, which is at once the smallest and the largest.

It is only when the fundamental monity divides and interacts with itself that outside becomes defined as a perspective on the boundary of interaction. The monity maintains its own subjectively inner perspective in interactions. What we call physical existence emerges as the interactions among monities compile into nested systems of systems of system of increasing complexity as viewed from the outside. What we call subjective experience and consciousness emerges as self-viewing from the inside, at each level of nested systems, evolves more complex subjective properties.

The important point is that these are all natural systems that create themselves through their own interactions. These interactions follow gradients that occur in environments that create themselves, in these compiling levels of complexity. For example, the property we measure as mass, emerges as the systems of interacting parts form dynamic subsystems that exist in the context of the whole unity, which is itself the Divine Self-Creating- Existence.

It is good to remember that even as it divides and re-divides into myriad interacting unities, the whole remains the unity of all that exists. This is not unlike the case in which the egg cell starts out as a single, whole entity, in this case, made of complex parts that are made of complex atoms, molecules and their processes. The unity of the egg perseveres through out embryology, and throughout the emergence of the whole human being as a coordinated unity. We have no idea why or how the unity divides itself into interacting parts or how or why it exists at all.

In a similar manner, in my photon theory, the S-photons interact and confine one another, even though the rest mass of a single photon is zero. When the S-photons are confined, the S-photons are not motionless, but to the contrary, they are moving very fast in a confined orbit. Thus a pair of confined S-photons taken as a whole system would define a rest mass greater than zero, even though a single photon would have a zero rest mass. When a T-photon is released it emerges already traveling at the greatest speed possible for a material object, and it has mass. It has a mass of motion, that is, a kinetic mass, because of its interaction with the totality of the cosmos through which it is moving. But the photon, or quanta of action, or unit of self-activity, has no location until it interacts with something. In some sense then it fills all and none of space and time before it interacts, since space and time do not exist except in the ways interaction creates and defines events.

In this way photons and their interactions create and define what we measure as space and time. Systems of S-photons define what we measure as mass and energy, both of which are systems properties. Atoms are comprised of subatomic entities that I hypothesize are built up of nested systems of interacting S-photons. At each level these whole natural systems compile to form more complex systems that gain new properties. In our monist theory, these nested systems also gain increasing noestemic, subjective abilities on the inside. That is to say, the subjective innerness of a photon, even though it is an innerness, does not have the complexity of human consciousness, which is an innerness of the complex brain and nervous system in the context of the living organism.

The subjective innerness of a single-celled organism has attributes and subjective qualities much more complex than the innerness of the atoms that comprise the molecules that self-create themselves into the organism in a dynamic organizational structure, through which the individual atoms and molecules are continuously flowing.

The qualities that evolve in more complex systems can include an inner experience of sight, taste, smell, hearing and touch for example. A single molecule, while having an innerness, does not have the advanced subjective experiences and perceptions of a complex animal. Thus we see that as evolution proceeds to develop more complex systems that from the outside have more and different physical properties, the same evolution results in the emergence of more qualities of subjective innerness from the inside.

Even within the complex human brain that is comprised of over eighty billion neurons, the various substructures of the brain have their own characteristic subjective qualities and capabilities that are accessible to themselves at each level. Just as the external systems compile to give greater and greater organizational complexity, so the internal subjective capabilities show more and more qualities of what becomes, at the highest levels, our perceptions, thoughts, memories and all the capacities of the brain that we have called consciousness.

In the opinion of the author, mechanical systems that are designed and built by something other than themselves do not have these coherent levels of subjectivity that compile. I think noestemia is only possible for natural systems that form themselves through the interaction of their parts in ways that are informed by the whole, in such a way that these subsystems are forming themselves in a circular self-creation.

Living systems are the most complex level of naturally occurring self-forming systems that we know of. So it is no surprise that living systems also exhibit the most developed and complex subjectivity of experience, which in the higher animals emerge as the conscious awareness of the living brain.

I've briefly outlined a coherent monistic model which preserves the self-creating that characterizes, in my view, the fundamental nature of all that exists and also adds to this the subjective innerness of being.

Since we have called that which creates and maintains all existence, the Divine, I have maintained that usage in order to capture the sense of reverence and sacred holiness that is associated with the Divine. This also serves to reconcile the spiritually transcendent with science and to illustrate that we are all speaking of the same thing, namely the mystery and miracle of existence in all its dimensions and at all its levels. The reason we thought it was supernatural is because it was beyond our understanding of nature. But now we see that Nature is self-creating and therefore is the Divine, we understand that the Divine Self-Creator is entirely Natural. And we understand Nature in a more expanded and enlightened way.

This is what I have called the Divine Self-Creating Miracle, DiMa and it operates from the very smallest to the very largest from the outside and from the inside that maintains an inner subjectivity of perspective and the outside or physical perspective on the same self-activities, in a paradoxical manner in which what is created is also what is creating, what is experienced is also experiencing each in its own way. This is the ultimate mystery and, when we come face to face with the fact that we have no idea how or why this incredible existence exists, we feel a sense of awe and come into a new appreciation of all being, and of each other, who are here poised between birth and death experiencing this miracle with every thought we think, every feeling we have and every atom of our being.

In this context we can reappraise the argument over evolution or intelligent design. Evolution simply means the way systems, including life-forms develop, and change over time. Intelligence, as we touched on in the essay on Information, has two meanings. The first meaning is that of subjective experience in which an intelligent being is consciously aware. The second meaning of intelligence is that of appropriate behaviours that conduce to maximizing the operational success of the organism in terms of its ability to function and to survive. Both meaning of intelligence connote the ability to solve problems either through behavior or through cognitive skills or both.

Design has two meanings, as well. Design simply means arrangement of component parts or patterns of operation or activity whether intentional or not, as in patterns in snowflakes or weather patterns. Design also means intentional actions in pursuit of some end goal, such as the boy has designs on the cookie jar, or the engineer designs an engine that works.

The contention of the author is that there is an intelligent design in nature but it is not the design of a supernatural being or deity. The intelligence in nature is twofold. The first sense in which nature is intelligent does not imply any subjective experience or conscious intent on the part of nature at all. The intelligence of nature in this context simply means its ability to self-pattern its own activities through interactions in ways that lead to the continued function of the system or organism. I have called this teleos or intellios and have related it to interaction and gradient following behaviors, keeping in mind that Nature, in its largest sense, has designed itself in such a manner that it's component parts can and do interact to form more complex systems with more complex properties. But this type of self-design does not involve what we would call a conscious intent on the part of nature or of natural systems to design themselves. Rather this type of natural design results from the self-formative capacities of natural systems.

Equally astounding is the fact of this subjective innerness of perspective at all levels of natural systems, including our own brains, which is the subjective experience of which we are aware and which identifies itself as us. In this sense intelligence implies a subjective experience and a conscious awareness that includes an ability to solve problems. This subjective innerness that I have called Noestemia in non-living systems like photons and molecules, Noesystemia in living systems, and Neuronoesystemia in animals with nervous systems, simply means that certain natural systems have an innerness of perspective on the changes they incur through their interactions and does not mean that these natural systems have any sort of conscious intent, as we experience it, to design themselves.

Seen in this context we see that evolution, that is, the

development of complexity over time, is, in fact part, of the intelligent design of Nature's modus operandi and that Nature is itself Divine. Intelligence here means, not a conscious intent, but rather means the self-formative capacity, or teleos or intellios of nature. The mystery and miracle is that All-that-Is is continuously creating itself everywhere at all times prior to time and space, matter and energy in a way that is not only physical as seen from the outside perspective but is also subjective from the inner perspective and that this Self-Creation is perfectly natural and not the work of some higher supernatural force or intelligence.

We thus have come to understand that Nature in its largest sense is Divine. All the waters of the earth are Natural and Holy. The planets, stars, and the entire universe is entirely natural and ultimately divinely miraculous. There is no division, no separation. Existence itself is supremely Divine and mysterious.

The concept of the supernatural is invoked only because we do not understand the full power and nature of All-that-Exists, in which what we have previously attributed to supernatural causes is seen to be perfectly natural. As we saw, when ancients invoked imaginary "fire gods" to explain fire, once we understood combustion, we saw that fire is a perfect natural phenomenon. But when we look closely at natural phenomena we see that they are miraculous, even more miraculous than the idea of invisible "fire deities." What could be more amazing and full of wonder than the realization that the Self-Creating Divine Matrice creates itself into what we perceive as atoms and molecules that interact to release electromagnetic radiation that we call fire.

This is where science and religion meet. This is the fundamental basis of all spiritual traditions and religions. This mystery of the Divine-Self Creating Matrice is the mountain up which all religions are paths. This is the individual direct communion we each have with the Divine every moment of our lives, before we live and after we die. Here is where all faiths harmonize. And this appreciation of DiMa is direct and personally available and must never be systematized or made into a religion, or have any type of worship or organizational structure around it. This is free for the taking — this understanding and appreciation of the wonder of existence.

There is no need of a supernatural being. This transcendent, Self-Experiencing-Self-Creativity is totally natural and given, and yet it is beyond nature as we have understood nature to be. This expands our view of Nature and brings all people together in a comprehension of the Divine, completely natural wonder of Being.

All that is necessary to experience this transcendent wonder is to come into the present moment and ask: How does all this get to be here? …. And then to realize that it is creating itself into existence, out of itself, into itself, by itself right now before our very eyes, and is also creating itself into our eyes and into us, in a miraculous way that we do not understand, which comes from an incomprehensible, ever-present love that is beyond our understanding that is the core of our own existence and of the existence of everyone, and of everything else.

The truth is that we have absolutely no idea how or why this miracle of existence comes into being. In fact, the miracle of existence cannot be expressed in words or concepts at all. This recognition that all this wonder and beauty exists and we do not know, and we have no words or concepts that even come close to it, leads us to an authentic sense of awe, wonder and love for our existence and for one another.

For me personally this sense of wonder is everywhere immanent and is full of love. Ever since I was a child under the chestnut tree in the back yard I've had a feeling of being surrounded by, and infused with a sacred sense of divine, loving presence. It is in the sunlight filtering down through the leaves and the gentle way the wind caressed all it touches. It's a feeling of the presence of love and holiness.

It's a feeling I found in my grandmother's love. It's a feeling of upwelling joy glittering and dancing in the moving leaves. It's as though I'm seeing through to a reality that is transcendent, a reality that is the very life of the creative force of the cosmos unfolding itself. It expresses itself in all the forms we see but is so much more. It is this sense of presence, which follows each of us and we follow it. It is this sense of joy which sends us sprinting across meadows, that sets the flowers to bloom, that unleashes the tiny stalks of grasses and makes them to sing in the winds tiny songs that you can hear if you linger a moment. And you realize that you are the Divine Self-Creating Miracle becoming itself as you and so is everyone else.

When you take the time to linger a moment and let the present become itself in your presence then you know it. This Divine Presence is unfolding itself into itself. And you know it is pure love. You know then that love is all there is. And you wonder why humans try so hard to make it seem otherwise.

This Presence is a gentle sense of peace that wells up into a fountain of joy inside. It is the eternal, infinite, Self-Creating, perfectly natural, Divine Existence that embodies a love so immense that is beyond our comprehension — and it is All that really Exists.

26.2 Essays

Bobbi Gibb Art

Bobbi Gibb is an exciting contemporary artist who creates bronze sculptures of the human form in action and portrait busts; vividly colored murals; and subtle, impressionistic landscapes, which reflect her deep love of both humanity and nature.

Bobbi's artwork reflects the human and divine spirit and her point of view on the transcendent source of all being. From life-like busts and full body sculptures detailing the human form in an exacting manner to expansive murals that display an explosion of nature as she sees it in her imagination, Bobbi's work explores all facets of nature.

For more information, or to commission artwork, visit:

http://www.bobbigibbart.net/

Bobbi Gibb
Marathon Sculpture Project

Join Joan Samuelson, Bill Rodgers, Meb Keflezighi, and a dozen other Boston Marathon winners by making a donation to the Bobbi Gibb Marathon Sculpture Project.

Boston currently has several sculptures of male marathon runners, but none of women runners. Your contribution will help support the creation of a sculpture by the Boston Marathon's first woman runner (Bobbi Gibb, 1966) that will honor women's running and the proud tradition of women in the Boston Marathon.

To donate, visit FirstGiving.com and search for "Gibb sculpture" or send a check to:

Bobbi Gibb Marathon Sculpture Project
c/o 26.2 Foundation
P.O. Box 820
Hopkinton, MA 01748

Thanks for your help!

Printed in Great Britain
by Amazon